CAXTON'S OWN PROSE

THE LANGUAGE LIBRARY

EDITED BY ERIC PARTRIDGE AND SIMEON POTTER

N. F. Blake

CAXTON'S OWN PROSE

ANDRE DEUTSCH

First published 1973 by
André Deutsch Limited
105 Great Russell Street London WC1

Printed in Great Britain by
William Clowes & Sons, Limited
London, Beccles and Colchester

ISBN 0 233 96475 4

Contents

🔤🔤🔤🔤🔤🔤

Preface

꘡꘡꘡꘡꘡꘡

THIS present book is designed as a companion volume to my
Caxton and his World, published in The Language Library in 1969.
The material should complement that in my other book, though
on occasions it may supersede it. Thus the dates given after the titles
of Caxton's books in *Caxton's Own Prose* sometimes differ from
those found in *Caxton and his World* on account of the results of
the investigation into dating recorded in this Introduction. As I
have not wished to duplicate material, I have not included a
bibliography in this book, since a substantial one was included in
Caxton and his World. As it happens, a bibliography of Caxton
scholarship by R. H. Wilson was published recently in *A Manual
of the Writings in Middle English*, vol. 3, ed A. E. Hartung (New
Haven: Connecticut Academy of Arts and Sciences, 1972), and a
further bibliography will be issued soon in volume one of *The New
Cambridge Bibliography of English Literature*, edited by G. Watson.

I am indebted to the Delegates of the Oxford University Press
for permission to re-use some of the material I included in my
Selections from William Caxton (Oxford: Clarendon Press, 1973);
this material consists of parts from No 72, 80 and 86. I am grate-
ful to the General Editor for including this volume in his series
and for his help with it. I would also like to thank my many
friends in Liverpool who have given me help and advice from
time to time.

Liverpool 1973.

7

Abbreviations

🔹🔹🔹🔹🔹🔹

BLAKE   N. F. Blake, *Caxton and his World*. London: Deutsch, 1969.

GODEFROY *Dictionnaire de l'ancienne langue française*, ed. F. Godefroy. Paris: Champion, 1881–1902.

MED   *Middle English Dictionary*, ed. H. Kurath and S. M. Kuhn. Ann Arbor: University of Michigan Press, 1954–.

OED   *The Oxford English Dictionary*, ed. J. A. H. Murray *et al*. Oxford: Clarendon Press, 1933.

Introduction

Dating the Editions

THE problems of dating Caxton's editions are considerable because one has to interpret what Caxton wrote in his prologues and epilogues, decide how busy he may have been at any time, and try to determine how long he took over his translations and the actual printing. As a first step it is necessary to provide a list of dates given in Caxton's editions of his various activities since this will provide us with a useful point of reference. Not everyone may agree with all the dates given, but I will discuss these disputed ones later.

1469	1 March	Begins translation of *History of Troy*
1471	19 Sept	Finishes translation of *History of Troy*
1474	31 March	Finishes *Game of Chess*
1477	18 Nov	Prints *Dicts or Sayings*
1478	10 Feb	Prints *Moral Proverbs*
1479	2 Feb	Receives *Cordial*
	3 Feb	Starts printing *Cordial*
	24 March	Finishes printing *Cordial*
1480	22 April	Translates and finishes *Ovid's Metamorphoses*
	10 June	Prints *Chronicles of England* (1st edn)
	18 August	Prints *Description of Britain*
1481	2 Jan	Starts translating *Mirror of the World*
	8 March	Finishes translating *Mirror of the World*
	12 March	Starts translating *Siege of Jerusalem*
	6 June	Finishes *Reynard the Fox*
	7 June	Finishes translating *Siege of Jerusalem*
	12 August	Prints *Of Old Age*
	10 Nov	Prints *Siege of Jerusalem*
1482	2 July	Ends *Polychronicon*
	8 Oct	Prints *Chronicles of England* (2nd edn)
1483	1 June	Finishes translating *Knight of the Tower*
	6 June	Prints *Pilgrimage of the Soul*
	30 June	Prints *Festial*
	2 Sept	Prints *Confessio Amantis*
	20 Nov	Finishes *Golden Legend*
	23 Dec	Translates *Caton*

During the year translates *Æsop*

1484	31 Jan	Prints *Knight of the Tower*
	26 March	Prints *Æsop*
	13 Sept	Finishes translating *Royal Book*
1485	18 June	Translates *Charles the Great*
	31 July	Prints *King Arthur*
	31 August	Translates *Paris and Vienne*
	1 Dec	Prints *Charles the Great*
	19 Dec	Prints *Paris and Vienne*
1486	8 June	Translates *Book of Good Manners*
1487	11 May	Prints *Book of Good Manners*
1489	23 Jan	Receives *Feats of Arms*
	7 May	Finishes *Doctrinal of Sapience*
	8 July	Translates *Feats of Arms*
	14 July	Prints *Feats of Arms*
1490	15 June	Translates *Art of Dieing*
	22 June	Translates *Eneydos*

Just before his death Caxton finishes translating *Lives of the Fathers*.

Before discussing some of the points raised by this list, I wish to consider the wording Caxton used in his prologues and epilogues, since there is some doubt whether particular texts were translated or printed on the dates he gives. For while there can be no dispute over such words as 'translated' or 'printed', other words like 'finished', 'achieved' or 'ended' are ambiguous. Even where he uses an expression like 'translated and finished' it is possible that he meant 'translated and printed' rather than simply 'translated'. In the following summary I have grouped together his uses of such words as 'finished' in different categories according to their probable meanings.

(a) In some texts which were not translated by Caxton 'finished' can refer only to the printing.

Cordial: 'Whiche werke present I begann . . ., and finisshed on the even of th'Annunciacion . . .' (24:68–71).

Description of Britain: 'Fynysshed by me William Caxton the xviii day of August . . .' (28b:11–13).

Dicts or Sayings: 'Whiche was fynisshed the xviii day of the moneth of Novembre . . .' (29b:6–8).

(b) This group is very similar to (a) in so far as most texts in it were not translated by Caxton. But they are put into a separate category because a reference to the printing makes it clear that 'finished' must mean the printing.

Chronicles of England: 'enprinted by me William Caxton in th'Abbey of Westmynstre by London; fynysshid and accomplisshid the x day of Juyn . . .' (17b: 14–16).

Confessio Amantis: 'Enprynted at Westmestre by me Willyam Caxton and fynysshed the ii day of Septembre . . .' (22b: 1–3).

King Arthur: 'and by me devyded into xxi bookes, chapytred and enprynted and fynysshed in th'Abbey [of] Westmestre the last day of Juyl . . .' (72b: 8–11).

Pilgrimage of the Soul: 'Emprynted at Westmestre by William Caxton and fynysshed the sixth day of Juyn . . .' (85b: 1–3).

In *Æsop* there are references both to the translating and printing. In the incipit the work is said to have been translated in 1483, so the epilogue's use of 'finished' in 1484 must refer to the printing, though the wording is not straightforward.

Æsop: 'translated and emprynted by me William Caxton at Westmynstre in th'abbey, and fynysshed the xxvi daye of Marche . . .' (2b: 62–5).

(c) This group is quite substantial and contains texts in which 'finished' almost certainly indicates the translation because either the printing is subsequently mentioned or else there are other details to indicate the printing was later.

Book of Good Manners: 'Fynysshed and translated out of Frenshe into Englysshe the viii day of Juyn . . .; and enprynted the xi day of Maye . . .' (9b: 2–5).

Charles the Great: 'The whyche werke was fynysshed in the reducyng of hit into Englysshe the xviii day of Juyn . . . and enprynted the fyrst day of Decembre' (16b: 15–18).

In *History of Troy* there is no reference at all to the printing, but the wording makes it clear that the translation is meant by 'finished'.

History of Troy: 'Whiche sayd translacion and werke was begonne in Brugis . . . and ended and fynysshid in the holy cyte of Colen . . .' (50a: 13–18); and 'Whiche werke was begonne in Brugis and contynued in Gaunt and finysshid in Coleyn' (50d: 9–11).

Knight of the Tower: 'Whiche book was ended and fynysshed the fyrst day of Juyn . . . and enprynted at Westmynstre the last day of Janyver . . .' (73b: 4–7).

Mirror of the World: 'Whiche book I began first to translate the second day of Janyver . . . and fynysshyd the viii day of Marche . . .' (75g: 32–4).

Paris and Vienne: 'translated out of Frensshe into Englysshe by Wylliam Caxton at Westmestre, fynysshed the last day of August . . . and enprynted the xix day of Decembre . . .' (82: 3–7).

Royal Book: 'Whiche translacion or reducyng oute of Frensshe into Englysshe was achyeved, fynysshed and accomplysshed the xiii day of Septembre . . .' (93b:23–5).

Siege of Jerusalem: 'Whiche book I began in Marche the xii daye and fynysshyd the vii day of Juyn . . . and in this maner sette in forme and enprynted the xx day of Novembre . . .' (96b:25–9).

(d) *Feats of Arms*, which presents other problems to be discussed later, is unusual in introducing 'finished' twice, referring respectively to the translation and the printing.

Feats of Arms: 'Whiche translacyon was finysshed the viii day of Juyll the sayd yere and enprynted the xiiii day of Juyll next folowyng and ful fynyshyd' (38:29–31).

(e) The final group contains those texts in which 'ended' or 'finished' could refer to either the translating or the printing.

Doctrinal of Sapience: 'Whyche is translated out of Frenshe into Englysshe by Wyllyam Caxton at Westmester. Fynysshed the vii day of May, . . .' (34b:2–4).

Game of Chess (1st edn): 'Fynysshid the last day of Marche the yer of Our Lord God a thousand, foure honderd and lxxiiii.' (45e: 20–1).

Golden Legend: 'Whiche werke I have accomplisshed at the commaundemente and requeste of . . . and have fynysshed it at Westmestre the twenty day of Novembre . . .' (47m:8–11).

Polychronicon: 'Ended the second day of Juyll, the xxii yere of the regne of Kynge Edward the Fourth . . . Fynysshed per Caxton.' (86d:12–15).

Reynard the Fox: 'and by me, William Caxton, translated into this rude and symple Englyssh in th'Abbey of Westmestre. Fynysshed the vi daye of Juyn . . .' (91:4–6).

Ovid's Metamorphoses: 'translated and fynysshed by me William Caxton at Westmestre the xxii day of Appryll . . .' (106:1–4).

In this group one ought perhaps to include Caxton's use of words like 'performed' or 'finished' when referring to texts he had issued previously. There are three examples:

Eneydos: 'After dyverse werkes made, translated and achieved,. . .' (36a:1).

Golden Legend: 'whan I had parfourmed and accomplisshed dyvers werkys and hystoryes translated out of Frensshe into Englysshe . . .' (47a:5–7).

King Arthur: 'After that I had accomplysshed and fynysshed dyvers hystoryes . . .' (72a:1–2).

In the *Golden Legend* 'parfourmed and accomplisshed' must mean 'printed' since the concept of 'translation' is introduced later. This fact is important in so far as *Ovid's Metamorphoses* is included in the list of books 'parfourmed and accomplisshed' and this provides the strongest evidence that this text was printed, even though no copies survive. The other two quotations are very similar except that the one from *Eneydos* introduces the word 'translated'. It is possible that 'achieved' is here a doublet of 'translated', but as all three passages are best understood to refer to the printing of his texts, it is more sensible to interpret 'translated and achieved' in *Eneydos* to mean 'translated and printed'. But as *Eneydos* and *King Arthur* do not mention specific titles, certainty is not possible.

As regards the previous six examples, it has always been assumed that as 'ended' in *Polychronicon* occurs in the epilogue to *Liber Ultimus* it means 'concluded the translation' and that consequently the book was printed after 2 July 1482. Yet we now know that there is little translation by Caxton in his *Liber Ultimus*, which particularly in its final half is almost identical with his edition of the *Chronicles of England*. Indeed, it is quite possible that this part of the *Liber Ultimus* was set up direct from the *Chronicles of England*, and so Caxton is unlikely to have used 'ended' in the sense 'concluded the translation' or even 'finished the editing'. It is more reasonable to assume that it has the sense 'printed', and the statement would thus be similar to the one made in the epilogue to *Description of Britain*. Since Caxton uses 'finished' to mean printed frequently, his use of 'ended' here may be taken to be identical.

In *Doctrinal of Sapience*, *Reynard the Fox* and *Ovid's Metamorphoses* it is accepted that 'finished' (following so closely on Caxton's reference to his 'translating' it) refers to the completion of the translation. But in the first two instances 'finished' is introduced as part of a separate phrase or sentence, and it might therefore refer to a different concept. As the examples in groups (a) and (b) prove that the word 'finished' often indicates the printing, the possibility that the same applies here should not be dismissed as readily as it has been. A consideration of the language by itself is not decisive, for 'finished' could refer to either the translation or the printing. But other evidence may help us to decide which is the more probable and this is where the list of Caxton's activities above may help. Let us consider the case of *Reynard the Fox* which he finished on 6 June 1481. A glance at the list reveals that in 1481 he translated *Mirror of the World* from 2 January to 8 March and *Siege of Jerusalem* from 12 March to 7 June. This looks like a well-regulated timetable of translation which does not allow for the translation of *Reynard the Fox* to be finished on 6 June. Admittedly

Caxton may have had two translations going at once and this is a possibility we have to accept when the evidence offers no alternative, as with the *Art of Dieing* and *Eneydos* which were translated on 15 and 22 June 1490 respectively. But the case of *Reynard the Fox* is different since the 'finished' there could refer to the translation or the printing. And the list of Caxton's work shows that he did a lot of translating in the first half of the year and a lot of printing in the second. So an interpretation which would allow for the printing of *Reynard the Fox* in the first half of the year is inherently more probable; so I would suggest that in this case 'finished' means 'printed'.

The case of the *Doctrinal of Sapience* is not so clear cut. In 1489 Caxton received the *Feats of Arms* from Henry VII through the agency of the Earl of Oxford on 23 January. The translation was completed on 8 July and the book was printed on 14 July. Yet on 7 May the *Doctrinal of Sapience* was 'finished'. If we interpret this to mean that he finished the translation on that date, then it implies that although he received *Feats of Arms* in January he may not have started translating it till May. Yet as he gives us a date for the reception of the work it seems more likely that he began his translation soon afterwards. After all, *Feats of Arms* was commissioned by the two most important men in the kingdom, and the *Doctrinal of Sapience* was to the best of our knowledge one of those texts which had no patron and which were turned out to keep the press working. It is perhaps more sensible to accept that this latter work was printed on 7 May 1489. This would mean that when Caxton started to translate *Feats of Arms*, the press was engaged in printing the *Doctrinal of Sapience*. When this text was completed on 7 May the printers would be able to start on that part of *Feats of Arms* which Caxton had finished. They were thus able to finish the printing only a week after he finished the translation.

In the case of *Ovid's Metamorphoses* the use of 'translated and finished' could be regarded as a doublet. Yet we saw earlier that in *Eneydos* the phrase 'translated and achieved' may mean 'translated and printed', and an interpretation along these lines should be considered for *Ovid's Metamorphoses*. In this case, however, the list of Caxton's activities marginally favours an interpretation that it was the translation which was completed on 22 April 1480. For the first edition of the *Chronicles of England* was printed on 10 June 1480, and as it is a fairly long text it is unlikely that its printing could have been completed between 22 April and 10 June. For if, as many assume, the second edition was printed immediately after *Polychronicon* in 1482, it took from 2 July to 8 October to be printed.

In the *Golden Legend* and the *Game of Chess* the reference to finishing the work is not associated with its translation, and so it is surprising perhaps that the dates have always been taken to indicate the completion of the translation. In the epilogue of the *Golden Legend* Caxton simply states that he 'accomplished' it at the request of the Earl of Arundel and 'finished' it on 20 November 1483. In his prologue, however, he implies he broke off his translation because of the work's length and he was encouraged to complete the work by the Earl who promised to 'take a resonable quantyte of them when they were achyeved and accomplisshed' (47a: 79–80). It is clear that Arundel encouraged him to print the book, and consequently Caxton's reference in his epilogue to finishing it might well refer to the printing rather than the translation. The evidence from the timetable of Caxton's work is not straightforward. If the translation of the *Golden Legend* was finished on 20 November 1483 it can hardly have been printed till late 1484 since *Knight of the Tower* was printed on 31 January and *Æsop* on 26 March 1484. The problem is whether, once he had got a patron to sponsor the volume who was prepared to dispose of some printed copies, he would finish the translation and then dally before he put it into print. Caxton would surely wish to make use of the offer as soon as he could, given the political situation in the latter half of 1483. However, this does raise a difficulty. The *Festial* was printed on 30 June and *Confessio Amantis* on 2 September 1483; so the *Golden Legend* would have had to be printed from 3 September to 20 November. The difficulty is whether such a large text could have been printed in such a short time. No answer can be provided to this question, but some of its implications will be considered later. In the meantime we must content ourselves with the conclusion that a case can be made out that the printing of *Golden Legend* was completed on 20 November 1483.

The assumption that in the epilogue to the first edition of the *Game of Chess* 'finished' refers to the translation is very insecurely based. Blades suggested that 'The word "fynysshed" has doubtless the same signification here as in the Epilogue to the Second Book of Caxton's translation of the Histories of Troy, "begonne in Brugis, contynued in Gaunt, and *finysshed* in Coleyn," which evidently refers to the translation only',[1] and his view seems to have been generally accepted since. But in the *History of Troy*

[1] W. Blades, *The Life and Typography of William Caxton* (London, 1863), II.9.

there is a clear reference to the translation which is not found in the *Game of Chess*. Furthermore, if *History of Troy* was printed in 1473 or even early 1474 as I have suggested (Blake p. 60), there is no reason why the *Game of Chess* should not have been printed on 31 March '1474'. It is only because scholars have placed the printing of *History of Troy* as late as 1475 that they are unwilling to accept the printing of the *Game of Chess* on 31 March '1474'.

I put 1474 in inverted commas in the previous paragraph because there has been some controversy as to what year is meant. Caxton wrote 31 March 1474 in his epilogue, but Blades understood this to mean 31 March 1475 and other scholars have followed him in this. Caxton used two methods of dating in his books: one by using the regnal year of the monarch and the other by giving the calendar year. Sometimes when he uses both methods we can see that, as was then common in England, he started his calendar year on 25 March, Lady Day, and not on 1 January. Thus the *Cordial* was delivered to Caxton by Earl Rivers on 'the secunde day of the moneth of Feverer in the yeer of Our Lord MCCCClxxviii' and the book was finished on 'the xxiiii daye of Marche in the xix yeer of Kyng Edwarde the Fourthe'. As Edward IV's nineteenth regnal year extended from 4 March 1479 to 3 March 1480, the book was finished on 24 March 1479. As Caxton can hardly have taken over a year to print this book and as there seems to be no question of a misprint here, his '2 February 1478' is our 2 February 1479. In the epilogue to the *Mirror of the World* Caxton wrote 'whiche book I began first to translate the second day of Janyver, the yere of Our Lord MCCCClxxx, and fynysshyd the viii day of Marche the same yere and the xxi yere of the regne of the most Crysten kynge, Kynge Edward the Fourthe.' Here there is a problem. The book was finished on 8 March 1481; yet the translation was commenced on '2 January 1480'. If one understands this to mean our 2 January 1481 it is difficult to see why Caxton wrote it was 'the same yere', for this interpretation demands that this year began on 25 March. In other words, the reading of 2 January 1480 as 2 January 1481 demands the use of one calendar and the interpretation of 'the same yere' demands the use of another. It would certainly be very confusing if Caxton was using two systems of reckoning within the one date. In his *Æsop* it is evident that his use of 26 March agrees with our own. *Æsop* was 'fynysshed the xxvi daye of Marche the yere of Oure Lord MCCCClxxxiiii and the fyrst yere of the regne of Kyng Rychard the Thyrdde.' His 26 March 1484 is our 26 March 1484. It is surprising therefore that his 31 March

1474 in the *Game of Chess* is interpreted as 31 March 1475. But Blades argued that Caxton was here using a system of dating the year from Easter, a system which was found in the Low Countries.[1] Whether this is so or not, as the book was destined for an English market (it was in English and it was dedicated to the Duke of Clarence), it is more likely that he used an English system of dating. There are consequently, in my opinion, no convincing grounds for interpreting his 31 March 1474 as 31 March 1475. Until better reasons are brought forward we must, I think, accept that 31 March 1474 is the right date. This is a matter of considerable interest, for if we understand Caxton's 'finished' to mean printed and if we accept the date 31 March 1474 as the correct one, we are provided with our first fixed point in the history of Caxton's press. Among other things it would help us to date the printing of the *History of Troy*, the first book printed in English, more exactly.

Two final questions remain. How long did it take Caxton to translate a book, and how long did it take his staff to print it? No definite answers can be given, for the conditions were constantly changing. The period of translation would depend on the difficulty of the language and the number of interruptions he suffered. The length of printing would depend on the quality and experience of the staff as well as their number. In 1479 he started printing *Cordial* on 3 February and finished on 24 March. That is a book of 76 leaves with 28/29 lines per page and it took him about seven weeks to print. But in 1483, if we can assume that the *Festial* was started as soon as the *Pilgrimage of the Soul* was completed, it was printed between 6 and 30 June. A book of 115 leaves with 38 lines per page was completed in 24 days. If the press then went on to *Confessio Amantis*, which was finished on 2 September, it took the printers about nine weeks to print a book of 218 leaves with 46 lines per page of double columns. In the last two cases the printing may have been even quicker than this, since other smaller pieces may have been printed before the major work was started. These times vary considerably, and are in any case based on the assumptions that Caxton had only one printing press and that one book was finished before the next was started. Even though the times taken for printing varied, one may well wonder whether the printers could have managed to complete *Golden Legend* in the

---

[1] *Ibid.* This system was found in France and spread to the Low Countries through the influence of the Dukes of Burgundy, but it was never the predominant system there. See R. L. Poole, 'The beginning of the year in the Middle Ages', *Proceedings of the British Academy*, 10 (1921–3), 113–37, and C. R. Cheney, *Handbook of dates for students of English history* (London, 1945), pp. 3–6.

space of 8½ weeks (2 September to 20 November 1483) since it consists of 447 leaves of 55 lines per two-column page.

For the time taken in translation we also have certain dates. In 1481 the *Mirror of the World* was translated between 2 January and 8 March and the *Siege of Jerusalem* between 12 March and 7 June. That gives 99 leaves of 29 lines in 9½ weeks and 142 leaves of 40 lines in 12½ weeks respectively. So the *Siege of Jerusalem* was translated very much quicker than the *Mirror of the World*. On the other hand, if we assume that the *Feats of Arms* was translated between 23 January and 8 July 1489, this would mean that a book of 143 leaves of 31 lines took 19½ weeks. But then we cannot tell what other engagements Caxton had, whether he was ill at all, or whether his pace of translation slowed down as he got older. Regrettably one cannot come to any conclusion as to the speed of translation or printing. It may however be suggested from the examples quoted in these two paragraphs that as a general rule the printers achieved a better daily output than the translator. This is hardly surprising since Caxton did so many other things apart from translation. It does mean, of course, that the press could never confine its activities to the works translated by Caxton, for if it did the printers would have been unoccupied for long periods of time. So in order to keep his press busy he was forced to publish a variety of texts which were already in existence.

Caxton's Reading

OWING to lack of evidence it is not possible to get an insight into Caxton's habitual reading. All we can do is to trace the sort of books he was familiar with from references to other works and from echoes of other writers in his own prose. The reader must remember that this collection does not contain the minor additions and alterations made by Caxton to the books he translated and printed so that it may sometimes be necessary to go beyond this volume. At the same time we have also to assume that all the literary echoes in Caxton's writings have not yet been identified so that this discussion will necessarily be incomplete. Another problem is how familiar Caxton was with the books he mentions or from which he borrowed. No general answer can be given to that question, and each reference must be judged on its own merits.

It seems probable that Caxton read most of the works he printed. Many of them he had himself translated. Some were abridged before printing and he may have been responsible for the editorial work. With several of the translations not made by Caxton, the language of the prologues and epilogues suggests that he read them through before passing them on to the printer. Thus he gives brief accounts of the three books which form the composite volume *Of Old Age*, and in the additions to that volume the use of such words as *juvente*, *senectute* and *virylyte* (words which do not occur elsewhere in his own prose) is best explained by the view that he took them from the body of the text. He was apparently familiar with the works of the English poets he printed for there are many echoes from them in his writings. It is only for works in Latin that evidence is lacking; but most of these are technical works like grammars and psalters which one would not read through as a whole.

As for the references to other works in Caxton's prologues and epilogues, one must first discount those in passages translated from French originals. Thus all the sources mentioned in the prologue to the *Doctrinal of Sapience* are taken direct from the French original. Some cases, however, are more difficult to decide. The reference to Aristotle's *Metaphysics* in the *Four Sons of Aymon* may have been introduced by one of the later printers or it may have come from Caxton's French version, for it is improbable that Caxton had read it. Likewise the story about Poggio in the prologue to *Caton* (15a:61ff) was probably taken from some French source as yet unidentified, for it may be significant that in this paragraph of the prologue the book is entitled *Cathon Glosed* whereas elsewhere it is called the *Book of Cathon*.

Some references to other works are of such a general nature that little weight can be attached to them. When in the epilogue to *Boethius* Caxton wrote that Boethius had translated many books from Greek into Latin we may assume that he was not familiar with any of these other translations, for this information he could easily have acquired from Chaucer's translation of the *De Consolatione*. In the *History of Troy* Caxton refers to such authors as Dictys Cretensis, Dares Phrygius and Homer, who had all written about the Trojan war. Their names were so well known that few would have had to read their works, even if they were available in fifteenth-century England, to realize that they were the main authorities for the war. Yet Caxton does refer to the bias adopted by individual authors and to the variety in the spelling of the names found in their accounts. Even this is hardly sufficient to show that Caxton had read these works, for there is no evidence, for example, that he modified his French source for the *Histoy of Troy* because of his knowledge of other works. Similarly when he refers in an addition to the *Golden Legend* to St Gregory's *Moralia* it is safe to assume that he knew only its title, for it was a work frequently quoted and cited in the Middle Ages and Caxton shows that he knows only what its main features are. The various Latin authors referred to in *Eneydos* were probably not known to him in their Latin texts. Thus his own book is ostensibly a version of Virgil's text, but he does not modify his French original by using a Latin text – an omission for which he was severely chided by Gavin Douglas.

The position with regard to English authors is somewhat different. In his prologue to *King Arthur*, for example, Caxton refers to Geoffrey of Monmouth. However, he gives no specific reference to the *Historia Regum Britanniae* as he does for the *Polychronicon* in that prologue. As he had discussed the problem of Arthur's authenticity with his clients, it seems probable that he heard of Geoffrey as an authority from them. There is no evidence that he had read his book. How familiar he was with Trevisa's translations is debatable. In his edition of Trevisa's translation of Higden's *Polychronicon* he mentions that Trevisa was vicar of Berkeley and that he had translated not only the *Polychronicon* but also *De Proprietatibus Rerum* by Bartholomaeus Anglicus and the Bible for Lord Berkeley. The *De Proprietatibus* was certainly translated by Trevisa and was well known in the fifteenth century since it was printed by Wynkyn de Worde, Caxton's successor. It is doubtful whether Trevisa made a translation of the Bible. If he did, it would have been as one of the helpers on the translation of the Wycliffite Bible and not at the request of Lord Berkeley. Caxton's reference is the only evidence we have for Trevisa's translation and it is unknown where he got this information from. The unreliability of his remarks suggests that he acquired this information from conversations with his clients rather than direct from the works in question.

It is unlikely that Caxton read any classical literature in the original language. References to such works as 'th'actes of Romayns' (15a: 28–9) are no doubt introduced to add authenticity and to give an impression of learning. Stories such as the one to which this reference is appended were borrowed freely from other vernacular works. The only classical book which Caxton might have read in the original Latin is the *Thebaid* of Statius, from which he introduced some details in his additions to *Jason* (71c). But as he used Boccaccio as his principal source for these passages and as Boccaccio also used Statius, it is possible that Caxton took the reference to Statius from there. Otherwise Caxton's familiarity with the classics would have come through French and English translations. He himself translated Ovid's *Metamorphoses* and Virgil's *Æneid* from French, and he may well have read other French versions of the classics. For example, in *Eneydos* he refers to the '*Pystles* of Ovyde' (36a: 78) which may have been known to him in a French form, for his reference suggests a certain acquaintance with the text. In the same prologue he mentions some of Skelton's translations such as those of Cicero's *Letters* and Diodorus's *Historical Library*. He may have read these. Certainly Virgil, Ovid and Cicero are the models which Caxton thinks one should follow. It is significant that he says Skelton had read many other classical works 'to me unknowen' (36a: 96), which implies that he was himself familiar with the three major Latin authors. Yet the impact made by the classics on Caxton's reading was minimal since he read them in medieval versions.

Caxton knew no Italian and his knowledge of works by Italians was slight. He mentions Poggio Bracciolini in his *Caton*, but he never read any of Poggio's works in Latin. His *Facetiae* which were included in *Æsop's Fables* were known to Caxton in the French version and he also used a French translation of Poggio's Latin version of the prologue to Diodorus's *Historical Library*. But Caxton seems not to have associated the 'noble clerke named Pogius of Florence' (15a:61) with *Æsop's Fables* or Diodorus Siculus and clearly knew little about him. Boccaccio, however, was a better known author in England who is praised by some English poets like Lydgate. Caxton knew some of his works. Thus he quotes extensively from his *De Genealogia Deorum* in his additions to *Jason* and he was well acquainted with the text. There is no reason to doubt that Caxton had read it in the original Latin. He also mentions Boccaccio as a source for Arthur in his prologue to *King Arthur*. But as the information about Arthur may have come from his clients and as an English poetic version of *De Casu Principum* was available in the fifteenth century, we cannot be certain that Caxton had read this work in Latin or even that he had read it at all. There is no reason to think that he knew other Italian works, and he was completely untouched by the new humanist ideals spreading from Italy.

The bulk of his reading in French consisted of historical and chivalric works. Indeed the French versions of the classics which he read might also be classified in this category since they had been given a medieval veneer. Caxton was principally interested in the history of the recent past and in the Arthurian story. His frequent references to the Nine Worthies underline his concern for heroism and feats of arms. When in his epilogue to the *Order of Chivalry* he mentions Froissart, we may assume that he had read the *Chronicles* for they portray that brilliant and chivalric society which was so quickly disappearing from Western Europe and which Caxton wanted to revive. It was from this work that he would have learned of the events and participants of the Hundred Years' War. In this epilogue he also refers to many Arthurian personages and stories. As this work was published before *King Arthur*, it is clear that he read Arthurian literature before he started printing it. And already in 1481 in his prologue to the *Siege of Jerusalem* he had mentioned 'the grete and many volumes of Seynt Graal, Ghalehot, and Launcelotte de Lake, Gawayn, Perceval, Lyonel, and Tristram, and many other of whom were overlonge to reherce and also to me unknowen' (96a: 67–70). The 'to me unknowen' is here indicative of his reading in Arthurian romance; and the form *Ghalehot* for Galahad suggests that he may have known Flemish versions. He claimed elsewhere that Arthurian tales were found in 'Dutch', Italian, Spanish and Greek as well as in Welsh and French (72a), and by 'Dutch' he probably meant Low German which would include Flemish. It is unlikely that he had read versions in languages other than Low German and French. Of the French texts he wrote on another occasion that they are found in many volumes 'which I have seen and redde beyonde the see' (72a: 88–9), which shows that while in the Low Countries he had read about Arthur and his knights. But he seems not to have known many English versions and even complains that the full Arthurian story is not found in English. It may even be significant that he printed Malory from a copy lent to him, as it may be that otherwise he would have remained ignorant of this version. The exploits of Charlemagne and Godfrey of Bouillon were also well known on the Continent. The deeds of the latter were available in both French and Latin, but according to Caxton they were not found in English. The Charlemagne epic was found in many volumes, but in what language Caxton does not say. However, enough has been said to show that chivalry and history were his favourite topics though like his contemporaries, he saw personal models to be emulated rather than general ideals.

In this connexion we may glance again at Caxton's printing of English works. He printed the *Brut* and the *Polychronicon*, but he printed no further works of English history or about English heroes, whether fictitious or not – apart from translating the missing life of the Earl of Oxford from French. He claimed in the prologue to the *Description of Britain* that the 'comyn cronicles of Englond' (28a: 1–2) were common enough, but when he came to add his contribution to the *Polychronicon* he could find only two works (which he called *Aureus de Universo* and *Fasciculus Temporum*) to help him. He added no stories about such famous English heroes as Henry v or about any of the other Englishmen whom he had praised in *Order of Chivalry*. He may have had some nationalistic feelings, but his reading was not guided by any nationalistic bias. Heroes sung in French works appealed to him whatever country they came from.

Caxton also read many religious and didactic works. These were, as far as we can tell, in Latin and French, for he gives no indication that he read English religious works and he certainly printed very few of them. But as a general rule he refers to few religious works apart from those he translated, though he likes to quote well-known sayings of the fathers. It may be that religious texts had little literary prestige and so there was little incentive to refer to them. It is consequently difficult to know how many texts he may have known other than those he printed. But since his additions to the *Golden Legend* show that he attended sermons and discussed religious matters with others, he may have read other books of a monitory nature. He knew the Vulgate well and translated parts of it for his additions to the *Golden Legend*. The French version of the *Game of Chess* came into his hands when he was in Bruges (46a: 16–17) and he possibly acquired and read other books like this while he was there. Indeed he says of the *Dicts or Sayings* that he had often read the French version (29a: 13–14) before he printed Earl Rivers's translation. Although he possessed and used the earlier English translation of the *Golden Legend*, it is noteworthy that he seems to have been ignorant of the existence of the earlier English versions of *Knight of the Tower* and *Dicts or Sayings*, for this implies that he was more interested in acquiring French than English texts.

Works by English authors are most frequently discussed by Caxton with regard to their previous production. This is natural since the foreign texts he printed were in his opinion now translated for the first time and, when he knew this was not the case as with the *Golden Legend*, he felt he had to justify his new translation. The English works had been in circulation for some time and the quality of the texts was therefore important. Of the English poets Chaucer is dealt with at the greatest length and receives the most praise. This suggests that any work not published by Caxton was probably unknown to him. Lydgate, however, was evidently much read by Caxton for allusions to his work occur frequently, but he printed relatively few of his poems. Thus Lydgate's *Troy-Book* and *Siege of Thebes* were certainly read by Caxton as may have been other of his poems; but they were not printed. Furthermore, Caxton gives us no personal details of Lydgate's life except that he was a monk of Bury (50d: 18–19) and rarely gives him any lavish praise. Personal details are included about Trevisa, Gower and Benedict Burgh. Echoes from *Confessio Amantis* are found in Caxton's writings and the poem must have been well known to him. Otherwise he probably knew only this poem by Gower and only the *Cato* by Burgh. No doubt Caxton read such fashionable poetry as he could lay his hands on, like the balades by Earl Rivers and the works of Skelton. He tells us nothing about Skelton's personal life though he recounts a great deal of his literary activity. But Skelton's work may have appeared too late in Caxton's life to be printed by him, though Caxton obviously felt he should keep abreast of new developments. By and large, echoes from English writings in Caxton's work come only from Chaucer, Gower and Lydgate – and their writings were doubtless the English works he read most often.

Introduction

To judge from his own writing, the bulk of Caxton's reading consisted of English poetry and French chivalric works. He also read didactic works, but little serious religious literature. He satisfied his religious needs by listening to sermons and attending churches and in discussions with others of religious topics.

The People of the Prologues and Epilogues

THE people who are mentioned by Caxton in his own writing fall into distinct groups. In fact one might go so far as to say that unless you were an author, a nobleman or a mercer you had little chance of appearing there. It is surprising, for example that none of his professional helpers such as Wynkyn de Worde are mentioned. Indeed, if de Worde had died before Caxton we should probably not have known that he had been Caxton's foreman. The technical side of book production was clearly not considered relevant to the literary works produced. Similarly there are very few references to clerics of any type, and those that do occur refer to non-literary matters. The Abbot of Westminster had asked Caxton to modernize a writ which caused him to reflect on the changing nature of English, and the High Canon of Waterford had discussed with him the truth of the legends of Tundale's cave. An anonymous 'worshipful preest and a parsone' (2b:19) was the source of the story about the proud dean and humble vicar in *Æsop's Fables*. Caxton seldom mentions events and people from his own past. In *Eneydos* he relates the story of the mercer Sheffelde and the eggs, but he does not say that he was present or that he was connected with the episode in any way. Otherwise he introduces no English people from his past life apart from an oblique reference to his parents. The people he mentions from his past life are Sir John Capons and Sir John de Banste who were both connected with the Duchy of Burgundy. Yet while Governor of the English Nation at Bruges he probably met many important Englishmen, and it is surprising that he had no stories to relate about them or which they had told him.

The majority of the people mentioned are authors. Foreign ones are either the authors of the books he translated or else their works are quoted and referred to. In the latter category are the authors of the classics and the fathers who were now respectable authorities. The authors of the books he translated were generally more recent since he likes to use up-to-date works. It is possible that he may have met some of these more recent authors, but he gives no indication that he had. Thus he refers in very respectful tones to Raoul Lefèvre, the author of the French versions of *History of Troy* and *Jason*. Raoul had been secretary to Duke Philip of Burgundy so that Caxton with his interest in literary works and the house of Burgundy might have known him while he was in Bruges. But there is no evidence that he did and the information he gives about him, like that for the other authors of the French originals, probably came from the manuscripts or books he was using for his translations. The English authors mentioned were from the fourteenth century, like Gower, Chaucer, and Trevisa; or from the fifteenth century, like Lydgate, Burgh, Malory and Tiptoft. It is unlikely that he had met any of the latter authors. It cannot even be shown that he met Skelton, whose work he praises so effusively in *Eneydos*. Details of Skelton's life are scarce and we do not know where he was in the late 1480s, but we may imagine that, had Caxton met him, he would have said so. The only English author Caxton seems to have known personally was Earl Rivers, whom he knew perhaps more as patron than as author. Caxton did know several Italians who were in England at this time. Pietro Carmeliano saw the *Sex Epistolae* through the press and Caxton published two works by Lorenzo Guglielmo Traversagni who taught for a time at Cambridge. Whether he met Stephano Surigone is more doubtful, though Surigone's epitaph to Chaucer is printed in Caxton's edition of Chaucer's translation of Boethius. It is perhaps surprising that Caxton knew so few authors, but this is explained partly by his interest in French rather than English literature and partly by his concern for books rather than for personalities.

Other Englishmen mentioned in the prologues and epilogues fall into fairly well-defined categories. First are the many heroes of the past who are held up as examples of chivalry. These include not only such famous men as Edward I and Edward III and their followers, but also more recent ones such as the Duke of Bedford, John Tiptoft and Sir John Fastolfe. The details provided of such heroes depend on the sources Caxton had available. His patrons form the other main group of Englishmen referred to in his writings. Some he never met, such as the Duke of Clarence and the Earl of Arundel. The kings, Edward IV, Richard III and Henry VII, he probably met in audience, but he was not a member of the court and his contacts with them were probably slight. Even his exact relationship to Margaret of Burgundy is uncertain, though he had audiences with her on several occasions. It is unlikely that he was on any terms of familiarity with her. He knew best his two special patrons, Elizabeth Woodville and Earl Rivers, though one must remember that their business may often have been conducted through intermediaries. In *Moral Proverbs*

we hear of Earl Rivers's secretary, who was presumably repre-
senting the Earl at the printer's office. After 1485 Caxton was
patronized by the Earl of Oxford as well as by the king's mother
and wife, but the personal contact with them would also have been
slight.

There are many references in Caxton's prologues and epilogues
to unnamed sponsors. Some can be identified, particularly where
the reference is to a single person. But when he refers vaguely to
'diverce gentlemen' it is difficult to know whether he was referring
to specific people or whether he was using a formula. For example,
in the prologue to *Charles the Great* Caxton wrote that 'somme
persones of noble estate and degree' (16a: 51) asked him to translate the life of Charles into English. Later in the same prologue he
states that he made the translation to satisfy the request of 'my
good synguler lordes and specyal maysters and frendes' (16a:
59–60). But in the epilogue he wrote that he had been asked to
make the translation by 'a good and synguler frende of myn,
Maister Wylliam Daubeney' (16b: 2–3). There is no reference to
Daubeney in the prologue and none to the lords and friends in the
epilogue. This discrepancy can be explained in several ways.
The translation was completed under Richard III and the printing
under Henry VII; it may be that a reference to Daubeney would
have been imprudent in Richard's reign and so he is mentioned
only in the epilogue. Or possibly Daubeney was associated with
the book at a late stage and so appeared only in the epilogue. But
these and other theories assume that Daubeney is the principal
patron and that the lords and friends are little more than a formula
which Caxton used to make his work seem more appealing. If
this is so here, it may equally apply elsewhere. Thus in the *History
of Troy* Caxton says that Margaret of Burgundy ordered him to
complete the translation, and the finished work is dedicated to her.
She would appear to be the principal sponsor of the work. Yet he
printed it because he had promised copies to 'dyverce gentilmen
and to my frendes' (50e: 9), which is hardly likely to be accurate
since he finished the translation in Cologne where he had gone to
learn the art of printing. Consequently where he refers to unnamed sponsors in the plural, it is better to assume that a particular patron was not involved and that he is using a formula to
make his work attractive to potential buyers.

It is undoubtedly among mercers and officials that Caxton had
his friends – and this is only natural. Both Pratt and Daubeney are
referred to as his special friends, and Bryce had also commissioned
and paid for a book. The nobility were his lords and masters, but

the mercers were his friends. It is easy enough to overlook this fact since the names of the nobility occur so frequently in his pages, but as I have tried to show he knew few of them personally and he was probably on good terms with only one or two. His friends and regular acquaintances came from his own class.

Caxton's Language

IT is now accepted that although Caxton was responsible for the introduction of many words into English, the bulk of them are direct translations of words in his sources. His own vocabulary was not very extensive and it appears that he did not go out of his way to enrich it. His own prose contains few examples of first occurrences in English. This difference between his own composition and his translated work can be recognized in this volume because several of his prologues and epilogues were modelled upon Continental sources. For example, parts of the prologues to *Charles the Great*, *Mirror of the World* and *Polychronicon* are translated from French originals. These sections contain many words of an exotic flavour which are found rarely, if at all, elsewhere in English. *Polychronicon* is worth considering in more detail. Caxton's prologue is based on a lost French version of Poggio's Latin translation of the prologue to the *Historical Library* by Diodorus Siculus. As the French text is not extant, it is uncertain that all the words introduced by Caxton were taken from there, but in most cases it remains the most reasonable interpretation. They are:

ASSERTRYCE The feminine form of an 'assertor' or advocate, not recorded in either OED or MED. The *-ice* ending from French was popular with Lydgate, on whose example Caxton could have modelled *assertryce*. But this form is almost certainly from the lost French original.

BRUTYSSH Caxton elsewhere uses *brute*, which entered English in the late fifteenth century for OED records it from c. 1460–70 and MED from 1475. But *brutish* is not recorded at all in MED, and not till 1555 in OED. *Brute* is the form based on French, and *brutish* is an English development with the addition of the native suffix *-ish*. Its introduction may be attributed to Caxton.

DYVULGACION OED does not record this word before 1540, though both *divulgen* and the past participle *divulgate* are found in Middle English.

INCONVENYTYS This occurs in the doublet 'errours and inconvenytys'. Possibly this form is a misprint for *inconvenientise*, recorded in MED as a borrowing from French; or it may simply be a variant.

MALEFAYTES Although *bienfait* (benefit) is common in Caxton and Middle English, *malefayte* is not recorded in OED. It may possibly have been more current than its omission from OED suggests for it is common in French.

MERYTORYOUSLY OED records this word from 1502 in the sense 'in a meritorious manner'. Caxton's sense of 'as a meritorious cause' is presumably taken over direct from the French original.

OCYOSYTE Caxton also used this word in 1483 in his translation of *Caton*, where it is a translation from the French.

VECORDYOUS This word is not recorded in OED and must be a loan from French, though only *vecorde* is listed in Godefroy.

Since many of these words are not recorded in OED, they were no doubt very rare. Caxton certainly did not use them again, and in *Polychronicon* he was influenced by the French source he was using.

Of more importance are the words found for the first time in Caxton's own prose. Unlike words in *Polychronicon*, these are of a more mundane quality. They are:

AMPLE Used adverbially in the phrase 'is more ample expowned' (79a:48). According to OED several of the first occurrences of the adjectival use are from Caxton's works where it is translated from French *ample*. The adverbial usage is not recorded in OED before 1549.

AOURNATE Used by Caxton of Chaucer's 'aournate writynges' (11:17–18), though elsewhere he uses the form *aourned* as in the 'fair and aourned volumes' (75a:13) of the *Mirror of the World*, where it is taken over from French. The verb *aournen* was common in late Middle English, and *aournate* is simply a Latinate form of the participial adjective.

BAGGE-BERARS This is not recorded in either OED or MED, but both elements of the compound are common enough. It is used of the messengers or legal attendants of the various courts mentioned in Caxton's tirade against the multiplicity of legal officers (45c:10). Since Caxton shows a close knowledge of the legal system, it may possibly be a technical term which is not recorded elsewhere.

CONJURYE This word, from French *conjuré*, is also possibly a technical term. It may have been used in the gilds, though it is the only reference in OED and is not recorded in MED. Caxton used it in the doublet 'cytezeyn and conjurye' of London (15a:13).

CONTEMPLARE This word should not really be included as Caxton used it also in book II of his *History of Troy*, from where he remembered it long enough to include it in the epilogue to that book.[1]

CROYSYNG 'A crusade'. The verb *croise* 'to go on crusade' is found in Middle English, and the noun was normally *croiserie*. It would seem that Caxton formed a verbal noun from the verb.

DEPARTE Used in the meaning 'to die' at 24:47. OED records this sense from 1501, though MED records the sense 'to cause to die' and such phrases as *departen from lif* much earlier.

DEPESSHED Used in the doublet 'depesshed and solde' (46a: 24) where it has the meaning 'distributed, sold'. Although this is the first recorded example in OED, Caxton also used the word elsewhere in his translations from French. It is taken from French *dépêcher*.

ENBELLISHER Used of Chaucer's contribution to the English language in *Boethius* (7:44). Although this is the first recorded instance of this noun, the verb *embellishen* is recorded quite often from the fifteenth century in MED, and it is used in passages in praise of Chaucer.

ENHERYTAGES 'Inheritance' (96a: 24). Borrowed from French, the word is not recorded by OED till 1559, but the verb was not infrequent in the fifteenth century.

EQUYVOCACIONS The sense in *History of Troy* (50e: 33) appears to be 'spellings'. This sense is not recorded elsewhere, although the meaning 'speaking in different ways of the same thing' which might be considered applicable in *History of Troy* is recorded by MED from 1450.

EXPERIMENTLY With the meaning 'by experience' (24:29), the word is not recorded before 1546 by OED and is not recorded at all in MED. But Caxton used *experiment* 'experience' in passages translated from French, and the adverbial use is a simple extension of that.

GENERALLY Used in the phrase 'in generally' (73a:25). OED records the usage with *in* from 1557 only, though the word *generally* by itself was common.

INTYTELYNG 'Title' (56d:5). It is recorded in OED from *a.* 1662; it is not in MED. The verb is found in Middle English and Caxton also uses it. This is another case of Caxton being the first to use a verbal noun of a verb already well established in the language.

[1] N. F. Blake, 'Word borrowings in Caxton's original writings', *English Language Notes*, 6 (1968), 87–90.

MATERNAL This word is used commonly in Caxton's prologues and epilogues after his epilogue to the *Cordial* (1479). He may indeed have learned the word from Earl Rivers who translated the *Cordial*. It is one of the few new words to enter Caxton's vocabulary permanently.

MUSICALLE The sense of 'of or pertaining to the muses', which is what Caxton appears to have meant by this word in *Eneydos* (36a:98), is not recorded elsewhere, though the word was already known in English in other senses. It may be a Caxton invention, though as he used it in reference to Skelton he could possibly have acquired it from that poet.

NECESSARILY Used in the phrase 'necessarily requysite' (79a: 54-5). OED records the adverb from 1488-9, but the adjective was common in Middle English. This is another example of the adverbial form of a common adjective being found first in Caxton's own prose.

OVERCHARGEABLE, OVERCURYOUS The use of *over-* as a prefix dates back to Old English times, though in late Middle English it was extended to many new words. Both the words to which Caxton prefixed *over-* were common.

PERCEYVYNGLY The adverb is not recorded in OED; but the verb and the participial adjective are both found earlier.

PROSPEROUSLY As with the previous form, the adjective was found before Caxton's time, but the adverb is first recorded in his own prose.

RECOVURE This form is not recorded in OED, but *recovery* was used from the fifteenth century in English. *Recovure* probably represents a French variant (see Godefroy *Recovre*), which Caxton may well have learned from Earl Rivers since it occurs in the prologue to the *Cordial* (24:47).

REGYSTRE At 15a:122 it is used in the sense 'table of contents', which is not recorded in OED before 1585. But the word existed already in other senses and Caxton himself used it elsewhere.

RYPYNG Used at 15a:51. The verbal noun is not recorded in OED, but the verb is common enough. Elsewhere in this prologue Caxton uses *rypenes*.

RUDEHEDE Used by Caxton in *Life of Our Lady* (74:4) to rhyme with *rede*. It may be considered a nonce word arising from the exigencies of rhyme instead of the more usual *rudeness*.

SEMPITERNALLY The adverb is not recorded in OED till 1509, but the adjective was current from the early fifteenth century.

SITUACION In the sense 'the place or location of something in relation to its surroundings' (75a:29) this word is first recorded in OED from Caxton's *Eneydos*. But the word also occurs in the *Mirror of the World* and Caxton no doubt took it from there for this prologue.

SLEYGHTLY In the sense 'indifferently' as at 2b: 34 this word is first recorded in 1599 in OED. But its other senses are recorded earlier.

SMATRE OED records the sense 'to dabble in' as at 73a: 48 only from 1530; but other senses of the word are found before.

VICEROYE Used of Sir John Capons who was 'viceroye and governour of Aragon' (47e: 4). Caxton has here probably anglicized the French titles which Capons had. OED records the word from *a.* 1524.

VIRYLYTE As in 'theyr myddle eage callyd virylyte' (79a: 75). Caxton may have found this word in *Of Old Age*; OED records it from 1586.

WELL-SAYENG A compound with the meaning 'eloquent writing' which is recorded only as a nonce word in Shakespeare by OED. The two constituent elements are common and compounds in *well-* are not infrequent.

This list reveals the following details. Very few loanwords have been introduced directly from French; and the few there are have simply been remembered from the text Caxton was issuing long enough to be included in the prologue or epilogue. There is no conscious attempt to enrich the language by using French words, which is perhaps surprising when one considers the admiration he felt for Lydgate and Skelton who both introduced many new words. In this respect Caxton was not an innovator, and in his own prose one tends to find words which were fashionable at the end of the fifteenth century but which were not brand new. The other words in the list represent either different grammatical categories of words already in the language or new senses of existing words. In many cases it may be considered fortuitous that Caxton provides the earliest example of a word since there is nothing unusual or personal about the new creations. Indeed as the *Middle English Dictionary* progresses it is probable that several words will be eliminated from the list. We may, I think, conclude that Caxton was not interested in enlarging his own vocabulary or even in enlarging the English wordstock. Most of the new words in his translations probably found their way there by chance, and when left to his own resources Caxton's vocabulary was certainly limited.

Another aspect of Caxton's language which has received some

comment is his sentence structure.[1] The comment has not often
been favourable because his sentences are considered too rambling
and unorganized. Any attempt to discuss his structure is compli-
cated by two complementary reasons. The first is that Caxton
lived at a time before English had been subjected to the gram-
marians' rules of syntax. We cannot therefore always tell what was
acceptable then and how far the tolerance of what we call 'loose-
ness' extended. The second is that Caxton's punctuation is confusing, perfunctory and misleading. So modern editors, as I too,
punctuate the text in the way they think most appropriate.
Unfortunately some modern punctuation is informed by modern
syntactical ideals and modern interpretations of fifteenth-century
words. Thus R. R. Aurner in his discussion of Caxton's structure
prints 7: 40–50 as one sentence which he calls a 'quaint rambling,
ununified sentence, in which three quite distinct ideas are made
structurally one'.[2] In my own edition I have started a new sentence at *Of whom* (7:46), for then it was quite in order to start a
new sentence with *who* or *which* or associated words (see below).
The decision how to punctuate the texts will clearly affect such
statistics as word-counts per sentence, which will in turn influence
the commentator's opinion about the quality of the prose.
Furthermore, surveys of Caxton's prose tend to assume that all
his work is in the same style. This is not so, for sometimes in a
prologue or epilogue he will aim at a high style, as often in the
openings, whereas elsewhere he is satisfied with a more colloquial
and informal style, particularly in the passages of reported
dialogue.

First we may consider the question of Caxton's rambling sentences. Some of them are indeed lengthy, but that does not mean
that they are unstructured. Consider, for example, this long
sentence in *Blanchardin and Englantine* (6:14–26):

> For, under correction, in my jugement it is as requesyte other-
> whyle to rede in auncyent hystoryes of noble fayttes and
> valyaunt actes of armes and warre, whiche have ben achyeved
> in olde tyme of many noble prynces, lordes and knyghtes, as
> wel for to see and knowe their valyauntnes for to stande in the
> specyal grace and love of their ladyes, and in lyke wyse for
> gentyl yonge ladyes and damoysellys for to lerne to be stedfaste
> and constaunt in their parte to theym that they ones have
> promysed and agreed to, suche as have putte their lyves ofte in

[1] See particularly R. R. Aurner, 'Caxton and the English sentence', *University of Wisconsin Studies in Language and Literature*, 18 (1923), 23–59.
[2] *Ibid.* p. 29.

jeopardye for to playse theym to stande in grace, as it is to
occupye theym and studye overmoche in bokes of contemplacion.

The sentence is built round the framework of the parallel clauses
it is as requesyte otherwhyle to . . . *as it is to,* though some readers may
fail to recognize this because of the large number of subordinate
clauses appended to the first of the two parallels. While the first
subordinate clause, a relative clause introduced by *whiche,* is
unambiguous, some difficulty may arise with the following ones.
The introduction of the *as wel* prompts a modern reader to anti-
cipate an *as,* which is not found since Caxton has used *in lyke wyse*
instead. This has the same sense as *as,* even though preceded by
and, and it is the difference between our own and fifteenth-century
usage which creates this difficulty. Furthermore, these two clauses
introduced by *as wel* and *in lyke wyse* do not seem strictly parallel.
This is simply because Caxton has inserted the *for gentyl yonge
ladyes and damoysellys* after *in lyke wyse,* for although all of us can
profit from the consideration of past heroism, it is only young
ladies who should remain constant to those to whom they have
betrothed themselves. Other difficulties for a modern reader may
be the *suche as,* which here has the sense both of 'which' referring
back to *theym* and of 'because of', and the use of the past tense in
have putte. Again these difficulties arise from our unfamiliarity
with fifteenth-century idiom. Once the sentence is broken down,
its structure is apparent. Caxton's ideas are logically and gram-
matically presented – though that is not to say that they could
not have been expounded more cogently and succinctly, for the
expansion of the first half of the sentence prevents it from being a
stylistically pleasing one.

In the previous sentence Caxton was motivated by a desire to
include a considerable amount of subordinate material. It is this
which normally leads him to depart from a grammatical base,
though this does not mean he could not organize his material
since one can see what the progression of his ideas is. A good
example is provided by a paragraph in the prologue to *Caton*
(15a:25–47). I have printed this paragraph as several sentences
in this edition. But everything in this paragraph is what Caxton
remembers and it all looks forward to the first sentence of the
following paragraph: 'O blessyd Lord, whanne I remembre this,
I am al abasshyd'. It would of course be possible to punctuate
the paragraph and the following sentence I have just quoted as
one sentence, which would then be a rambling one in the extreme.

But it is doubtful whether Caxton meant it to be read in this way, since he introduces several disparate ideas. Not to do so, however, does mean that some of the sentences are ungrammatical by our standards. Thus the opening sentence consists of a protasis without an apodosis:

> O whan I remembre the noble Romayns that for the comyn wele of the cyte of Rome they spente not only theyr moevable goodes, but they put theyr bodyes and lyves in jeopardy and to the deth, as by many a noble ensample we may see in th'actes of Romayns, as of the two noble Scipions, Affrican and Asyan, Actilius and many other, and amonge al other the noble Catho, auctour and maker of this book whiche he hath lefte for to remayne ever to all the peple for to lerne in hit and to knowe how every man ought to rewle and governe hym in this lyf.

This *whan* looks forward to the next paragraph *whanne I remembre this*. This latter 'when' is the recapitulation of all that has gone before and stylistically the brevity of this sentence contrasts well with the prolixity of the preceding paragraph. Yet it is unlikely that the first sentence of this paragraph which I have just quoted should be extended so far that it included the second 'when'. This could be done only quite arbitrarily by using semi-colons instead of fullstops and by including in a sentence many different ideas. And even if this were done, there would still be parts of the sentence which would remain ungrammatical by our standards. The sentence introduced by *And bycause* is not grammatical for there is no main clause to follow the subordinate clause thus created; but this is so whether this sentence remains a complete sentence or is punctuated as part of another. It is more reasonable to assume that just as there was more tolerance of variety in spelling and vocabulary, so also there was more freedom in syntactical construction. This may mean that Caxton was not a profound stylist, but it does not mean that he could not organize what he wrote or that he necessarily lost himself in his prose. The organization of the paragraph is clear enough, and his inclusion of the second 'when' shows he had not lost control.

That there was more syntactical freedom then than now is further indicated by similar constructions elsewhere. The opening of the prologue to *Jason* (71a: 1–16) is parallel to the paragraph in *Caton*. This opens *For as moche as*, a construction which in Caxton's prose is normally followed by a 'therefore'. In *Jason* this is not found till after a second *for as moche as*. Thus as in the case of the 'when' in *Caton*, Caxton leaves the first 'as much as' isolated for

it has no main clause to follow it. Again I have not punctuated
the text in a way that would bring these two examples of 'as
much as' into the same sentence since they are separated by quite
different ideas which clearly form independent sentences in their
own right. And again it must be pointed out that the development
of the thought of the passage is logical and coherent.

More rambling in style possibly is the first section of Caxton's
original part of the prologue to *Polychronicon* (86a: 116–39). Once
more it is relatively easy to follow the sense of the passage; the
major difficulty stems from the lack of complete parallelism in the
piece, which in its turn leads to some possible ambiguity. Thus
the sentence opens:

> Thenne syth historye is so precious and also prouffytable, I
> have delybered to wryte twoo bookes notable, retenyng in them
> many noble historyes as the lyves, myracles, passyons, and deth
> of dyverse hooly sayntes, whiche shal be comprysed by th'ayde
> and suffraunce of Almyghty God in one of them whiche is
> named *Legenda Aurea*, that is the *Golden Legende*, and that other
> book is named *Polycronycon*, in whiche book ben comprised
> briefly many wonderful historyees . . .'.

The difficulty here lies in the *retenyng in them* which applies not
only to the *many noble historyes as the lyves* immediately following,
but also to the *many wonderful historyees* at the end of this part of
the sentence. This is obscured by the change in construction half-
way through, for the second part is introduced *and that other book
is named*. If, however, Caxton had written 'retenyng in them
many noble historyes . . . *Golden Legende*, and many wonderful
historyees in that other book which is named *Polycronycon* . . .' his
meaning would be less obscure. But Caxton used his own construction for a good reason: he wanted to qualify his *many wonderful historyees* with a long list of the contents of the *Polychronicon*
for that was the book he was printing. Therefore he wanted to
leave the *many wonderful historyees* to the end of this part of the
sentence so that the details of the contents which follow would
stand in apposition. So the progression of the sentence is this: I
intend to write two books: contents of one and its name, name
of the other and its contents. The basis of a balanced contrast is
there, but it is not achieved because of the expansion of the
second list of contents and because there is not sufficient verbal
echo between the two halves. The rest of the complete sentence
follows a clear path. Caxton mentions the original author and then
the translator. Finally he includes his printing and his own con-

tributions to the text. Stylistically we might say that having started out by comparing two books, Caxton ought not to have spent the rest of the sentence giving details about only one of them. But his meaning is clear even though his style is far from polished.

Long sentences sometimes occur in passages where Caxton is giving information: the contents of a volume, the causes which led him to print a text, etc. It is partly this wish to include so much material that leads to the infelicities of his style. But such sentences occur only sporadically. Equally typical are passages of reported speech and rhetorical colouring. The former are quite common and are naturally much simpler in style. The sentences are shorter and the piece is usually constructed on a 'he said . . . I said' framework. These passages are found particularly in texts printed for the nobility: *History of Troy* for Margaret, *Dicts or Sayings* for Earl Rivers, and the second edition of the *Canterbury Tales* for an anonymous patron. They describe the conversations Caxton had with his patrons about the text. In *Eneydos* we are presented with a variant form, for the narrative passage about the mercer Sheffelde relapses into reported speech between him and the lady of the house. Perhaps more typical of Caxton are the passages of rhetoric with which he seeks to impress his readers. Consequently they are found particularly at the beginning of his prologues. In most cases he has not so much arranged his sentences in a rhetorical pattern as increased the number of his adjectives and nouns to make the piece more heavy and pompous. Thus in the opening of *Blanchardin and Eglantine* we find

> Unto the right noble, puyssaunt and excellent pryncesse, my redoubted lady, my Lady Margarete, Duchesse of Somercete, moder unto our naturel and soverayn lord and most Crysten kynge, Henry the Seventh, by the grace of God Kyng of Englonde and of Fraunce, Lord of Yrelond etc., I Wyllyam Caxton, his most indygne, humble subgette and lytil servaunt, presente this lytyl book unto the noble grace of my sayd lady. (6:1–8)

Here one may notice the many doublets and triplets (*noble, puyssaunt and excellent*; or *humble subgette and lytil servaunt*), the use of titles to give weight, the inverted word order to bring the reader's attention directly to the patron, and the otherwise simple thought. Passages like this were found in contemporary French works and were no doubt imitated by Caxton. The same applies to the more rhetorical openings which introduce an abstract idea, such as that to the second edition of the *Canterbury Tales*. That is itself an imitation of the opening to the prologue of *Polychronicon*, which is a translation from French. These passages are even weightier, but the rhetorical colour comes more from the lexis than the syntax even here.

Other features of Caxton's syntax will be given only summary treatment. Only those features which might cause a little hesitation in a modern reader are outlined below.

(1) Opening a sentence

The majority of the sentences have a coordinate construction so that *and* appears frequently. But a relative may be used to begin a sentence and then it approximates in meaning to modern 'this'.

> Whiche Boecius was an excellente auctour (7: 10–11);
> Wherein in myne oppynyon he hath (7:27);
> Of whom emong all other (11:24).

It will be seen that there is as yet no specialization in the use of the relatives. Caxton also commonly uses a participle to open a sentence:

> Bysechynge my sayd ladyes bountyuous grace (6:39–40);
> Fynysshed and translated (9b:2).

(2) Connectives

Caxton's use of connectives to link one clause with another may sometimes cause difficulties. An *and* may be omitted where we would include it:

> for the erudicion and lernyng of suche as ben ignoraunt and not knowyng of it, atte requeste of ... (7:34–5).

On the other hand it may be included where we today would not use it. Caxton's 'as much as' is followed in the next clause by 'therefore', but occasionally this appears as 'and therefore' as at 47a:53. Caxton's use of *and* in some instances approximates to modern 'who' as in:

> There was a noble clerke named Pogius of Florence, and was secretary ... (15a:61–2).

Which has a much wider range of uses than today. At 29a:46 one may take it either as redundant or in the sense 'although':

> he thought that Socrates spared the sothe and wrote of women more than trouthe, whyche I cannot thinke that so trewe a man and ...

Which and *that* are used indiscriminately:

> they had axyd of hym whiche was the best boke of them alle and
> that he reputed for best (15a: 66–7).

That may occur frequently with some examples being redundant:

> to th'entent that yf my sayd lord or ony other persone whatsom-
> ever he or she be that shal rede or here it that if they be not wel
> plesyd wythall that they . . . (29a: 146–8);
> So after longe tyme that this worshipful man (2b: 28–9).

The use of *ne* is in some cases redundant:

> Wherof I mervaylle that my sayd lord hath not wreton them, ne
> what hath mevyd hym so to do, ne what cause he hadde at that
> tyme (29a: 38–40).

(3) Pronouns

As commonly in the fifteenth century the subject personal pronoun is often omitted:

> Also hath procured (24:19);
> happened that to my hande cam (36a:3).

A subject pronoun may also be superfluous:

> that al they that shal rede or here it that they may (9a: 30–1).

A redundant object pronoun may be found associated with *which*:

> bookes whyche wryters have abrydgyd it (11: 34).

(4) Verbs

The main verb may be omitted:

> and had ben senatour of that noble and famous cite Rome, and
> also his two sones senatours for their prudence and wisedom
> (7: 13–15);
> whiche to me I repute a comandement and verili glad to obeye
> (38:18–19).

The use of tenses is often different from our own:

> Whiche Boecius was an excellente auctour . . . and also had
> translated (7: 10–12).

(5) Word order

Variation from modern word order is found particularly in plac-
ing the subject after the verb:

> therby more surely myght be remembred the four last thingis
> (24:11–12);
> And what worship had he at Rome (79f: 31–2).

Themes and Critical Vocabulary

In his prologues and epilogues Caxton turns time and again to the question of the value of the books he printed. Although he had definite ideas as to what he should print, his critical vocabulary was not well developed and he had no general theory as to what constitutes a work of literature. He relies on the critical language and themes of the fifteenth century and on occasions this can lead to contradictions. In discussing the structure of a work, he does not consider what constitutes a literary whole, for he is concerned simply with the inviolability of the received text. In *Dicts or Sayings* Earl Rivers had decided to leave out certain letters which were 'lytil appertinent' (29a:29) to the work as a whole, presumably because they were letters and not proverbial sayings. Caxton agreed with this decision. But he insisted on including the sayings of Socrates which Rivers had also left out, for otherwise those who knew the work in French might complain of the omission. So he reinstated this passage, though he included it with his prologue as a separate section. He never considered whether these two principles of operation were reconcilable: one section is included for completeness and the other is left out for incompatibility. This example underlines his normal method of procedure. He had no fixed theory about literary works, but he dealt with each problem as it arose and justified it by resort to traditional themes and language.

The majority of Caxton's remarks about his books concern either the purpose and contents of his book or their style. The contents of each book are described at varying length. Sometimes he will give what is a short summary of the book, as he does in *Of Old Age*. Generally he is less specific. The contents of *Blanchardin and Eglantine* are described in this way:

Whiche boke specyfyeth of the noble actes and fayttes of warre achyeved by a noble and victorious prynce named Blanchardin, sone unto the Kynge of Fryse, for the love of a noble pryncesse callyd Eglantyne, otherwyse named in Frensche *l'orguylleuse d'amours*, whiche is as moche to saye in Englyshe as 'the proude lady of love', Quene of Tormaday; and of the grete adventures, labours, anguysshes and many other grete dyseases of theym

44

bothe tofore they myghte atteyne for to come to the fynall conclusion of their desired love, as al alonge by the grace of God it
shall be shewed in th'istorye of thys present book (6:29–39).

This description could with an adjustment of the proper nouns be
used for almost any romance for it lacks any concrete details
which distinguish this story from others. It is typical that he
should describe a book's content in such a general way, often
indeed by employing many abstract nouns. Thus the *Canterbury
Tales* consists of 'tales, whyche ben of noblesse, wysedom,
gentylesse, myrthe, and also of veray holynesse and vertue,
wherin he fynysshyth thys sayd booke' (11:29–31); and in *King
Arthur* one can find 'many joyous and playsaunt hystoryes and
noble and renomed actes of humanyte, gentylnesse and chyvalryes.
For herein may be seen noble chyvalrye, curtosye, humanyte,
frendlynesse, hardynesse, love, frendshyp, cowardyse, murdre,
hate, vertue and synne.' (72a:109–13). This use of abstract nouns
in enumerating the contents suggests he was more concerned with
the tone and moral implications of his books than with their
specific narrative details. It was not the story but what it stood for
that was important. Hence in commending his books be may say
of their contents that they are 'joyefull' (6:13), 'strange
and mervayllous' (50b:7) or 'vertuous good' (73a:23),
but it is clear that of these qualities entertainment was of
least, and moral character of most importance. It is certainly
the latter attribute which is selected most frequently for comment.

   It is the moral utility of the works which is also stressed as the
reason for their being printed. Instruction and not enjoyment is
the motive for publication. One might expect this reason to be a
strong one for recommending didactic and religious books. In
these the theme of avoiding sin and amending one's life is common. The *Book of Good Manners* will be 'used emonge the people
for th'amendement of their maners and to th'encreace of vertuous
lyvyng' (9a:17–18); *Caton* will teach a man to 'eschewe alle
vyces and ensiewe vertue' (15a:72); and *Cordial* will help people
to 'knowe themself herafter the better and amende thair lyvyng
or they departe and lose this tyme of grace to the recouvure of their
salvacion' (24:45–8). However, the ideal of instruction lies behind
the printing of the chivalric works as well. Knights should know
how they ought to behave and stories of the past should inspire
them to emulate the heroes of the past. Thus such works as *Feats
of Arms* and *Order of Chivalry* teach a knight the code of chivalric

behaviour by outlining the rules of courtly conduct. *King Arthur*, on the other hand, shows present-day nobles how people behaved in the past so that they can emulate their actions. This attitude is reinforced by the themes of the nine worthies and a past golden age.

The theme of the nine worthies occurs only in those works which deal with one of their number, *King Arthur*, *Charles the Great* and *Siege of Jerusalem*. In *Charles the Great* only the three Christian worthies are mentioned, but in the other two all nine are enumerated. No attempt is made to distinguish between the actions performed by these heroes or in what ways one is distinguished from another, for Caxton concentrates more upon the sources in which their stories are preserved than upon what they actually did. Caxton never develops this theme. Other writers, such as the author of *The Squire of Low Degree* and Skelton in *Phyllyp Sparowe*, introduce a far greater range of heroes including many remembered in English romances. Caxton is quite content with the theme of the nine worthies, for whom there are respectable authorities. The concept of a past golden age which can be compared with the present is a more general one which is not developed uniformly in the various prologues and epilogues. In terms of chivalry it is discussed by Caxton in the epilogue to *Order of Chivalry*. Here he seems to think that all past ages produced their heroes, for he mentions not only Brenius and Belinus but also many English warriors since the Conquest. It is only in the recent past that chivalry has fallen into desuetude and knights have become lazy. It is partly for this reason that he feels it necessary to arouse his contemporaries to go on crusade against the Turks. Indeed, the absence of any united action against the Turks is one of the reasons for his conviction that chivalry is dead. Otherwise the past is regarded as a time when people worked for the public good in distinction to his own time when everyone is out to line his own pocket. In London men seek to increase their own wealth and take no interest in corporate affairs; lawyers go to the courts for personal profit and not for justice; and England which had been great in the past has fallen into a period of weakness and decay. Naturally there is no attempt to localize the past when everything was ideal, though the Roman republic is occasionally held out as an example when men furthered the good of the state. The past is not of much interest in itself except as a scourge to goad contemporary people to better and nobler deeds. Thus in the *Book of Good Manners* it is not only in comparison with the past that London is found wanting, but also in comparison with other

major cities abroad. The golden age is almost any other place and
time than late fifteenth-century England.

It is rarely that the reason for a book's publication is more
specific. But the *Rule of St Benet* was printed so that Benedictines
could observe their rule more strictly, the *Description of Britain* so
that Englishmen would know the geography of these islands
better, and the *Vocabulary* that people could learn French and
English more easily. These are more technical books and a more
practical reason was therefore necessary. The more general books
of all kinds are to improve the readers' behaviour. It is somewhat
strange therefore that Caxton should insist on the elitist character
of his books. They are not for ordinary people, but for the nobles
and the educated. This theme occurs in several of his works and
not only in courtly works like *Order of Chivalry*, but also in translations of the classics such as *Eneydos* and *Of Old Age*. Who he
meant by his noble readers he never defined, and probably such
remarks were meant to indicate that his works were fashionable
rather than provincial.

The desire to emphasize the moral character of his work may
have led Caxton to include a number of proverbial sayings,
though many of them are found in prologues and epilogues in
French and other English works. His claim that he printed so
many of his books to avoid idleness, the 'moder of lyes and stepdame of vertues' (47a:17), which appears so frequently in his
works, could readily be paralleled from other writers. Similarly
the insistence that all literary works are written for our instruction, a saying which is attributed to various fathers, is common
enough. Caxton used it as his justification for printing romances
and other seemingly secular works, since they could thus be read
as allegories and parables.

His comments on style consist of complaints about the English
language and about his own lack of rhetorical training and remarks concerning his sources. English was an impoverished
language which had been greatly enriched by Chaucer. His own
translations attempted to emulate the language of Chaucer, but
they often failed in this because of his lack of rhetorical expertise.
In *Eneydos* and *Polychronicon* he remarks how wretched English
had been in the past. It had been 'rude and old' and it had contained so many words no longer intelligible that it was difficult to
make old texts comprehensible any more. *Rude* is his favourite
word of disapproval, and his own writings are characterized as
'rude', though it usually occurs in a doublet with 'simple',
'broad', 'imperfect' or 'common'. A statement to this effect can

be found in almost every prologue and epilogue because he con-
tinually felt called on to apologize for the style of his translations.
Probably the words had little particular significance other than a
vague disapproval. If anything, they are used to imply 'provincial'
and 'uncultured' as against 'fashionable' and 'elegant'. Elegance
springs from rhetoric and eloquence, two terms which Caxton
used indiscriminately. He apologizes for his lack of these on three
occasions. In *Blanchardin and Eglantine* he laments 'ne knowynge
the arte of rethoryk ne of suche gaye termes as now be sayd in
these dayes and used' (6: 43–4). In *Charles the Great* there are 'no
gaye termes ne subtyl ne newe eloquence' (16a: 66–7). Similarly
Feats of Arms contains no 'curyous ne gaye termes of rethoryk'
(38: 35). The phrase 'gay terms' occurs in all examples. The terms
were of course the figures of rhetoric with which one decorated
a work. Although 'gay' was used frequently to describe works of
literature – it was used by Lydgate in his *Troy-Book* of Chaucer's
style – the phrase 'gay terms' is not recorded outside Caxton's
works. By it Caxton meant 'eloquent and pleasing rhetorical
figures'.

He did not use this phrase to describe either Chaucer's works or
the style of his French sources. Chaucer had enriched the English
language, and Caxton usually expressed this by using other
expressions. Chaucer had *embellished, ornated* or *made fair* the
English language with his *fair* and *ornate* style. Skelton likewise
had translated the classics into English with 'polysshed and ornate
termes' (36: 94–5). One must necessarily suppose that by these
expressions he meant that both had used an elaborate vocabulary
which was Latin or French based. The enrichment consisted in
replacing old and unfashionable words with new and more elegant
ones. As it happens, *ornate* is not a word he used of the style of his
French sources, and its use only with reference to the works by
Skelton and Chaucer suggests a particular regard for the style of
these authors. The French works were written in a *fair* language,
though often with *honest* and *strange* terms. These are words of
general approval, though *strange* is somewhat ambiguous for in
Eneydos, together with *overcurious*, it implies overelaboration and
overrefinement.

Two other favourite words are *briefly* and *compendiously*. The
former is used of *King Arthur* in which French tales 'have late ben
drawen oute bryefly into Englysshe' (72a: 91–2), and of *Polychronicon* 'in whiche book ben comprised briefly many wonderful
historyees' (86a: 122–3). The continuation of *Polychronicon* is
included to 'contynue the sayd werk bryefly' (86c: 3). Both these

books are among the largest printed by Caxton and he can hardly have intended us to understand *briefly* in its common sense of 'in a short space or time'. It approximates in meaning to 'succinctly', though with the implication that a great deal is said in the words used. It was in this sense and also as a term of approval that he included *shortly* in that list of adverbs used to describe how effectively the *Royal Book* presented its didactic material – 'so subtylly, so shortly, so perceyvyngly and so parfyghtly' (93b: 14–15). *Compendiously* has the same range of meaning as *briefly* but, unlike that word, it was found commonly in fifteenth-century literature to describe style. Possibly Caxton picked up *compendiously* from Lydgate, but used the more familiar *briefly* and *shortly* as alternatives on his own initiative. The meaning of these words is perhaps best defined by Caxton himself when he writes of Chaucer that 'he wrytteth no voyde wordes, but alle hys mater is ful of hye and quycke sentence' (59b: 22–3). Presumably Caxton felt that the use of words for their own sake rather than as a means of expressing the thought as beautifully as possible amounted to overrefinement of style. Other words of approval in his critical vocabulary include *craftily*, *cunningly* and *curiously*, which have the sense of 'with great skill and workmanship', though *curiously* may have the added sense of 'elaborately'. All were used interchangeably and could indeed be used of artifacts as well as of books.

Despite the use of words which seem to imply that elaboration was desirable, Caxton also used *plain* as a word of approval. This may be because some of the original Latin works of which he printed English translations were in a difficult style so that the thought was hard to follow. *Boethius* was written in a style 'harde and difficile to be understonde of simple persones' (7: 21–2). Similarly once *Of Old Age* had been translated into English it was 'more ample expowned and more swetter to the reder' (79a: 48–9). On being turned into English these works were easier to understand, and the necessity of intelligibility is something which Caxton insists upon time and again. We should not be misled into thinking he was simply interested in decorative verbiage for its own sake, for he was always too much concerned with the meaning of his texts.

However, one must conclude that Caxton's critical vocabulary is not very well developed and his remarks often appear to be contradictory. He used the expressions which were current at the time and many of them were used emotively and with little critical meaning. Nevertheless, we can discern the basis of his attitudes to literature. Meaning was paramount, but that meaning could be and indeed should be expressed in as elegant a way as possible. But it was wrong to introduce words which did not help one to understand the meaning of the text: the elaboration must always serve a practical end.

The Texts

THE intention of this edition is to assemble all Caxton's own writings in one volume. As Caxton did not compose any works of his own, but only translated texts from French, Latin or Dutch, and printed works already available in English, his own contributions take the form of prologues, epilogues, colophons and interpolations. Where a text has only a very brief implicit or explicit I have usually not bothered to include it unless it contains a detail worth recording or unless some other part of the same text is included. Likewise I have not included Caxton's tables of contents or indices. Several of Caxton's prologues and epilogues are based to a greater or lesser extent on existing French prologues and epilogues. I have included these in full because it is easier to read them as a connected whole and because Caxton's modifications are included piecemeal. I have also included the passage about Socrates in the *Dicts or Sayings* (No 29) since it forms part of the complete epilogue. I have not, however, included such things as the balade at the end of the *Curial* (No 26), even though it may have been translated by Caxton, since it stands apart from the colophon. As for interpolations made by Caxton in the texts, I have included only those of a reasonable length, for the book would be too fragmented if all Caxton's little insertions were included. Furthermore, not all of his texts have yet been properly edited so that it is uncertain how much he altered some of them. I hope, nevertheless, that all his major interpolations are to be found here, though later research may well uncover others.

It was difficult to decide how to arrange the texts. A strict chronological arrangement has certain drawbacks. First, the dates of some texts are disputed and certain currently accepted dates may be modified by later research. Secondly, a chronological arrangement would lead to the separation of the different editions of individual texts. Since this book is intended as a companion volume to my *Caxton and his World*, I have decided to follow the arrangement of Caxton's texts found in pp. 224–39 of that work. The arabic numbers before each title correspond to the numbers given there. This will enable the reader who wishes for further details about a text to consult the equivalent number in *Caxton and his World.* The absence of numbers in the sequence naturally implies that those texts contain no original writing by Caxton.

The texts have been edited in the following way. The original spelling is preserved, but *u/v* and *i/j* are normalized in accordance with modern practice and ʒ is transliterated as *gh*. Word-division, punctuation and paragraphing are editorial. Additions to the texts are indicated by the use of square brackets; other emendations are recorded in footnotes. I have generally based my text on a single copy of Caxton's edition so that variant readings between different copies are not recorded. The base copy is, where possible, that found in the *Short Title Catalogue* series of microfilms issued by Ann Arbor, Michigan.

Caxton's Own Prose

1. ADVERTISEMENT (*c.* 1477)

If it plese ony man spirituel or temporel to bye ony pyes of
two and thre comemoracions of Salisburi Use enpryntid
after the forme of this present lettre, whiche ben wel and truly
correct, late hym com to Westmonester into the Almonesrye
at the Reed Pale and he shal have them good chepe.   5

Supplico stet cedula

2. AESOP (26 March 1484)

(a) *Incipit*

Here begynneth the book of the subtyl historyes and fables
of Esope, whiche were translated out of Frensshe into
Englysshe by Wylliam Caxton at Westmynstre in the yere of
Oure Lorde MCCCClxxxiii.

(b) *Conclusion*

There was in a certayne towne a wydower wowed a wydowe
for to have and wedde her to his wyf, and at the last they
were agreed and sured togyder. And whan a yonge woman
beynge servaunt with the wydowe herd therof, she came to
her maystresse and sayd to her: 'Allas, maystresse, what have   5
ye doo?'
'Why?' sayd she.
'I have herd say,' sayd the mayde, 'that ye be assured and
shalle wedde suche a man.'
'And what thenne?' sayd the wydowe.   10
'Allas,' sayd the mayde. 'I am sory for yow, bycause I have
herd saye that he is a peryllous man, for he laye so ofte and
knewe so moch his other wyf that she deyde therof; and I am
sory therof that yf ye shold falle in lyke caas.'
To whome the wydowe answerd and sayd: 'Forsothe, I   15
wold be dede, for ther is but sorowe and care in this world'.

This was a curteys excuse of a wydowe.

Now thenne I wylle fynysshe alle these fables wyth this tale that foloweth, whiche a worshipful preest and a parsone told me late. He sayd that there were duellynge in Oxenford two 20 prestes, bothe Maystres of Arte, of whome that one was quyck and coude putte hymself forth, and that other was a good, symple preest. And soo it happed that the mayster that was perte and quyck was anone promoted to a benefyce or tweyne, and after to prebendys, and for to be a dene of a 25 grete pryncess chappel, supposynge and wenynge that his felaw, the symple preest, shold never have be promoted, but be alwey an annuel or at the most a parysshe preest. So after longe tyme that this worshipful man, this dene, came rydynge into a good paryssh with a x or xii horses lyke a 30 prelate, and came into the chirche of the sayd parysshe and fond there this good symple man, somtyme his felawe, whiche cam and welcomed hym lowely. And that other badde hym 'Good morowe, Mayster Johan', and toke hym sleyghtly by the hand and axyd hym where he dwellyd. 35

And the good man sayd: 'In this paryssh'.

'How?' sayd he. 'Are ye here a sowle preest or a paryssh preste?'

'Nay, sir,' said he. 'For lack of a better, though I be not able ne worthy I am parson and curate of this parysshe.' 40

And thenne that other avaled his bonet and said: 'Mayster Parson, I praye yow to be not displeasyd, I had supposed ye had not be benefyced. But, mayster,' sayd he, 'I pray yow, what is this benefyce worth to yow a yere?'

'Forsothe,' sayd the good, symple man, 'I wote never, for 45 I make never accomptes therof, how wel I have had hit four or fyve yere.'

'And knowe ye not,' said he, 'what it is worth? It shold seme a good benefyce.'

'No, forsothe,' sayd he, 'but I wote wel what it shalle be 50 worth to me.'

'Why?' sayd he. 'What shalle hit be worth?'

'Forsothe,' sayd he, 'yf I doo my trewe dylygence in the cure of my parysshens in prechyng and techynge and doo my parte longynge to my cure, I shalle have heven therfore. 55 And yf theyre sowles ben lost or ony of them by my defawte, I shall be punysshed therfore. And herof am I sure.'

And with that word the ryche dene was abasshed and

thought he shold be the better and take more hede to his
cures and benefyces than he had done. This was a good   60
answere of a good preest and an honest.

And herewith I fynysshe this book translated and emprynted by me William Caxton at Westmynstre in th'abbey,
and fynysshed the xxvi daye of Marche the yere of Oure Lord
MCCCClxxxiiii and the fyrst yere of the regne of Kyng   65
Rychard the Thyrdde.

5. ART OF DIEING (*c.* 1490)

(a) *Incipit*

Here begynneth a lityll treatise shorte and abredged spekynge
of the arte and crafte to knowe well to dye.

(b) *Explicit*

Thus endeth the trayttye abredged of the arte to lerne well to
deye, translated oute of Frenshe into Englysshe by William
Caxton the xv day of Juyn, the yere of Our Lord a M iiiiC
lxxxx.

6. BLANCHARDIN AND EGLANTINE (*c.* 1489)

Prologue

Unto the right noble, puyssaunt and excellent pryncesse, my
redoubted lady, my Lady Margarete, Duchesse of Somercete,
moder unto our naturel and soverayn lord and most
Crysten kynge, Henry the Seventh, by the grace of God Kyng
of Englonde and of Fraunce, Lord of Yrelond etc., I   5
Wyllyam Caxton, his most indygne, humble subgette and
lytil servaunt, presente this lytyl book unto the noble grace
of my sayd lady; whiche boke I late receyved in Frenshe
from her good grace, and her commaundement wythalle for
to reduce and translate it into our maternal and Englysh   10
tonge; whiche boke I had longe tofore solde to my sayd
lady, and knewe wel that the storye of hit was honeste and
joyefull to all vertuouse yong noble gentylmen and wymmen
for to rede therin, as for their passe-tyme. For, under correction, in my jugement it is as requesyte otherwhyle to rede 15
in auncyent hystoryes of noble fayttes and valyaunt actes of
armes and warre, whiche have ben achyeved in olde tyme of
many noble prynces, lordes and knyghtes, as wel for to see

and knowe their valyauntnes[1] for to stande in the specyal
grace and love of their ladyes, and in lyke wyse for gentyl   20
yonge ladyes and damoysellys for to lerne to be stedfaste
and constaunt in their parte to theym that they ones have
promysed and agreed to, suche as have putte their lyves ofte
in jeopardye for to playse theym to stande in grace, as it is to
occupye theym and studye overmoche in bokes of contempla-   25
cion. Wherfore, at th'ynstaunce and requeste of my sayd
lady, whiche I repute as for a commaundemente, I have
reduced this sayd boke out of Frenshe into our Englyshe.
Whiche boke specyfyeth of the noble actes and fayttes of
warre achyeved by a noble and victorious prynce named   30
Blanchardin, sone unto the Kynge of Fryse, for the love of a
noble pryncesse callyd Eglantyne, otherwyse named in
Frensche *l'orguylleuse d'amours*, whiche is as moche to saye in
Englyshe as 'the proude lady of love', Quene of Tormaday;
and of the grete adventures, labours, anguysshes and many   35
other grete dyseases of theym bothe tofore they myghte
atteyne for to come to the fynall conclusion of their desired
love, as a[l a]longe by the grace of God it shall be shewed
in th'istorye of thys present book. Bysechynge my sayd
ladyes bountyuous grace to receyve this lityll boke in gree of   40
me, her humble servaunt, and to pardoune me of the rude
and comyn Englyshe, where as shall be found faulte; for I
confesse me not lerned ne knowynge the arte of rethoryk ne
of suche gaye termes as now be sayd in these dayes and used.
But[2] I hope that it shall be understonden of the redars and   45
herers – and that shall suffyse.

Besechynge Allmyghty God to graunte to her moste noble
goode grace longe lyffe and th'accomplysshement of hir hihe,
noble and joyes desires in thys present lyff; and after this
short and transytorye lyff, everlastynge lyff in heven. Amen.   50

Here begynneth the table of the victoryous prynce,
Blanchardyn, sone of the noble Kyng of Fryse, and of
Eglantyne, Quene of Tormaday, otherwyse callyd *l'orgoyl-
leuse d'amours*, whiche is to saye 'the proude lady in love'.

7. BOETHIUS (*c.* 1478)

Epilogue

Thus endeth this boke whiche is named the *Boke of Consolacion
of Philosophie*, whiche that Boecius made for his comforte and

---

¹ walyauntnes   ² Bat

consolacion, he beyng in exile for the comynn and publick
wele, havyng grete hevynes and thoughtes and in maner of
despayr, rehercing in the sayde boke howe Philosophie   5
appiered to him shewyng the mutabilite of this transitorie
lyfe, and also enformyng howe fortune and happe shold be
understonden with the predestynacion and prescience of
God as moche as maye and ys possible to bee knowen
naturelly, as afore ys sayd in this sayd boke. Whiche Boecius   10
was an excellente auctour of dyverce bookes craftely and
curiously maad in prose and metre, and also had translated
dyverce bookes oute of Greke into Latynn and had ben
senatour of that noble and famous cite Rome, and also his
two sones senatours for their prudence and wisedom. And   15
for as moche as he withstode to his power the tyrannye of
Theodorik, thenne Emperour, and wold have defended the
sayde cite and senate from his wicked hondes, wherupon he
was convict and putte in prison, in whiche prisonn he made
this forsaide *Boke of Consolacion* for his singuler comfort. And   20
for as moche as the stile of it is harde and difficile to be
understonde of simple persones, therfore the worshipful
fader and first foundeur and enbelissher of ornate eloquence
in our Englissh, I mene Maister Geffrey Chaucer, hath
translated this sayd werke oute of Latyn into oure usual and   25
moder tonge, folowyng the Latyn as neygh as is possible to
be understande. Wherein in myne oppynyon he hath deservid
a perpetuell lawde and thanke of al this noble royame of
Englond, and in especiall of them that shall rede and understande it. For in the sayd boke they may see what this   30
transitorie and mutable worlde is and wherto every mann
livyng in hit ought to entende. Thenne for as moche as this
sayd boke so translated is rare and not spred ne knowen, as it
is digne and worthy, for the erudicion and lernyng of suche
as ben ignoraunt and not knowyng of it, atte requeste of a   35
singuler frende and gossib of myne I, William Caxton, have
done my debuoir and payne t'enprynte it in fourme as is
hereafore made, in hopyng that it shal prouffite moche peple
to the wele and helth of theire soules and for to lerne to have
and kepe the better pacience in adversitees. And furthermore   40
I desire and require you that of your charite ye wold praye
for the soule of the sayd worshipful mann, Geffrey Chaucer,
first translatour of this sayde boke into Englissh and enbelissher in making the sayd langage ornate and fayr, whiche
shal endure perpetuelly and therfore he ought eternelly to be 45

remembrid. Of whom the body and corps lieth buried in th'Abbay of Westmestre beside London tofore the Chapele of Seynte Benet, by whos sepulture is wreton on a table hongyng on a pylere his epitaphye maad by a poete laureat, whereof the copye foloweth etc.   50

Epitaphium Galfridi Chaucer per poetam laureatum
    Stephanum
Surigonum Mediolanensem, in decretis licenciatum.
[Here follow the thirty lines in Latin of the epitaph]

Post obitum Caxton voluit te vivere cura
    Willelmi, Chaucer clare poeta, tui;
Nam tua non solum compressit opuscula formis   55
    Has quoque sed laudes iussit hic esse tuas.

9. BOOK OF GOOD MANNERS (11 May 1487)

(a) *Prologue*

Whan I consydere the condycions and maners of the comyn people whiche without enformacion and lernyng ben rude and not manerd, lyke unto beestis brute (acordyng to an olde proverbe he that is not manerd is no man, for maners make man), thenne it is requesite and necessary that every man use   5
good and vertuous maners. And to th'ende that every man shold have knowleche of good maners, an honest man and a specyal frende of myn, a mercer of London named Wylliam Praat, which late departed out of this lyf on whos soule God have mercy, not longe tofore his deth delyverd to me in   10
Frenshe a lytel book named the *Book of Good Maners*, whiche book is of auctoryte for as moche as there is nothyng sayd therin but for the moost parte it is aledged by scrypture of the Byble or ellis by sayeng of holy sayntes, doctours, philosophres and poetes, and desyred me instantly to trans-   15
late it into Englyssh, our maternal tonge, to th'ende that it myght be had and used emonge the people for th'amende-ment of their maners and to th'encreace of vertuous lyvyng. Thenne I, at the request and desyre of hym whyche was my synguler frende and of olde knowlege, have put myself in   20
devoyr for t'accomplysshe his desyre and have after the lytel connyng that God hath lent me translated out of Frenshe into our Englyssh this sayd *Book of Good Maners*; besechyng Almyghty God that it may prouffyte bothe the redars and

herers therof, for that is th'entent of hym that was fyrst   25
cause that brought the boke to my hande and also of me that
have accomplysshed it; prayeng al them that shal rede and
here it to correcte where as they fynde faulte and to holde me
excused of the rude and unparfyght Englyssh. And I beseche
Almyghty God that it so may be understonden that al they   30
that shal rede or here it that they may the better lyve in this
present lyf that after this lyf they and I may come to the
everlastyng lyf in heven where as is joye and blysse per-
durable. Amen.

(b) *Colophon*

Explicit et hic est finis per Caxton et cetera.
Fynysshed and translated out of Frenshe into Englysshe the
viii day of Juyn, the yere of Our Lord M iiiiC lxxxvi and the
first yere of the regne of Kyng Harry the vii; and enprynted
the xi day of Maye after, et cetera.   5
  Laus Deo.

11. CANTERBURY TALES (Second Edition) (*c.* 1484)

Prologue

Grete thankes, lawde and honour ought to be gyven unto the
clerkes, poetes and historiographs that have wreton many
noble bokes of wysedom, of the lyves, passions and myracles
of holy sayntes, of hystoryes of noble and famous actes and
faittes, and of the cronycles sith the begynnyng of the creacion   5
of the world unto thys present tyme, by whyche we ben dayly
enformed and have knowleche of many thynges of whom we
shold not have knowen, yf they had not left to us theyr
monumentis wreton. Emong whom and in especial tofore
alle other we ought to gyve a syngular laude unto that noble   10
and grete philosopher, Gefferey Chaucer, the whiche for his
ornate wrytyng in our tongue maye wel have the name of a
laureate poete. For tofore that he by hys labour enbelysshyd,
ornated and made faire our Englisshe, in thys royame was
had rude speche and incongrue, as yet it appiereth by olde   15
bookes whyche at thys day ought not to have place ne be
compared emong ne to hys beauteuous volumes and aournate
writynges. Of whom he made many bokes and treatyces of
many a noble historye as wel in metre as in ryme and prose;
and them so craftyly made that he comprehended hys maters   20

in short, quyck and hye sentences, eschewyng prolyxyte, castyng away the chaf of superfluyte, and shewyng the pyked grayn of sentence utteryd by crafty and sugred eloquence.

Of whom emong all other of hys bokes I purpose t'emprynte by the grace of God the *Book of the Tales of Cauntyrburye*, in whiche I fynde many a noble hystorye of every astate and degre: fyrst rehercyng the condicions and th'arraye of eche of them as properly as possyble is to be sayd, and after theyr tales, whyche ben of noblesse, wysedom, gentylesse, myrthe, and also of veray holynesse and vertue, wherin he fynysshyth thys sayd booke. Whyche book I have dylygently oversen and duly examyned to th'ende that it be made acordyng unto his owen makyng, for I fynde many of the sayd bookes whyche wryters have abrydgyd it and many thynges left out, and in somme place have sette certayn versys that he never made ne sette in hys booke.

Of whyche bookes so incorrecte was one brought to me vi yere passyd, whyche I supposed had ben veray true and correcte. And accordyng to the same I dyde do enprynte a certayn nombre of them, whyche anon were sold to many and dyverse gentylmen. Of whome one gentylman cam to me and said that this book was not accordyng in many places unto the book that Gefferey Chaucer had made. To whom I answerd that I had made it accordyng to my copye, and by me was nothyng added ne mynusshyd. Thenne he sayd he knewe a book whyche hys fader had and moche lovyd that was very trewe and accordyng unto hys owen first book by hym made; and sayd more yf I wold enprynte it agayn, he wold gete me the same book for a copye, how be it he wyst wel that hys fader wold not gladly departe fro it. To whom I said in caas that he coude gete me suche a book trewe and correcte, yet I wold ones endevoyre me to enprynte it agayn for to satysfye th'auctour, where as tofore by ygnouraunce I erryd in hurtyng and dyffamyng his book in dyverce places, in settyng in somme thynges that he never sayd ne made and levyng out many thynges that he made whyche ben requysite to be sette in it. And thus we fyll at accord. And he ful gentylly gate of hys fader the said book and delyverd it to me, by whiche I have corrected my book as hereafter alle alonge by th'ayde of Almyghty God shal folowe. Whom I humbly beseche to gyve me grace and ayde to achyeve and accomplysshe to hys lawde, honour and glorye; and that alle ye that shal in thys book rede or heere wyll of your charyte emong

your dedes of mercy remember the sowle of the sayd Gefferey
Chaucer, first auctour and maker of thys book; and also that   65
alle we that shal see and rede therin may so take and understonde the good and vertuous tales that it may so prouffyte
unto the helthe of our sowles, that after thys short and
transitorye lyf we may come to everlastyng lyf in heven.
Amen.   70

        By Wylliam Caxton.

15. CATON (*c.* 1484)

(a) *Prologue*

Here begynneth the prologue or prohemye of the book callid
Caton. Whiche booke hath ben translated into Englysshe by
Mayster Benet Burgh, late Archedeken of Colchestre and Hye
Chanon of Saint Stephen's at Westmestre, which ful craftly
hath made it in balade ryal for the erudicion of my Lord   5
Bousher, sone and heyr at that tyme to my lord, the Erle of
Estsex. And bycause of late cam to my hand a book of the
said *Caton* in Frensshe, whiche reherceth many a fayr lernynge
and notable ensamples, I have translated it oute of Frensshe
into Englysshe, as al along hereafter shalle appiere; whiche   10
I presente unto the cyte of London.

    Unto the noble, auncyent and renommed cyte, the Cyte of
London in Englond, I William Caxton, cytezeyn and conjurye
of the same and of the fraternyte and felauship of the
mercerye, owe of ryght my servyse and good wyll and of very   15
dute am bounden naturelly to assiste, ayde and counceille as
ferforth as I can to my power as to my moder, of whom I
have receyved my noureture and lyvynge; and shal praye for
the good prosperite and polecye of the same duryng my lyf.
For, as me semeth, it is of grete nede, bycause I have knowen   20
it in my yong age moche more welthy, prosperous and rycher
than it is at this day. And the cause is that ther is almost none
that entendeth to the comyn wele, but only every man for
his singuler prouffyte.

    O whan I remember the noble Romayns that for the comyn   25
wele of the cyte of Rome they spente not only theyr moevable
goodes, but they put theyr bodyes and lyves in jeopardy and
to the deth, as by many a noble ensample we may see in th'actes
of Romayns, as of the two noble Scipions, Affrican and Asyan,
Actilius and many other, and amonge al other the noble   30

Catho, auctor and maker of this book whiche he hath lefte
for to remayne ever to all the peple for to lerne in hit and to
knowe how every man ought to rewle and governe hym in
this lyf. And as in my jugement it is the beste book for to be
taught to yonge children in scole; and also to peple of every   35
age it is ful convenient, yf it be wel understanden. And
bycause I see that the children that ben borne within the sayd
cyte encreace and prouffyte not lyke theyr faders and olders,
but for the moost parte after that they ben comen to theyr
parfight yeres of discrecion and rypenes of age, how wel that   40
theyre faders have lefte to them grete quantite of goodes, yet
scarcely amonge ten two thryve. I have sene and knowen in
other londes in dyverse cytees that of one name and lygnage
successyvely have endured prosperously many heyres, ye a v
or vi hondred yere, and somme a thousand. And in this noble   45
cyte of London it can unnethe contynue unto the thyrd heyr
or scarcely to the second.

O blessyd Lord, whanne I remembre this, I am al abasshyd.
I cannot juge the cause. But fayrer ne wyser ne bet-bespoken
children in theyre yongthe ben nowher than ther ben in   50
London; but at their ful rypyng ther is no carnel ne good
corn founden, but chaff for the moost parte. I wote wel there
be many noble and wyse, and prove wel and ben better and
rycher than ever were theyr faders. And to th'ende that
many myght come to honoure and worshyppe, I entende to   55
translate this sayd *Book of Cathon*. In whiche I doubte not, and
yf they wylle rede it and understande, they shal moche the
better conne rewle themself therby. For among all other
bookes this is a synguler book and may well be callyd 'The
Regyment or Governaunce of the Body and Sowle'.   60

There was a noble clerke named Pogius of Florence, and
was secretary to Pope Eugenye and also to Pope Nycholas,
whiche had in the cyte of Florence a noble and well-stuffed
lybrarye whiche alle noble straungyers comynge to Florence
desyred to see; and therin they fonde many noble and rare   65
bookes. And whanne they had axyd of hym whiche was the
best boke of them alle and that he reputed for best, he sayd
that he helde *Cathon Glosed* for the best book of his lyberarye.
Thenne syth that he that was so noble a clerke helde this
book for the best, doubtles hit must folowe that this is a   70
noble booke and a vertuous, and suche one that a man may
eschewe alle vyces and ensiewe vertue. Thenne to th'ende
that this sayd book may prouffyte unto the herars of it, I

byseche Almyghty God that I may ach[y]eve and accomplysshe it unto his laude and glorye, and to th'erudicion and   75
lernynge of them that ben ygnoraunt that they maye thereby
prouffyte and be the better. And I requyre and byseche alle
suche that fynde faute or errour that of theyr charyte they
correcte and amende hit; and I shalle hertely praye for them
to Almyghty God that he rewarde them.   80

In this smal lytyl booke is conteyned a short and prouffitable doctryne for all maner of peple, the whiche is taken and
composed upon the said *Book of Cathon* with some addicions
and auctoritees of holy doctours and prophetes, and also
many historyes and ensamples autentyke of holy faders and   85
auncyent cronycles trewe and approuved.

Item, this lytell booke shalle be devyded in two partyes
pryncipal. The fyrst partye pryncipal is the proheme, whiche
begynneth *Cum animadverterem* and endureth unto *Itaque Deo
supplica*. The second partye pryncipal is the trayttye and alle   90
the maner of this present book, whiche begynneth *Itaque Deo
supplica* and[1] endureth unto the ende of the sayd lytel booke.
Item, this second partye pryncipal is devyded in two partyes,
the fyrst is in prose and the second in verse. The fyrst partye,
whiche is in prose, begynneth *Itaque Deo supplica* and endureth   95
unto *Si Deus est animus*, the whiche conteyneth lvi commaundements. Item, the second partye, whiche is in verse,
is subdyvyded into foure partyes. The fyrst begynneth at *Si
Deus est animus* and endureth unto *Telluris si forte*, the whiche
conteyneth fourty commaundements. The second partye   100
begynneth at *Telluris si forte* and endureth unto *Hoc quicunquibus velis*, whiche conteyneth xxxv commaundements. The
third partye begynneth at *Hoc quicunquibus* and endureth to
Securam quicunque, whiche conteyneth xxvi commaundements.
The fourthe partye begynneth at *Securam* and endureth unto   105
th'ende of the book and conteyneth lvi commaundements.
And soo this present lytel booke conteyneth in somme two
honderd xiii commaundments as wel in prose as in verse.

But to th'ende that th'ystoryes and examples that ben
conteyned in this lytel book may be lygh[t]ly founden and   110
also for to knowe upon what commaundementes they ben
adjousted and alledged, they shalle be sette and entytled by
maner of rubrysshe in commaundement upon whiche eche
shalle be conteyned and alledged. And they shalle be signed

---

[1] an-

as that, folowed of the nombre of leves where they shalle be 115
wreton.

[Table of Contents]

Thus endeth the table and the rubrishes of this present
boke, whiche is called *Caton* in Englysshe, ryght singuler and
prouffytable. And over and above these that be comprysed
in this sayd table is many a notable commaundement, lern- 120
ynge and counceylle moche prouffitable, whiche is not sette
in the sayd regystre or rubrysshe.

(b) *Colophon*

Here fynyssheth this present book whiche is sayd or called
Cathon, translated oute of Frensshe into Englysshe by
William Caxton in th'Abbay of Westmynstre the yere of
Oure Lord MCCCClxxxiii and the fyrst yere of the regne of
Kynge Rychard the Thyrd the xxiii day of Decembre.   5

16. CHARLES THE GREAT (1 December 1485)

(a) *Prologue*

Saynt Poul, doctour of veryte, sayth to us that al thynges that
ben reduced by wrytyng ben wryton to our doctryne; and
Boece maketh mencion that the helthe of every persone
procedeth dyvercely. Thenne sythe it is soo that the Cristen
feyth is affermed and corrobered by the doctours of Holy   5
Chyrche, nevertheles the thynges passed dyversly reduced to
remembraunce engendre in us correction of unlauful lyf. For
the werkes of the auncient and olde peple ben for to gyve to
us ensaumple to lyve in good and vertuous operacions digne
and worthy of helth in folowyng the good and eschewyng   10
the evyl; and also in recountyng of hye hystoryes the comune
understondyng is better content to the ymagynacion local
than to symple auctoryte, to which it is submysed.

I saye this gladly for oftymes I have ben excyted of the
venerable man, Messire Henry Bolomyer, Chanonne of   15
Lausanne, for to reduce for his playsyr somme hystoryes as
wel in Latyn and in Romaunce, as in other facion wryton;
that is to say of the ryght puyssaunt, vertuous and noble
Charles the Grete, Kyng of Fraunce and Emperour of Rome,
sone of the grete Pepyn, and of his prynces and barons, as   20
Rolland, Olyver and other, touchyng somme werkes haultayne doon and commysed by their grete strength and ryght
ardaunt courage to the exaltacyon of the Crysten fayth and

to the confusyon of the hethen sarazyns and myscreaunts,
whiche is a werk wel contemplatyf for to lyve wel. And   25
bycause the sayd Henry Bolomyer hath seen of thys mater and
the hystoryes dysjoyned wythoute ordre, therfor at his
request after the capacyte of my lytel entendement and after
th'ystoryes and mater that I have founden, I have ordeyned
this book folowyng. And it myght soo have ben that yf I had   30
ben more largely enformed and al playn, I had better[1]
made it, for I have not sayd ony matere but I have therof ben
enformed, fyrst by an autentyke book named *Myrrour
Hystoryal* as by the canonnes and somme other bookes whiche
make mencyon of the werke folowyng. And bycause I may   35
have a lytel parte of honourable foundement I shal touche of
the first Cristen Kyng of Fraunce. For the moste parte of
this book is made to th'onour of the Frensshmen and for
prouffyte of every man. And after the desyre of the redar and
herer there shalle be founden in the table all playne the mater   40
of whyche the persone shal have desyre to here or rede wythoute grete atedyacyon, by the playsyr of God; to whome I
submytte al myn entente to write nothyng that ought to be
blamed ne but that it be to the helthe and savacion of every
persone.   45

Thenne for as moche I late had fynysshed in enprynte the
book of the noble and vyctoryous Kyng Arthur, fyrst of the
thre moost noble and worthy of Crysten kynges, and also
tofore had reduced into Englisshe the noble hystorye and lyf
of Godefroy of Boloyn, Kyng of Jherusalem, last of the said   50
iii worthy, somme persones of noble estate and degree have
desyred me to reduce th'ystorye and lyf of the noble and
Crysten prynce, Charles the Grete, Kyng of Fraunce and
Emperour of Rome, the second of the thre worthy, to th'ende
that th'ystoryes, actes and lyves may be had in our maternal   55
tongue lyke as they be in Latyn or in Frensshe, for the moost
quantyte of the people understonde not Latyn ne Frensshe
here in this noble royame of Englond.

And for to satysfye the desyre and requeste of my good
synguler lordes and specyal maysters and frendes, I have   60
enprysed and concluded in myself to reduce this sayd book
into our Englysshe, as all alonge and playnely ye may rede,
here and see in thys book here folowyng; besechyng al them
that shal fynde faute in the same to correcte and amende it,
and also to pardone me of the rude and symple reducyng.   65

[1] letter

And though so be there be no gaye termes ne subtyl ne newe eloquence, yet I hope that it shal be understonden, and to that entente I have specyally reduced it after the symple connyng that God hath lente to me. Wherof I humbly and wyth al my herte thanke hym, and also am bounden to praye 70 for my fader and moder's soules that in my youthe sette me to scole, by whyche by the suffraunce of God I gete my lyvyng – I hope truly. And that I may so do and contynue I byseche hym to graunte me of his grace, and so to laboure and occupye myself vertuously that I may come oute of dette 75 and dedely synne, that after this lyf I may come to hys blysse in heven. Amen.

Here begynnen the chapytres and tytles of this book folowyng nombred for to fynde the more lyghtly the mater therin comprised. 80

(b) *Epilogue*

And bycause I Wylliam Caxton was desyred and requyred by a good and synguler frende of myn, Maister Wylliam Daubeney, one of the Tresorers of the Jewellys of the noble and moost Crysten kyng, our naturel and soverayn lord late of noble memorye, Kyng Edward the Fourth, on whos soule 5 Jhesu have mercy, to reduce al these sayd hystoryes into our Englysshe tongue, I have put me in devoyr to translate thys sayd book as ye here tofore may see al alonge and pl[a]yn; prayeng alle them that shal rede, see or here it to pardon me of thys symple and rude trans[l]acyon and reducyng; bysechyng 10 theym that shal fynde faute to correcte it, and in so doyng they shal deserve thankynges; and I shal praye God for them, who brynge them and me after this short and transytorye lyf to everlastyng blysse. Amen.

The whyche werke was fynysshed in the reducyng of hit 15 into Englysshe the xviii day of Juyn the second yere of Kyng Rychard the Thyrd and the yere of Our Lord MCCCClxxxv, and enprynted the fyrst day of Decembre the same yere of Our Lord and the fyrst yere of Kyng Harry the Seventh.

Explicit per William Caxton 20

17 CHRONICLES OF ENGLAND (First Edition) (10 June 1480)

(a) *Prologue*

In the yere of th'yncarnacion of Our Lord Jhesu Crist MCCCClxxx and in the xx yere of the regne of Kyng Edward

the Fourthe atte requeste of dyverce gentilmen I have
endevourd me to enprinte the Cronicles of Englond as in this
booke shall by the suffraunce of God folowe. And to th'ende   5
that every man may see and shortly fynde suche mater as it
shall plese hym to see or rede, I have ordeyned a table of the
maters shortly compiled and chapitred as here shall folowe.
Which booke begynneth at Albyne how she with her susters
fonde this land first and named it Albion and endeth at the   10
beginnyng of the regne of our said soverain lord, Kyng
Edward the iiii.

(b) *Conclusion*

Whom I pray God save and kepe and sende hym the accomplisshement of the remenaunt of his rightfull enheritaunce
beyonde the see; and that he may regne in them to the
playsir of Almyghty God, helthe of his soule, honour and
wurship in this present lyfe, and well and prouffyt of alle his   5
subgettis; and that ther may be a verray finall pees in all
Cristen reames that the infidelis and mysscreauntes may be
withstanden and destroied and our faith enhaunced, which
in thise dayes is sore mynusshed by the puissaunce of the
Turkes and hethen men; and that after this present and short   10
lyfe we may come to the everlasting lyfe in the blisse of heven.
Amen.

Thus endeth this present booke of the Cronicles of
Englond, enprinted by me William Caxton in th'Abbey of
Westmynstre by London; fynysshid and accomplisshid the   15
x day of Juyn the yere of th'incarnacion of Our Lord God
MCCCClxxx and in the xx yere of the regne of Kyng Edward
the Fourth.

22. CONFESSIO AMANTIS (2 September 1483)

(a) *Prologue*

This book is intituled *Confessio Amantis*, that is to saye in
Englysshe 'The Confessyon of the Lover', maad and compyled by Johan Gower squyer, borne in Walys, in the tyme
of Kyng Richard the Second. Which boke treteth how he was
confessyd to Genyus, preest of Venus, upon the causes of   5
love in his fyve wyttes and seven dedely synnes, as in thys
sayd book al alonge appyereth. And bycause there been comprysed therin dyvers hystoryes and fables towchyng every

matere, I have ordeyned a table here folowyng of al suche
hystoryes and fables where and in what book and leef they   10
stande in, as hereafter foloweth.

(b) *Colophon*

Enprynted at Westmestre by me Willyam Caxton and
fynysshed the ii day of Septembre the fyrst yere of the regne
of Kyng Richard the Thyrd, the yere of Our Lord a thousand
CCCClxxxiii.[1]

24. CORDIAL (24 March 1479)

Epilogue

This book is thus translated out of Frenshe into our maternal
tongue by the noble and vertuouse lord, Anthoine Erle
Ryviers, Lord [of] Scales and of the Isle of Wight, Defenseur
and Directeur of the Causes Apostolique for our Holy Fader
the Pope in this royame of Englonde, uncle and governour   5
to my lorde Prince of Wales. Which book was delivered to me
William Caxton by my saide noble Lorde Ryviers on the day
of Purification of Our Blissid Lady, fallyng the Tewsday the
secunde day of the moneth of Feverer in the yeer of Our
Lord MCCCClxxviii, for to be enprinted and so multiplied to   10
goo abrood emonge the peple that therby more surely myght
be remembred the four last thingis undoubtably comyng.

And it is to be noted that sythen the tyme of the grete
tribulacion and adversite of my saide lord he hath been ful
vertuously occupied, as in goyng of pilgremagis to Seint   15
James in Galice, to Rome, to Seint Bartylmew, to Seint
Andrew, to Seint Mathew in the royalme of Naples, and to
Seint Nicholas de Bar in Puyle, and other dyverse holy
places. Also hath procured and goten of our Holy Fader the
Pope a greet and a large indulgence and grace unto the chapel   20
of Our Lady of the Piewe by Seint Stephen's at Westmestre
for the relief and helpe of Cristen sowles passed out of this
transitorie world; whiche grace is of like vertue to th'indulgence of *Scala celi*.

And notwithstonding the greet labours and charges that   25
he hath had in the service of the Kyng and of my said Lord
Prince as wel in Wales as in Englonde, which hath be to him
no litle thought and besines bothe in spirite and in body, as

[1] CCCClxxxiii

the fruit therof[1] experimently sheweth, yet over that t'enriche
his vertuous disposicion he hath put him in devoyr at all tymes   30
whenn he might have a leyser, whiche was but startemele, to
translate diverse bookes out of Frensh into English. Emong
other passid thurgh mynn honde the booke of the wise
sayinges or dictes of philosophers, the wise and holsomm
proverbis of Christine[2] of Pyse, set in metre; over that hath   35
made diverse balades ayenst the seven dedely synnes. Furthermore it semeth that he conceiveth wel the mutabilite and the
unstablenes of this present lyf and that he desireth with a greet
zele and spirituell love our goostly helpe and perpetuel
salvacion and that we shal abhorre and utterely forsake   40
th'abhominable and dampnable synnes whiche comunely be
used nowadayes, as pride, perjurye, terrible swering, thefte,
murdre, and many other. Wherfore he took upon hym the
translating of this present werke named *Cordyale*, trusting
that bothe the reders and the herers therof sholde knowe   45
themself herafter the better and amende thair lyvyng or they
departe and lose this tyme of grace to the recovure of their
salvacion. Whiche translating in my jugement is a noble and a
meritorious dede, wherfor he is worthy to be greetly com-
mended and also singulerly remembred with our goode   50
prayers. For certaynely as well the reders as the herers well
conceyvyng in their hertes the forsayd foure last thinges
may therby greetly be provoqued and called from sinne to the
greet and plentiuouse mercy of our blissid Saveour, whiche
mercy is above all his werkis. And no man beyng contrite   55
and confessed nedeth to fere th'obteyning therof, as in the
preface of my saide lordes booke made by hym more playnly
it appereth.

Thenne in obeying and folowyng my said lordes comandement, in whiche I am bounden so to do for the manifolde   60
benefetes and large rewardes of hym had and receyved of me
undeservid, I have put me in devoyr t'accomplisshe his saide
desire and comaundement, whom I beseche Almighty God
to kepe and mayntene in his vertuous and laudable actes and
werkis and sende hym th'accomplisshement of his noble and   65
joyous desirs and playsirs in this worlde, and after this short,
daungerous and transitory lyf everlasting permanence in
heven. Amen. Whiche werke present I begann the mornn after
the saide Purificacion of Our Blissid Lady, whiche was the[3]
daye of Seint Blase, bisshop and martir, and finisshed on the   70

[1] Thrrof   [2] xpristine   [3] the the

even of th'Annunciacion of Our Said Blissid[1] Lady, fallyng
on the Wednesday the xxiiii daye of Marche in the xix yeer of
Kyng Edwarde the Fourthe.

26. CURIAL (*c.* 1484)

(a) *Prologue*

Here foloweth the copye of a lettre whyche Maistre Alayn
Charetier wrote to hys brother whyche desired to come
dwelle in court, in whyche he reherseth many myseryes and
wretchydnesses therin used, for t'advyse hym not to entre
into it leste he after repente, like as hierafter folowe; and   5
late translated out of Frensshe into Englysshe. Whyche copye
was delyverid to me by a noble and vertuous Erle, at whos
instance and requeste I have reduced it into Englyssh.

(b) *Colophon*

Thus endeth the *Curial,* made by Maystre Alain Charretier;
translated thus in Englyssh by Wylliam Caxton.

28. DESCRIPTION OF BRITAIN (18 August 1480)

(a) *Prologue*

Hit is so that in many and diverse places the comyn cronicles
of Englond ben had and also now late enprinted at Westmynstre; and for as moche as the descripcion of this londe, whiche
of olde tyme was named Albyon and after Britayne, is not
descrived ne comynly had ne the noblenesse and worthynesse   5
of the same is not knowen, therfor I entende to sette in this
booke the discripcion of this said ile of Britayne with the
commoditees of the same.

(b) *Epilogue*

Here endeth the[2] *Discripcion of Britayne,* the whiche conteyneth Englond, Wales and Scotland; and also bicause
Irlonde is under the reule of Englond and of olde tyme it
hath so continued, therfore I have sette the descripcion of the
same after the said Britayne which I have taken oute of   5
Policronicon. And bicause it is necessarie to alle Englisshmen
to knowe the propretees, commoditees and mervailles of
them, therfore I have sette them in enprinte according to the

---

[1] bilissid   [2] het

translacion of Trevisa, whiche atte request of the Lord
Barkeley translated the book of *Policronicon* into Englissh.   10
Fynysshed by me William Caxton[1] the xviii day of August,
the yere of Our Lord God MCCCClxxx and the xx yere of
the regne of Kyng Edward the Fourthe.

29. DICTS OR SAYINGS (First Edition) (18 November 1477)

(a) *Epilogue*

Here endeth the book named the *Dictes or Sayengis of the
Philosophres*,[2] enprynted by me William Caxton at Westmestre
the yere of Our Lord MCCCClxxvii. Whiche book is late
translated out of Frenshe into Englyssh by the noble and
puissant lord, Lord Antone Erle of Ryvyers, Lord of Scales   5
and of the Ile of Wyght, Defendour and Directour of the
Siege Apostolique for our holy fader the pope in this royame of Englond, and governour of my Lord Prynce of
Wales. And it is so that at suche tyme as he had accom-
plysshid this sayd werke, it liked him to sende it to me in   10
certayn quayers to oversee; whiche forthwith I sawe and
fonde therin many grete, notable and wyse sayengis of the
philosophres acordyng unto the bookes made in Frenshe
whiche I had ofte afore redd; but certaynly I had seen none in
Englissh til that tyme.   15
And so afterward I cam unto my sayd lord and told him
how I had red and seen his book, and that he had don a
meritory dede in the labour of the translacion therof into our
Englissh tunge, wherin he had deservid a singuler lawde and
thank, etc. Thenne my sayd lord desired me to oversee it and   20
where as I sholde fynde faute to correcte it. Wherein I
answerd unto his lordship that I coude not amende it, but if I
sholde so presume I might apaire it, for it was right wel and
connyngly made and translated into right good and fayr
Englissh. Notwithstondyng he willed me to oversee it and   25
shewid me dyverce thinges whiche as him semed myght be
left out, as diverce lettres missives sent from Alisander to
Darius and Aristotle, and eche to other—whiche lettres were
lytil appertinent unto t[h]o dictes and sayenges aforsayd for
as moche as they specifye of other maters—and also desired   30
me, that don, to put the sayd booke in enprinte.
And thus obeying hys request and comaundement I have

---

[1] Ca&ton   [2] philosophhres

put me in devoyr to oversee this hys sayd book and beholden as nyghe as I coude howe it accordeth wyth
th'origynal, beyng in Frensh. And I fynde nothyng dyscor-   35
daunt therin, sauf onely in the dyctes and sayengys of
Socrates, wherin I fynde that my saide lord hath left out
certayn and dyverce conclusions towchyng women. Wherof
I mervaylle that my sayd lord hath not wreton them, ne what
hath mevyd hym so to do, ne what cause he hadde at that tyme.   40
But I suppose that som fayr lady hath desired hym to leve it
out of his booke; or ellys he was amerous on somme noble
lady, for whos love he wold not sette yt in hys book; or
ellys for the very affeccyon, love and good wylle that he hath
unto alle ladyes and gentylwomen, he thought that Socrates   45
spared the sothe and wrote of women more than trouthe,
whyche I cannot thinke that so trewe a man and so noble a
phylosophre as Socrates was shold wryte otherwyse than
trouthe. For if he had made fawte in wryting of women, he
ought not ne shold not be belevyd in hys other dyctes and   50
sayinges. But I apperceyve that my sayd lord knoweth
veryly that suche defautes ben not had ne founden in the
women born and dwellyng in these partyes ne regyons of
the world. Socrates was a Greke boren in a ferre contre from
hens, whyche contre is alle of othre condycions than thys is   55
and men and women of other nature than they ben here in this
contre, for I wote well of whatsomever condicion women ben
in Grece, the women of this contre ben right good, wyse,
playsant, humble, discrete, sobre, chast, obedient to their
husbondis, trewe, secrete, stedfast, ever besy and never ydle,   60
attemperat in speking, and vertuous in alle their werkis – or
atte leste sholde be soo. For whiche causes so evydent my sayd
lord, as I suppose, thoughte it was not of necessite to sette in
his book the saiengis of his auctor Socrates touchyng women.
But for as moche as I had comandement of my sayd lord to   65
correcte and amende where as I sholde fynde fawte, and
other fynde I none sauf that he hath left out these dictes and
saynges of the women of Grece; therfore in accomplisshing
his comandement for as moche as I am not in certayn wheder
it was in my lordis copye or not, or ellis peraventure that the   70
wynde had blowe over the leef at the tyme of translacion of
his booke, I purpose to wryte tho same saynges of that Greke
Socrates, whiche wrote of tho women of Grece and nothyng
of them of this royame, whom I suppose he never knewe. For
if he had I dar plainly saye that he wold have reserved them   75

in especiall in his sayd dictes. Alway not presumyng to put
and sette them in my sayd lordes book, but in th'ende aparte
in the rehersayll of the werkis, humbly requiryng al them that
shal rede this lytyl rehersayll that yf they fynde ony faulte
t'arette it to Socrates and not to me whiche wryteth as here- 80
after foloweth.

Socrates sayde that women ben th'apparaylles to cacche men,
but they take none but them that wil be poure, or els them
that knowe hem not. And he sayde that ther is none so grete
empeshement unto a man as ignoraunce and women. And he 85
sawe a woman that bare fyre, of whom he saide that the
hotter bare the colder. And he sawe a woman seke, of whom
he sayd that the evyl restyth and dwellyth with the evyll. And
he sawe a woman brought to the justyce and many other
women folowed her weping, of whome he said: 'The evyll 90
ben sory and angry bicause the evyll shal perisshe'. And he
sawe a iong mayde that lerned to wryte, of whom he sayde that
me multiplied evyl upon evyll. And he sayd that the ignoraunce of a man is knowen in thre thinges, that is to wete,
whan he hath no thought to use reason, whan he cannot 95
refrayne hys covetises, and whan he is governed by the
conceyll of women in that he knoweth that they knowe not.
And he sayd unto hys dyscyples: 'Wylle ye that I enseygne
and teche you howe ye shal mowe escape from alle
evyll?' 100
And they ansuerd 'Ye'.

And thenne he sayde to them: 'For whatsomever thing
that it be, kepe you and be wel waar that ye obeye not to
women'.

Who ansuerd to hym agayn: 'And what sayest thou by our 105
good moders and susters?'

He sayd to hem: 'Suffice you with that I have sayd to you,
for alle ben semblable in malice'. And he sayde: 'Whosomever wyll acquere and gete scyence, late hym never put hym
in the governaunce of a woman'. 110

And he sawe a woman that made her fresshe and gaye, to
whom he sayd: 'Thou resemblest the fyre, for the more wode
is leyd to the fyre, the more wole it brenne, and the gretter is
the hete.'

And on a tyme one axyd hym what hym semed of women. 115
He ansuerd that the women resemble unto a tre called
Edelfla, whyche ys the fayrest tre to beholde and see that may
be, but wythin it ys ful of venym. And they sayd to hym and

75

demanded wherfore he blamed so women and that he
hymself had not comen into thys world ne none other men 120
also wythoute hem. He ansuerd: 'The woman ys like unto a
tre named Chassoygnet, on whyche tre ther ben many
thynges sharpe and pryckyng whiche hurte and prycke them
that approche unto hyt; and yet neverthelesse that same tre
bringeth forth good dates and swete'. 125

And they demanded hym why he fled from the women.
And he ansuerd: 'For as moche as I see them flee and
eschewe the good and comenly do evyll'.

And a woman sayde to hym: 'Wylt thou have ony other
woman than me?' 130

And he ansuerde to her: 'Arte not thou ashamed t'offre
thyself to hym that demandeth ner desireth the not?'

Lo these ben the dictes and sayengis of the phylosophre
Socrates, whiche he wrote in his book; and certaynly he wrote
no worse than afore is rehersed. And for as moche as it is 135
acordaunt that his dyctes and sayengis shold be had as wel
as others, therfore I have sette it in th'ende of this booke.
And also somme persones peraventure that have red this
booke in Frensshe wold have arette a grete defaulte in me that
I had not do my devoir in visiting and overseeyng of my 140
lordes book acording to his desir. And somme other also
happely might have supposed that Socrates had wreton
moche more ylle of women than hereafore is specifyed.
Wherfore in satisfyeng of all parties and also for excuse of the
saide Socrates I have sette these saide dyctes and sayengis 145
aparte in th'ende of this book to th'entent that yf my sayd
lord or ony other persone whatsomever he or she be that shal
rede or here it that if they be not wel plesyd wythall that
they wyth a penne race it out or ellys rente the leef out of the
booke. 150

Humbly requyryng and besechyng my sayd lord to take no
displaysir on me so presumyng, but to pardone where as he
shal fynde faulte, and that it plese hym to take the labour of
th'enpryntyng in gre and thanke; whiche gladly have don my
dyligence in th'accomplysshyng of his desire and com- 155
mandement in whyche I am bounden so to do for the good
reward that I have resseyvyd of his sayd lordship. Whom I
beseche Almyghty God t'encrece and to contynue in his vertuous disposicion in this world, and after thys lyf to lyve
everlastyngly in heven. Amen. 160

Et sic est finis.

(b) *Colophon*

Thus endeth this book of the dyctes and notable wyse
sayenges of the phylosophers, late translated and drawen out
of Frenshe into our Englisshe tonge by my forsaide lord,
th'Erle of Ryvers and Lord Skales, and by hys comandement
sette in forme and emprynted in this manere as ye maye here   5
in this booke see. Whiche was fynisshed the xviii day of the
moneth of Novembre and the sevententh yere of the regne
of Kyng Edward the Fourth.

34. DOCTRINAL OF SAPIENCE (7 May 1489)

(a) *Prologue*

This that is writen in this lytyl book ought the prestes[1] to
lerne and teche to theyr parysshens and also it is necessary
for symple prestes that understonde not the scriptures. And
it is made for symple peple and put into Englissh. Whiche
treates was made by grete counseyl and deliberacion and is   5
approuved, as it is sayd in the table. And bycause that for to
here examples styreth and moveth the peple that ben symple
more to devocion than that grete auctorite of scyence as it
appereth by the right reverend fader and doctour Bede, preste,
whiche sayth in th'ystoryes of England that a bysshop of   10
Scotland, a subtyl and a grete clerk, was sent by the clerks of
Scotland into England for to preche the word of God. But
bycause he used in hys sermons subtyll auctorytees suche as
symple peple hadde ne toke therin no savour, he retourned
wythout doyng of ony grete good ne proffyt. Wherfore they   15
sente another of lasse scyence, the whiche was more playn and
used comynly in hys sermons examples and parables by
whyche he prouffyted moche more unto the erudicion of the
symple peple than dyd that other. Then Maystre Jaques de
Vytry, an holy man and clerke whyche was a cardynal, in   20
prechyng comynly thrugh the royame of Fraunce usyd in
hys sermons examples the whyche meved in suche wyse alle
the royame of Fraunce that it is not in mynde of ony man that
tofore hym was ne syth that styred and moeved the peple to
devocion as he dyde. For as it is redde accordyng to suche   25
examples that Seint Austyn, doctour of the chirche, was
more moeved to converte hymself to the Crysten feyth by
th'examples that were recounted to hym by Symplicien,

[1] prestres

77

Vyctoryn and by th'examples of the merveyllouse lyf and
conversacion of Seynt Anthonye th'ermyte than he was by   30
the prayers and bewayllynges of hys moder ne by the sermons
of Seynt Ambrose ne also than he was for the grete maladyes
that he suffred as hys legende maketh mencion. We rede in the
holy scrypture that Our Lord Jhesu Cryst preched to his
discyples oftymes by examples and parables, wherfore we   35
have entencion to saye and wryte somme good examples in
this matere for the better to styre and moeve the symple peple
to devocion lyke as dyde they abovesayd. And bycause this
boke shold be the better redde, herd and understanden, hit is
made short to be the more clerely undrestond to th'ende that   40
ther may be found therin helthe for our soules.

(b) *Colophon*

Thus endeth the *Doctrinal of Sapyence*, the whyche is ryght
utile and prouffytable to alle Crysten men. Whyche is translated out of Frenshe into Englysshe by Wyllyam Caxton at
Westmester.[1] Fynysshed the vii day of May, the yere of Our
Lord MCCCClxxxix.   5

Caxton me fieri fecit.

(c) *Addition in Windsor Copy*

This chapitre tofore I durst not sette in the boke bycause it
is not convenyent ne aparteynyng that every layeman sholde
knowe it, et cetera.

36. ENEYDOS (*c.* 1490)

(a) *Prologue*

After dyverse werkes made, translated and achieved, havyng
noo werke in hande I sittyng in my studye where as laye many
dyverse paunflettis and bookys, happened that to my hande
cam a lytyl booke in Frenshe whiche late was translated oute
of Latyn by some noble clerke of Fraunce, whiche booke is   5
named *Eneydos* made in Latyn by that noble poete and grete
clerke Vyrgyle. Whiche booke I sawe over and redde therin
how after the generall destruccyon of the grete Troye Eneas
departed berynge his olde fader Anchises upon his sholdres,
his lityl son Yolus on his honde, his wyfe wyth moche other   10
people folowynge; and how he shypped and departed – wyth

1 Westmestter

78

alle th'ystorye of his adventures that he had er he cam to the
achievement of his conquest of Ytalye, as all alonge shall be
shewed in this present boke. In whiche booke I had grete
playsyr bycause of the fayr and honest termes and wordes in   15
Frenshe, whyche I never sawe tofore lyke ne none so playsaunt ne so wel ordred. Whiche booke, as me semed, sholde
be moche requysyte to noble men to see as wel for the
eloquence as the historyes, how wel that many honderd
yerys passed was the sayd *Booke of Eneydos* wyth other werkes   20
made and lerned dayly in scolis specyally in Ytalye and other
places; whiche historye the sayd Vyrgyle made in metre.

And whan I had advysed me in this sayd boke, I delybered
and concluded to translate it into Englysshe, and forthwyth
toke a penne and ynke and wrote a leef or tweyne whyche I   25
oversawe agayn to corecte it. And whan I sawe the fayr and
straunge termes therin, I doubted that it sholde not please
some gentylmen whiche late blamed me sayeng that in my
translacyons I had over-curyous termes whiche coude not be
understande of comyn peple and desired me to use olde and   30
homely termes in my translacyons. And fayn wolde I satysfye
every man, and so to doo toke an olde boke and redde therin;
and certaynly the Englysshe was so rude and brood that I
coude not wele understande it. And also my lorde Abbot of
Westmynster ded do shewe to me late certayn evydences   35
wryton in olde Englysshe for to reduce it into our Englysshe
now usid. And certaynly it was wreton in suche wyse that it
was more lyke to Dutche than Englysshe: I coude not
reduce ne brynge it to be understonden. And certaynly our
langage now used varyeth ferre from that whiche was used   40
and spoken whan I was borne, for we Englysshemen ben
borne under the domynacyon of the mone whiche is never
stedfaste but ever waverynge: wexynge one season, and
waneth and dyscreaseth another season.

And that comyn Englysshe that is spoken in one shyre   45
varyeth from another. In so moche that in my dayes happened
that certayn marchauntes were in a shippe in Tamyse for to
have sayled over the see into Zelande. And for lacke of
wynde thai taryed atte forlond and wente to lande for to
refreshe them. And one of theym named Sheffelde, a mercer,   50
cam into an hows and axed for mete and specyally he axyd after
eggys. And the goode wyf answerde that she coude speke no
Frenshe. And the marchaunt was angry for he also coude
speke no Frenshe, but wolde have hadde egges; and she

understode hym not. And thenne at laste another sayd that he 55
wolde have eyren; then the good wyf sayd that she under-
stod hym wel. Loo! what sholde a man in thyse dayes now
wryte, 'egges' or 'eyren'? Certaynly it is harde to playse
every man bycause of dyversite and chaunge of langage.

For in these days every man that is in ony reputacyon in 60
his countre wyll utter his commynycacyon and maters in
suche maners and termes that fewe men shall understonde
theym. And som honest and grete clerkes have ben wyth me
and desired me to wryte the moste curyous termes that I coude
fynde. And thus bytwene playn rude and curyous I stande 65
abasshed. But in my judgemente the comyn termes that be
dayli used ben lyghter to be understonde than the olde and
aunċyent Englysshe. And for as moche as this present booke
is not for a rude, uplondyssh man to laboure therin ne rede it,
but onely for a clerke and a noble gentylman that feleth and 70
understondeth in faytes of armes, in love and in noble
chyvalrye, therfor in a meane bytwene bothe I have reduced
and translated this sayd booke into our Englysshe not over-
rude ne curyous, but in suche termes as shall be understanden
by Goddys grace accordynge to my copye. And yf ony man 75
wyll entermete in redyng of hit and fyndeth suche termes that
he cannot understande, late hym goo rede and lerne Vyrgyll
or the *Pystles* of Ovyde, and ther he shall see and understonde
lyghtly all yf he have a good redar and enformer. For this
booke is not for every rude and[1] unconnynge man to see, but 80
to clerkys and very gentylmen that understande gentylnes and
scyence.

Thenne I praye alle theym that shall rede in this lytyl
treatys to holde me for excused for the translatynge of hit, for
I knowleche myselfe ignorant of connynge to enpryse on me 85
so hie and noble a werke. But I praye Mayster John Skelton,
late created poete laureate in the Unyversite of Oxenforde, to
oversee and correcte this sayd booke and t'addresse and
expowne where as shalle be founde faulte to theym that shall
requyre it. For hym I knowe for suffycyent to expowne and 90
englysshe every dyffyculte that is therin, for he hath late
translated the *Epystlys* of Tulle, and the *Boke of Dyodorus
Syculus* and diverse other werkes oute of Latyn into Englysshe,
not in rude and olde langage but in polysshed and ornate
termes craftely, as he that hath redde Vyrgyle, Ovyde, Tullye 95
and all the other noble poetes and oratours to me unknowen.

[1] dna

And also he hath redde the ix muses and understande theyr musicalle scyences and to whom of theym eche scyence is appropred. I suppose he hath dronken of Elycon's well. Then I praye hym and suche other to correcte, adde or mynysshe 100 where as he or they shall fynde faulte, for I have but folowed my copye in Frenshe as nygh as me is possyble. And yf ony worde be sayd therin well I am glad, and yf otherwyse I submytte my sayd boke to theyr correctyon.

Whiche boke I presente unto the hye born, my tocomynge 105 naturell and soverayn lord, Arthur by the grace of God Prynce of Walys, Duc of Cornewayll and Erle of Chester, fyrst bygoten sone and heyer unto our most dradde naturall and soverayn lorde and most Crysten kynge, Henry the vii by the grace of God Kynge of Englonde and of Fraunce and 110 Lord of Irelonde, byseching his noble grace to receyve it in thanke of me, his moste humble subget and servaunt. And I shall praye unto Almyghty God for his prosperous encreasyng in vertue, wysedom and humanyte that he may be egal wyth the most renommed of alle his noble progenytours; and so 115 to lyve in this present lyf that after this transitorye lyfe he and we alle may come to everlastynge lyf in heven. Amen.

(b) *Colophon*

Here fynyssheth the *Boke of¹Eneydos* compyled by Vyrgyle, whiche hathe be translated oute of Latyne into Frenshe, and oute of Frenshe reduced into Englysshe by me, Wylliam Caxton, the xxii daye of Juyn, the yere of Our Lord M^{iiii}Clxxxx, the fy[f]the yere of the regne of Kynge Henry the Seventh.   5

38. FEATS OF ARMS (14 July 1489)

Epilogue

Thus endeth this boke whiche Christyne of Pyse made and drewe out of the boke named *Vegecius: De Re Militari* and out of th'*Arbre of Batayles* wyth many other thynges sett into the same requisite to werre and batailles. Whiche boke beyng in Frenshe was delyvered to me, William Caxton, by the most   5 Crysten kynge and redoubted prynce, my naturel and soverayn lord, Kyng Henry the vii Kyng of Englond and of Fraunce, in his palais of Westmestre the xxiii day of Janyvere, the iiii yere of his regne, and desired and wylled me to trans-

¹ yf

late this said boke and reduce it into our English and natural   10
tonge, and to put it in enprynte to th'ende that every gentylman born to armes and all manere men of werre, captayns,
souldiours, vytayllers and all other, shold have knowlege
how they ought to behave theym in the fayttes of warre and
of bat02ylles; and so delyvered me the said book thenne my   15
lord th'Erle of Oxenford awayting on his said grace. Whiche
volume conteynyng four bokes I receyved of his said grace
and according to his desire, whiche to me I repute a comandement and verili glad to obeye, and after the lityl
connyng that God hath lente me I have endevoyrd me to the   20
utterest of my power to fulfylle and accomplisshe his desire
and comaundement as wel to reduce it into Englyshe as to
put it in enprinte to th'ende that it may come to the sight and
knowlege of every gentylman and man of warre. And for
certayn in myn oppinyon it is as necessary a boke and as   25
requysite as ony may be for every estate hye and lowe that
entende to the fayttes of werre, whether it be in bat02ylles,
sieges, rescowse and all other fayttes, subtyltees and re-
medyes for meschieves. Whiche translacyon was finysshed
the viii day of Juyll the sayd yere and enprynted the xiiii day   30
of Juyll next folowyng and ful fynyshyd.

    Thenne syth I have obeyed his most dredeful comaunde-
ment, I humbly byseche[1] his most exellent and bounteuous
Hyenes to pardone me of this symple and rude translacion
wherein be no curyous ne gaye termes of rethoryk; but I hope   35
to Almighti God that it shal be entendyble and understanden
to every man and also that it shal not moche varye in sentence
fro the copye receyved of my said soverayn lord. And where
as I have erryd or made defaulte, I beseche them that fynde
suche to correcte it, and so dooyng I shal praye for them. And   40
yf ther be onything therin to his pleasir I am glad and thinke
my labour wel enployed for to have the name to be one of the
litel servantes to the hiest and most Cristen kyng and prince
of the world, whom I byseche Almyghty God to preserve,
kepe and contynue in his noble and most redoubted enter-   45
pryses as wel in Bretayn, Flaundres and other placis that he
may have victorie, honour and renommee to his perpetual
glorye. For I have not herd ne redde that ony prynce hath
subdued his subgettis with lasse hurte et cetera, and also
holpen his neighbours and frendis out of this londe. In   50
whyche hye enterprises I byseche Almyghty God that he may

[1] bysecle

82

remayne alleway vyctoryous and dayly encreace fro vertu to
vertue and fro better to better to his laude and honour in this
present lyf that after thys short and transitorye lyf he may
atteyne to everlastyng lyf in heven, whiche God g[r]aunte to   55
hym and to alle his lyege peple. Amen.

Per Caxton

43. FIFTEEN OES (*c.* 1491)

Epilogue

Thiese prayers tofore wreton ben enprinted bi the commaundementes of the moste hye and vertuous pryncesse, our
liege lady Elizabeth by the grace of God Quene of Englonde
and of Fraunce, and also of the right hye and most noble
pryncesse Margarete, moder unto our soverayn lorde the   5
kyng, etc.

By their most humble subget and servaunt William Caxton.

44. FOUR SONS OF AYMON (*c.* 1489)

(a) *Prologue*

[Reprinted from W. Copland's print of 1554]

As the philosopher in the fyrst booke of hys *Methafysyque* sayth
that every man naturally desireth to know and to con newe
thynges, and therfore have the clerkes and people of great
understandynge desyred and coveite to lerne[1] sciences and
to know vertues of thinges, some by phylosophy, other by   5
poetrye, and other by historyes and cronyckes of thynges
passed. And upon these three they have greatly laboured in
suche that, thanked be God, by theyr good dylygence and
laboures they have had greate knowledge by innumerable
volumes of bookes whiche have be made and compyled by   10
great studye and payne unto thys daye. And bycause that
above all thinges the princes and lordes of hie estate and
entendement desyre to see th'ystoryes of the ryght noble and
hye vertues of the predecessours[2] whiche ben digne and
worthy of remembraunce of perpetuall recommendacion,   15
therfore late at the request and commaundement of the ryght
noble and vertus erle, John Erle of Oxeforde, my good

[1] lerned   [2] prodecessours

synguler and especial lorde, I reduced and translated out of
Frenche into our maternall and Englyshe tongue the lyfe of
one of his predecessoures named Robert Erle of Oxeforde   20
toforesayd with[1] diverse and many great myracles, whiche God
shewed for him as wel in his lyfe as after his death as it is
shewed all alonge in hys sayde booke.

And also that my sayd lorde desyreth to have other
hystories of olde tyme passed of vertues chyvalry reduced in   25
lykewyse into our Englishe tongue, he late sent to me a booke
in Frenche conteynyng th'actes and faytes of warre doone and
made agaynst the great Emperour and King of Fraunce,
Charlemayne, by the iiii sonnes of Aymon, otherwyse named
in Frenche *Les Quatre Fylz Aymon.* Whyche booke, accordynge   30
to hys request, I have endevorde me to accomplyshe and to
reduce it into our Englyshe, to my great coste and charges as
in the translatinge as in enprynting of the same; hopyng and
not doubtyng but that hys good grace shall rewarde me in
suche wise that I shal have cause to pray for his good and   35
prosperus welfare. And besechynge his said noble good grace
to pardon me of the rude [translatynge] and this simple worke,
for accordyng to the coppy whyche he sent to me I have
folowed as nigh as I can; and where as any defaute shall be
founde I submyt me to the correccion of them that under-   40
stande the cronycle and hystory, besechyng[2] them to correcte
it and amende there as they shall fynde faute. And I shall
praye Almighty God for them that so doo to rewarde them
in suche wyse that after this shorte and transytory lyfe we all
may come to everlastyng lyfe in heven. Amen.   45

Thus endeth the prologue.

(b) *Colophon*

[Reprinted from W. Copland's print of 1554]
Here finissheth the hystory of the noble and valiaunt knyght,
Reynawde of Mountawban, and his three bretheren. Im-
printed at London by Wynkyn de Worde the viii daye of Maye
and the yere of Our Lorde MCCCCiiii at the request and
commaundement of the noble and puissaunt erle, the Erle of   5
Oxenforde; and now emprinted in the yere of Our Lorde
MCCCCliiii, the vi daye of Maye, by Wylliam Copland for
Thomas Petet.

[1] ẇ
[2] besethyng

45. GAME OF CHESS (First Edition) (31 March 1474)

(a) *Prologue*

To the right noble, right excellent and vertuous prince, George Duc of Clarence, Erle of Warwyk and of Salisburye, Grete Chamberlayn of Englond, and Leutenant of Irelond, oldest broder of Kynge Edward by the grace of God Kynge of England and of Fraunce, your most humble servant William Caxton amonge other of your servantes sendes unto yow peas, helthe, joye and victorye upon your enemyes.

Right highe, puyssant and redoubted Prynce, for as moche as I have understand and knowe that ye are enclined unto the comyn wele of the Kynge, our sayd soveryn[1] lord, his nobles, lordes and comyn peple of his noble royame of Englond, and that ye sawe gladly the inhabitans of the same enformed in good, vertuous, prouffitable and honeste maners, in whiche your noble persone wyth guydyng of your hows haboundeth gyvyng light and ensample unto all other, therfore I have put me in devour to translate a lityll book late comen into myn handes out of Frensh into Englisshe, in which I fynde th'auctorites, dictees and stories of auncient doctours, philosophes, poetes and of other wyse men whiche been recounted and applied unto the moralite of the publique wele as well of the nobles as of the comyn peple after the game and playe of the chesse. Whiche booke, right puyssant and redoubtid Lord, I have made in the name and under the shadewe of your noble protection not presumyng to correcte or enpoigne onythynge ayenst your noblesse, for God be thankyd your excellent renome shyneth as well in strange regions as within the royame of England gloriously unto your honour and laude, whiche God multeplye and encrece, but to th'entent that other, of what estate or degre he or they stande in, may see in this sayd lityll book yf they governed themself as they ought to doo.

Wherfor, my right dere redoubted Lord, I requyre and supplye your good grace not to desdaygne to resseyve this lityll sayd book in gree and thanke as well of me your humble and unknowen servant as of a better and gretter man than I am, for the right good wylle that I have had to make this lityll werk in the best wyse I can ought to be reputed for the fayte and dede.

[1] saueryn

And for more clerely to procede in this sayd book I have ordeyned that the chapitres ben sette in the begynnynge to 40
th'ende that ye may see more playnly the mater wherof the
book treteth, etc.

(b) *Book III ch. 2*

And also hit is to be supposyd that suche as have theyr goodes
comune and not propre is most acceptable to God, for ellys
wold not thise religious men as monkes, freris, chanons,
observantes, and all other avowe hem and kepe the wilfull
poverte that they ben professid too. For in trouth I have 5
myself ben conversant in a religious hous of White Freris
at Gaunt whiche have alle thynge in comyn amonge them and
not one richer than another, in so moche that yf a man gaf to
a frere iii d. or iiii d. to praye for hym in his masse, as sone as
the masse is doon he deliverith hit to his overest or pro- 10
curatour; in whyche hows ben many vertuous and devoute
freris. And yf that lyf were not the beste and the most
holiest, Holy Church wold never suffre hit in religion.

(c) *Book III ch. 3*

Alas, and in Engeland what hurte doon the advocats, men of
lawe and attorneyes of court to the comyn peple of the
royame as well in the spirituell lawe as in the temporall: how
torne they the lawe and statutes at their pleasir; how ete they
the peple; how enpovere they the comynte. I suppose that in 5
alle Cristendom ar not so many pletars, attorneys and men of
the lawe as ben in Englond onely. For yf they were nombrid,
all that lange to the courtes of the Chauncery, Kinges
Benche, Comyn Place, Cheker, Ressayt and Helle, and the
bagge-berars of the same, hit shold amounte to a grete 10
multitude. And how all thyse lyve and of whome, yf hit shold
be uttrid and told, hit shold not be bylevyd, for they entende
to theyr synguler wele and prouffyt and not to the comyn.

(d) *Book IV ch. 1*

Alas, what haboundance was sometymes in the royames and
what prosperite, in whiche was justice and every man in his
office contente; how stood the cytees that tyme in worship
and renome; how was renomed the noble royame of Englond, alle the world dredde hit and spack worship of hit. How 5
hit now standeth and in what haboundance I reporte me to
them that knowe hit: yf ther ben theevis wythin the royame

or on the see, they knowe that laboure in the royame and sayle
on the see; I wote well the fame is grete therof. I pray God
save that noble royame and sende good, true and politicque   10
counceyllours to the governours of the same.

(e) *Epilogue*

And therfore, my ryght redoubted Lord, I pray Almighty God
to save the Kyng our soverain lord and to gyve him grace to
issue as a kynge and t'abounde in all vertues and to be assisted
with all other his lordes in such wyse that his noble royame of
Englond may prospere and habounde in vertues, and that   5
synne may be eschewid, justice kepte, the royame defended,
good men rewarded, malefactours punysshid, and the ydle
peple to be put to laboure, that he wyth the nobles of the
royame may regne gloriously in conquerynge his rightfull
enheritaunce that verray peas and charite may endure in bothe   10
his royames and that marchandise may have his cours in suche
wise that every man eschewe synne and encrece in vertuous
occupacions. Praynge your good grace to resseyve this lityll
and symple book, made under the hope and shadowe of your
noble protection by hym that is your most humble servant,   15
in gree and thanke. And I shall praye Almighty God for your
longe lyf and welfare, whiche he preserve and sende yow
th'accomplisshement of your hye, noble, joyous and vertuous
desirs. Amen.

Fynysshid the last day of Marche the yer of Our Lord God   20
a thousand, foure honderd and lxxiiii.

46. GAME OF CHESS (Second Edition) (*c.* 1483)

(a) *Prologue*

The holy appostle and doctour of the peple, Saynt Poule,
sayth in his epystle: alle that is wryten is wryten unto our
doctryne and for our lernyng. Wherfore many noble clerkes
have endevoyred them to wryte and compyle many notable
werkys and historyes to the ende that it myght come to the   5
knowlege and understondyng of suche as ben ygnoraunt, of
which the nombre is infenyte; and accordyng to the same
saith Salamon that the nombre of foles is infenyte. And emong
alle other good werkys it is a werke of ryght special recomendacion to enforme and to late understonde wysedom and   10
vertue unto them that be not lernyd ne cannot dyscerne

wysedom fro folye. Thenne emonge whom there was an excellent doctour of dyvynyte in the royame of Fraunce of the ordre of th'ospytal of Saynt John's of Jherusalem whiche entended the same and hath made a book of the chesse 15 moralysed, whiche at suche tyme as I was resident in Brudgys in the counte of Flaundres cam into my handes. Whiche whan I had redde and overseen, me[1] semed ful necessarye for to be had in Englisshe, and in eschewyng of ydlenes and to th'ende that somme which have not seen it ne understonde 20 Frenssh ne Latyn, I delybered in myself to translate it into our maternal tonge. And whan I so had achyeved the sayd translacion I dyde doo sette in enprynte a certeyn nombre of theym, whiche anone were depesshed and solde.

Wherfore bycause thys sayd book is ful of holsom wysedom 25 and requysyte unto every astate and degree, I have purposed to enprynte it, shewyng therin the figures of suche persons as longen to the playe, in whom al astates and degrees ben comprysed. Besechyng al them that this litel werke shal see, here or rede to have me for excused for the rude and symple 30 makyng and reducyn[g] into our Englisshe, and where as is defaute to correcte and amende, and in so doyng they shal deserve meryte and thanke; and I shal pray for them that God of his grete mercy shal rewarde them in his everlastyng blisse in heven, to the whiche he brynge us that wyth his 35 precious blood redemed us. Amen.

This book is devyded and departed into four traytyes and partyes.

(b) *Conclusion*

Thenne late every man of what condycion he be that redyth or herith this litel book redde take therby ensaumple to amende hym.

Explicit per Caxton

47. GOLDEN LEGEND (20 November 1481?)

(a) *Prologue*

The holy and blessed doctour Saynt Jerom sayth thys auctoryte: Do alweye somme good werke to th'ende that the devyl fynde the not ydle. And the holy doctour Saynt Austyn sayth in the *Book of the Labour of Monkes* that no man stronge or myghty to laboure ought to be ydle. For which cause whan 5

---
[1] ne

I had parfourmed and accomplisshed dyvers werkys and
hystoryes translated out of Frensshe into Englysshe at the
requeste of certeyn lordes, ladyes and gentylmen, as th'
Ystorye of the Recuyel of Troye, the *Book of the Chesse*, the
Hystorye of Jason, the *Hystorye of the Myrrour of the World*, the   10
xv bookes of *Metamorpheseos* in whyche been conteyned the
fables of Ovyde, and the *Hystorye of Godefroy of Boloyn in the
Conqueste of Jherusalem*, wyth other dyvers werkys and bookes,
I nyste what werke to begynne and put forth after the said
werkys tofore made; and for as moche as ydelnesse is so   15
moche blamed, as sayth Saynt Bernard the myllyfluous
doctour that she is moder of lyes and stepdame of vertues and
it is she that overthroweth stronge men into synne, quenchyth
vertue, nouryssheth pryde and maketh the waye redy to goo
to helle; and Johan Cassyodore sayth that the thought of hym   20
that is ydle thynketh on none other thynge but on lychorous
metys and vyandes for his bely; and the holy Saynt Bernard
aforesayd sayth in an epystle whan the tyme shal come that it
shal behove us to rendre and gyve acomptes of our ydle
tyme, what reson may we rendre or what answer shal we   25
gyve whan in ydlenes is none excuse; and Prosper sayth that
whosomever lyveth in ydlenesse lyveth in manere of a dombe
beest; and bycause I have seen the auctorytees that blame and
despyse so moche ydlenes and also knowe wel that it is one of
the capytal and dedely synnes moche hateful unto God ther-   30
fore I have concluded and fermelye purposed in myself no
more to be ydle, but wyl applye myself to laboure and suche
ocupacion as I have be acustomed to do.

And for as moche as Saynt Austyn aforesayd sayth upon a
psalme that good werke ought not be doon for fere of payne   35
but for the love of rightwysnesse and that it be of veray and
soverayn fraunchyse, and bycause me semeth to be a soverayn
wele to incyte and exhorte men and wymmen to kepe them
from slouthe and ydlenesse and to lete to be understonden to
suche peple as been not letterd the natyvytees, the lyves, the   40
passyons, the myracles, and the dethe of the holy sayntes and
also somme other notorye dedes and actes of tymes passed, I
have submysed myself to translate into Englysshe[1] the
Legende of Sayntes which is callyd *Legenda Aurea* in Latyn –
that is to say the 'Golden Legende' for in lyke wyse as golde   45
is moste noble above al other metalles in lyke wyse is thys
legende holden moost noble above al other werkys. Ageynst

[1] Englyssle

me here myght somme persones saye that thys *Legende* hath be
translated tofore; and trouthe it is. But for as moche as I had by
me a *Legende* in Frensshe, another in Latyn, and the thyrd in   50
Englysshe whiche varyed in many and dyvers places, and also
many hystoryes were comprysed in the two other bookes
whiche were not in the Englysshe book, and therfore I have
wryton one oute of the sayd thre bookes, which I have
ordryd otherwyse than the sayd Englysshe *Legende* is whiche   55
was so tofore made. Besechyng alle theym that shall see or
here it redde to pardone me where I have erryd or made fawte,
whyche yf ony be is of ygnoraunce and ageyn my wylle; and
submytte it hooly of suche as can and may to correcte it,
humbly bysechyng them so to doo. And in so doyng they shal   60
deserve a synguler lawde and meryte. And I shal praye for
them unto Almyghty God that he of his benygne grace
rewarde them etc., and that it prouffyte to alle them that shal
rede or here it redde, and may encreace in them vertue and
expelle vyce and synne that by the ensaumple of the holy   65
sayntes amende theyr lyvyng here in thys shorte lyf that by
their merytes they and I may come to everlastyng lyf and
blysse in heven. Amen.

And for as moche as this sayd werke was grete and overchargeable to me t'accomplisshe, I feryd me in the begynnyng   70
of the translacyon to have contynued it bycause of the longe
tyme of the translacion and also in th'enpryntyng of the
same; and in maner halfe desperate to have accompliss[he]d
it was in purpose to have lefte it after that I had begonne to
translate it and to have layed it aparte, ne had it be at   75
th'ynstaunce and requeste of the puyssant, noble and
vertuous erle, my Lord Wyllyam Erle of Arondel, whiche
desyred me to procede and contynue the said werke and
promysed me to take a resonable quantyte of them when they
were achyeved and accomplisshed. And sente to me a   80
worshypful gentylman, a servaunte of his named John
Stanney, whych solycyted me in my lordes name that I shold
in no wyse leve it but accomplisshe it, promysyng that my sayd
lord shold duryng my lyf yeve and graunte to me a yerely fee,
that is to wete a bucke in sommer and a doo in wynter; with   85
whiche fee I holde me wel contente. Thenne atte contemplacion[1] and reverence of my sayd lord I have endevoyred
me to make an ende and fynysshe thys sayd translacion, and
also have enprynted it in the moost best wyse that I have

[1] centemplacion

coude or myght; and presente this sayd book[1] to his good   90
and noble lordshyp as chyef causer of the achyevyng of hit,
prayeng hym to take it in gree of me Wyllyam Caxton, hys
poure servaunte, and that it lyke hym to remembre my fee.
And I shal praye unto Almyghty God for his longe lyf and
welfare and after this shorte and transytorye lyf to come into   95
everlastyng joye in heven, the whiche he sende to hym and
me and unto al them that shal rede and here this sayd book,
that for the love and feythe of whome al these holy sayntes
hath suffred deth and passyon. Amen.

And to th'ende eche hystorye,[2] lyf and passyon may be   100
shortely founden I have ordeyned this table folowyng where
and in what leef he shal fynde suche as shal be desyred, and
have sette the nombre of every leef in the margyne.

(b) *Nativity of Our Lord*

[Fol. 5ᵛ] This Feste of Natyvyte of Our Lord is one of the
grettest feestes of all the yere, and for to telle alle the myracles
that Our Lord hath shewde it shold conteyne an hole booke.
But at this tyme I shal leve and passe over sauf one thynge that
I have herde ones prechyd of a worshipeful doctour that   5
what persone beyng in clene lyf desire on this day a bone of
God, as fer as it is rightful and good for hym, Our Lord atte
reverence of this blessyd and hie feste of his Natyvyte wyll
graunte it to hym. Thenne lete us alway make us in clene lyf
at this feste that we may so plese hym that after this short lyf   10
we may come unto his blysse. Amen.

(c) *Circumcision of Our Lord*

[Fol. 8ʳ] Also it is said that it is in the chirche of Our Lady at
Andwarp in Braband. And there I knowe well that on
Trynyte Sonday they shewe it with grete reverence and is
there born abowte with a grete and a solempne procession,
and that though I be unworthy have seen dyverse tymes, and   5
have rede and herd thereof many myracles that God hath
shewd there for it. And as towchyng [this] I have herd saye
there that there was a cardynal sente fro Rome for to see it;
and as he was at his masse solempnly it was leyd on the
corporas, at whiche tyme it bled thre dropes of blood on the   10
said corporas. There they worshippe it as fore the flessh of
Our Lord whiche was cutte of at his circunsicion and named
it there *prepucium Domini*. Yf it be trewe to somme it semeth

---

[1] boook   [2] hystoryy

merveyll bycause it is so that the flessh that was cut of was of
the very flessh that was cutte of his body humayne. 15

(d) *History of Joshua*

[Fol. 63ʳ] And dyverse dukes after hym juged and demed
Israhel of whom ben noble hystoryes, as of Jepte, Gedeon
and Sampson, whiche I passe over unto th'*Ystoryes of the
Kynges* whiche is redde in holy chyrche fro the fyrst Sonday
after Trynyte Sonday unto the first Sonday of August. And 5
in the moneth of August is redde the *Book of Sapience*; and in
the moneth of Septembre ben redde th'ystoryes of Job, of
Thobye and of Judith;[1] and in Octobre the *Hystorye of the
Machabeis*; and in Novembre the *Book of Ezechiel* and his
visions; and in Decembre the hystorye of Advent; and the 10
Book of Ysaye unto Crystemasse. And after the fest of Epyph-
anye unto Septuagesme ben red th'*Epistles of Paule*. And this is
the rewle of the Temporal thurgh the yere, etc.

(e) *History of David*

[Fol. 70ʳ] For as I ones was byyonde the see rydyng in the
companye of a noble knyght named Syr John Capons, and
was also doctour in bothe lawes and was born in Malyorke
and had ben Viceroye and Governour of Aragon and
Catelone and that tyme Counceyllour unto the Duc of 5
Bourgonye Charloys, it happend we comened of the hystorye
of David. And this said noble man told me that he had redde
that David dyde this penaunce folowyng for thyse said
synnes: that he dalf hym in the ground standyng nakyd unto
the heed so longe that the wormes began to crepe in his 10
flesshe, and made a verse of this psalme *Miserere* and thenne
cam out. And whan he was hole therof, he wente in agayn and
stode so agayn as longe as afore is said and made the second
verse. And so as many tymes he was dolven in the erth as ben
verse in the said psalme of *Miserere mei, Deus*; and every tyme 15
was abydyng therin tyl he felte the wormes crepe in his
flesshe. This was a grete penaunce and a token of grete
repentaunce, for ther ben in the psalme xx verses and xx
tymes he was dolven. Thus thys noble man told me rydyng
bytwene the toun of Gaunt in Flaundres and the toun of 20
Bruxellis in Braband.
[Fol. 71ᵛ] This David was an holy man and made the holy
Psawter, whiche is an holy booke, and is conteyned therin the

[1] Judich

olde lawe and newe lawe. He was a grete prophete, for he
prophecyed the comyng of Cryst, his natyvyte, his passyon   25
and resurrection, and also his ascencion, and was grete with
God. Yet God wold not suffre hym to bylde a temple for hym,
for he had shedde man's blood. But God said to hym his sone
that shold regne after hym shold be a man pesyble and he shold
bylde the temple to God. And whan David had regned xl yere   30
Kynge of Jherusalem over Juda and Israhel, he deyed in
good mynde and was buryed with his faders in the cyte of
David.

(f) *History of Solomon*

[Fol. 72ᵛ] And for to wryte the curiosyte and werke of the
temple and the necessaryes, the tables and cost that was don
in gold, sylver and laton, it passeth my connynge to expresse
and englysshe them. Ye that ben clerkys may see it in the
Second Book of Kynges and the *Seconde Book of Paralipomenon*. It is   5
wondre to here the costes and expencis that was made in that
temple, but I passe over.
[Fol. 73ᵛ] What shal I aldaye wryte of the rychesses, glorye
and magnyfycence of Kynge Salamon? It was so grete that it
cannot be expressyd, for ther was never none lyke tofore hym   10
ne never shal none come after hym lyke unto hym. He made
the *Book of the Parables*, conteynyng xxxi chapytres, the *Booke
of the Canticles*, the *Book of Ecclesiastes*, conteynyng xii chapytres, and the *Booke of Sapience*, conteynyng xix chapytres.
[Fol. 73ᵛ] It is said, but I fynde it not in the Byble, that   15
Salamon repentyd hym moche of thys synne of ydolatrye and
dyde moche penaunce therfor, for he lete hym be drawe
thurgh Jherusalem and bete hymself wyth roddes and
scorgys that the blood folowed in the syght of alle the peple.

(g) *History of Rehoboam*

[Fol. 74ʳ] And here I leve alle th'ystorye and make an ende of
Booke of Kynges for thys tyme, etc. For ye that lyste to knowe
how every kyng regned after other, ye may fynde it in the
fyrst chapytre of Saynt Mathew, whyche is redde on Crystemas
day in the mornyng tofore *Te Deum* whyche is the genelagye of   5
Our Lady.

(h) *History of Job*

[Fol. 75ʳ] Thenne after that Job and they talked and spoken
togydre of hys sorowe and myserye, of whyche Seynt

Gregory hath made a grete book callyd the *Morallys of Seynt Gregory*, whiche is a noble book and a grete werk. But I passe over all tho maters and retorne unto the ende how God 5 restored Job agayn to prosperyte.

(i) *Life of St George*

[Fol. 158ᵛ] Thys blessyd and holy marter Saynt George is patrone of this royame of Englond and the crye of men of warre, in the worshyp of whome is founded the noble Ordre of the Garter and also a noble college in the castell of Wyndesore by kynges of Englond. In whiche college is the 5 herte of Saynt George whyche Sygysmond the Emperour of Almayn broughte and gafe for a grete and a precious relyque to Kyng Harry the fyfthe; and also the sayd Sygismonde was a broder of the sayd Garter; and also there is a pyece of his heed. Which college is nobly endowed to th'onoure and 10 worshyp of Almyghty God and hys blessyd marter Saynt George. Thenne lete us praye unto hym that he be special protectour and defendour of thys royame.

(j) *Life of St Augustine*

[Fol. 276ᵛ–277ʳ] Many other myracles hath God shewed by his lyfe and also after his deth whiche were overlonge to wryte in this booke, for they wold (I suppose) conteyne a book as moche as al this and more. But among other [under] correction I wylle sette here in one myracle whiche I have 5 sene paynted on an aulter of Saynt Austyn at the Blacke Freres at Andwerpe how be it I fynde hit not in the *Legende*, myn exempler, neyther in Englysshe, Frensshe ne in Latyn.

It was soo that this gloryous doctor made and compyled many volumes as afore is sayd among whome he made a book 10 of the Trynyte. In whiche he studyed and mused sore in his mynde soo ferforthe that on a tyme as he wente by the see-syde in Auffryke studyeng on the Trynyte, he fonde by the see-syde a lytel childe whiche hadde made a lytel pytte in the sonde, and in his honde a lytel spone. And wyth the spone he tooke 15 oute water of the large see and poured hit into the pytte. And whanne Saynt Augustyn behelde hym he merveyled and demaunded hym what he dyde. And he answerd and sayde: 'I wylle lade oute and brynge alle this water of this see into thys pytte.' 20

'What,' sayd he, 'hit is impossyble. How maye hit be done

sythe the see is soo greete and large and thy pytte and spone
soo lytylle?'

'Yes, forsothe,' sayd he. 'I shalle lyghtlyer and sonner
drawe alle the water of the see and brynge hit into this pytte   25
than thow shalt brynge the mysterye of the Trynyte and his
dyvynyte into thy lytel understandynge as to the regard therof,
for the mysterye of the Trynyte is greter and larger to the
comparyson of thy wytte and brayne than is this grete see
unto this lytel pytte.' And therwyth the childe vanysshed   30
awey.

Thenne here may every man take ensample that no man,
and specially symple lettred men ne unlerned, presume to
entermete ne to muse on hyghe thynges of the godhede
ferther than we be enfourmed by our faythe, for our only   35
feyth shalle suffyse us.

Thenne herewith I make an ende of the lyf of this gloryous
doctor Saynt Austyn, to whome late us devoutely praye that
he be a medyatour and advocate unto the blessyd Trynyte
that we maye amende oure synful lyfe in this transytorye   40
world that whan we shalle departe we may come to everlastyng blysse in heven. Amen.

(k) *Nativity of Our Lady*

[Fol. 287ʳ⁻ᵛ] Thenne late us contynuelly gyve laude and
praysyng to her as moche as we maye and late us saye with
Saynt Jeromme this response: *Sancta et inmaculata vyrginitas.*
And how this hooly response was made I purpose under
correction to wryte here. It is so that I was at Coleyn and   5
herd reherced there by a noble doctour that the hooly and
devoute Saynt Jeromme had a custome to vysyte the chirches
at Rome. And so he cam into a chirche where an ymage of our
blessyd Lady stoode in a chappell by the dore as he entryd
and passyd forthe by withoute ony salutacion to Our Lady   10
and wente forthe to every aulter and made his prayers to all
the sayntes in the chirche eche after other, and retourned
ageyne by the same ymage without ony saleweng to her.
Thenne our blessyd Lady called hym and spak to hym by the
sayd ymage and demaunded of hym the cause why he made   15
no salutacion to her seyng that he had done honoure and
worship to alle the other sayntes of whom the ymages were
in that chirche.

And thenne Saynt Jeromme kneled doune and sayd thus:

'*Sancta et inmaculata vyrginitas quibus te*[1] *laudibus referam* 20
nescio; quia quem celi capere non poterant tuo gremio contulisti;'
whiche is to say 'Holy and undefowled virgynyte, I wote
never what lawde and praysynges I shalle gyve unto the, for
hym that alle the hevenes myght not take ne conteyne thou
hast borne in thy wombe.' 25

So syth this holy man thought hymself insuffycyent to gyve
to her lawde thenne what shal we synful wretches doo but put
us hooly in her mercy, knowlechyng us insufficient to gyve
to her due law[d]e and praysyng? But late us mekely byseche
her t'accepte oure good entente and wylle, and that by her 30
merytes we maye atteyne after this lyf to come to her in
everlastyng lyf in heven. Amen.

(l) *Life of St Ursula*

[Fol. 337ᵛ] Hit is to be remembryd that amonge these
enleven thousand vyrgyns were many men, for the Pope
Cyryaque and other bisshops and Ethereus Kynge with other
lordes and knyghtes hadde moche peple to serve them. And
as I have ben enformed in Coleyn that there were men besyde 5
wymmen that thylke tyme suffryd martirdome fyften thousand. So the nombre of this hooly multitude as of the hooly
vyrgyns and men were xxviM; to whom late us praye to Our
Lord that he have mercy on us.

(m) *Epilogue*

Thus endeth the legende named in Latyn *Legenda Aurea,* that
is to saye in Englysshe the *Golden Legende,* for lyke as golde
passeth in valewe alle other metalles so thys legende
excedeth alle other bookes. Wherin ben conteyned alle the
hygh and grete festys of Our Lord, the festys of our blessyd 5
Lady, the lyves, passyons and myracles of many other
sayntes, and other hystoryes and actes as al allonge hereafore
is made mencyon. Whiche werke I have accomplisshed at the
commaundemente and requeste of the noble and puyssaunte
erle and my special good lord, Wyllyam Erle of Arondel, and 10
have fynysshed it at Westmestre the twenty day of Novembre,
the yere of Our Lord MCCCClxxxiii and the fyrst yere of the
reygne of Kyng Rychard the Thyrd.
    By me Wyllyam Caxton.

[1] the

50. HISTORY OF TROY (*c.* 1473)

(a) *Preface*

Here begynneth the volume intituled and named the
Recuyell of the Historyes of Troye, composed and drawen out of
dyverce bookes of Latyn into Frensshe by the ryght venerable
persone and worshipfull man, Raoul Lefevre, preest and
chapelayn unto the ryght noble, gloryous and myghty   5
prynce in his tyme, Phelip Duc of Bourgoyne, of Braband et
cetera, in the yere of the incarnacion of Our Lord God a
thousand, foure honderd, sixty and foure; and translated and
drawen out of Frenshe into Englisshe by Willyam Caxton,
mercer of the cyte of London, at the comaundement of the   10
right hye, myghty and vertuouse pryncesse, hys redoubtyd
lady, Margarete by the grace of God Duchesse of Bourgoyne,
of Lotryk, of Braband et cetera. Whiche sayd translacion and
werke was begonne in Brugis in the countee of Flaundres the
fyrst day of Marche, the yere of the incarnacion of our said   15
Lord God a thousand, foure honderd, sixty and eyghte, and
ended and fynysshid in the holy cyte of Colen the xix day of
Septembre the yere of our sayd Lord God a thousand foure
honderd, sixty and enleven et cetera.

And on that other side of this leef foloweth the prologe.   20

(b) *Prologue*

Whan I remembre that every man is bounden by the comandement and counceyll of the wyse man to eschewe slouth
and ydlenes, whyche is moder and nourysshar of vyces, and
ought to put myself unto vertuous ocupacion and besynesse
than I, havynge no grete charge of ocupacion, folowynge the   5
sayd counceyll toke a Frenche booke and redde therin many
strange and mervayllous historyes wherein I had grete pleasyr
and delyte as well for the novelte of the same as for the fayr
langage of Frenshe; whyche was in prose so well and compendiously sette and wreton whiche me thought I understood   10
the sentence and substance of every mater. And for so moche
as this booke was newe and late maad and drawen into
Frenshe and never had seen hit in oure Englissh tonge, I
thought in myself hit shold be a good besynes to translate
hyt into oure Englissh to th'ende that hyt myght be had as   15
well in the royame of Englond as in other landes, and also for
to passe therwyth the tyme; and thus concluded in myself to

97

begynne this sayd w[e]rke. And forthwith toke penne and
ynke and began boldly to renne forth as blynde Bayard in thys
presente werke whyche is named the *Recuyell of the Trojan*   20
Historyes.

   And afterward whan I rememberyd myself of my symplenes
and unperfightnes that I had in bothe langages, that is to wete
in Frenshe and in Englisshe, for in France was I never, and
was born and lerned myn Englissh in Kente in the Weeld,   25
where I doubte not is spoken as brode and rude Englissh as is
in ony place of Englond; and have contynued by the space of
xxx yere for the most parte in the contres of Braband, Flandres,
Holand and Zeland; and thus whan alle thyse thynges cam
tofore me aftyr that Y had made and wretyn a fyve or six   30
quayers, Y fyll in dispayr of thys werke and purposid no
more to have contynuyd therin, and tho quayers leyd apart;
and in two yere aftyr laboured no more in thys werke. And
was fully in wyll to have lefte hyt tyll on a tyme hit fortuned
that the ryght hyghe excellent and right vertuous prynces,   35
my ryght redoughted lady, my Lady Margarete by the grace
of God suster unto the Kynge of Englond and of France, my
soverayn lord, Duchesse of Bourgoine, of Lotryk, of
Brabant, of Lymburgh and of Luxenburgh, Countes of
Flandres, of Artoys and of Bourgoine, Palatynee of Heynawd,   40
of Holand, of Zeland and of Namur, Marquesse of the Holy
Empire, Lady of Fryse, of Salius and of Mechlyn, sente for
me to speke wyth her good grace of dyverce maters. Among
the whyche Y lete her Hyenes have knowleche of the
forsayd begynnyng of thys werke, whiche anone comanded   45
me to shewe the sayd v or vi quayers to her sayd grace. And
whan she had seen hem, anone she fonde a defaute in myn
Englissh whiche sche comanded me to amende and moreover
comanded me straytli to contynue and make an ende of the
resydue than not translated. Whos dredefull comandement Y   50
durste in no wyse disobey because Y am a servant unto her
sayde grace and resseive of her yerly fee and other many goode
and grete benefetes and also hope many moo to resseyve of
her Hyenes; but forthwyth wente and labouryde in the sayde
translacion aftyr my symple and pour connyng also nigh as Y   55
can folouyng myn auctour, mekeli beseching the bounteuous
hyenes of my said lady that of her benyvolence liste to accepte
and take in gree this symple and rude werke here folowyng.
And yf ther be onythyng wreton or sayd to her playsir Y shall
thynke my labour well enployed; and where as ther is   60

defawte that she arette hyt to the symplenes of my connyng
whiche is ful small in this behalve; and requyre and praye
alle them that shall rede this sayd werke to correcte hyt and
to hold me excusid of the rude and symple translacion. And
thus Y ende my prologe.   65

Here foloweth the prologue of that worshipful man Raoul
Lefevre, whiche was auctor of this present book in the
Frensh tonge.

(c) *Conclusion of Book II*

Besechyng her that is cause of this translacion out of Frenshe
into this symple and rude Englissh, that is to wete my right
redoubtyd lady, Margarete by the grace of God suster of my
soverayn lord the Kynge of Englond and of France et cetera,
Duchesse of Bourgoyne and of Brabant et cetera, that she   5
wole resseyve my rude labour in thanke and in gree.

(d) *Epilogue to Book II*

Thus endeth the seconde book of the *Recule of the Historyes of
Troyes,* whiche bookes were late translated into Frenshe out
of Latyn by the labour of the venerable persone Raoul
Lefevre, preest, as afore is said, and by me indigne and
unworthy translated into this rude Englissh by the comande-   5
ment of my said redoubtid lady, Duches of Bourgone. And
for as moche as I suppose the said two bokes ben not had
tofore this tyme in oure Englissh langage, therfor I had the
better will to accomplisshe this said werke. Whiche werke was
begonne in Brugis and contynued in Gaunt and finysshid in   10
Coleyn in the tyme of the troublous world and of the grete
devysions beyng and reygnyng as well in the royames of
Englond and Fraunce as in all other places unyversally
thurgh the world, that is to wete the yere of Our Lord a
thousand, four honderd lxxi.   15

And as for the thirde book whiche treteth of the generall
and last destruccion of Troye, hit nedeth not to translate hit
into Englissh for as moche as that worshi[p]full and religyous
man Dan John Lidgate, monke of Burye, dide translate hit
but late, after whos werke I fere to take upon me, that am not 20
worthy to bere his penner and ynkehorne after hym, to
medle me in that werke. But yet for as moche as I am bounde
to contemplare my sayd ladyes good grace and also that his
werke is in ryme, and as ferre as I knowe hit is not had in
prose in our tonge; and also paraventure he translated after   25

99

some other auctor than this is. And yet for as moche as
dyverce men ben of dyverce desyres, some to rede in ryme
and metre and some in prose, and also because that I have
now good leyzer beyng in Coleyn and have none other thynge
to doo at this tyme, in eschewyng of ydlenes, moder of all   30
vices, I have delibered in myself for the contemplacion of my
sayd redoubtid lady to take this laboure in hand by the
suffrance and helpe of Almyghty God, whome I mekely
supplye to gyve me grace to accomplysshe hit to the playsir
of her that is causer therof and that she resseyve hit in gre of   35
me her faithfull, trewe and moste humble servant et cetera.
    Thus endeth the seconde book.

(e) *Epilogue*

Thus ende I this book whyche I have translated after myn
auctor as nyghe as God hath gyven me connyng, to whom be
gyven the laude and preysyng. And for as moche as in the
wrytyng of the same my penne is worn, myn hande wery and
not stedfast, myn eyen dimmed with overmoche lokyng on   5
the whit paper, and my corage not so prone and redy to
laboure as hit hath ben, and that age crepeth on me dayly and
febleth all the bodye, and also because I have promysid to
dyverce gentilmen and to my frendes to adresse to hem as
hastely as I myght this sayd book, therfore I have practysed   10
and lerned at my grete charge and dispense to ordeyne this
said book in prynte after the maner and forme as ye may here
see; and is not wreton with penne and ynke as other bokes
ben to th'ende that every man may have them attones. For
all the bookes of this storye named the *Recule of the Historyes*   15
of Troyes thus enpryntid as ye here see were begonne in oon
day and also fynysshid in oon day. Whiche book I have
presented to my sayd redoubtid lady as afore is sayd. And
she hath well acceptid hit and largely rewarded me, wherfore
I besche Almyghty God to rewarde her [with] everlastyng   20
blisse after this lyf.
    Prayng her said grace and all them that shall rede this
book not to desdaigne the symple and rude werke nether to
replye agaynst the sayyng of the maters towchyd in this book,
thauwh hyt acorde not unto the translacion of other whiche   25
have wreton hit. For dyverce men have made dyverce bookes
whiche in all poyntes acorde not, as Dictes, Dares and
Homerus. For Dictes and Homerus, as Grekes, sayn and wryten favorably for the Grekes and gyve to them more worship

than to the Trojans. And Dares wryteth otherwyse than they   30
doo. And also as for the propre names hit is no wonder that
they acorde not, for somme oon name in thyse dayes have
dyverce equyvocacions after the contrees that they dw[e]lle
in. But alle acorde in conclusion the generall destruccion of
that noble cyte of Troye and the deth of so many noble   35
prynces as kynges, dukes, erles, barons, knyghtes and comyn
peple, and the ruyne irreperable of that cyte that never syn
was reedefyed; whiche may be ensample to all men duryng
the world how dredefull and jeopardous it is to begynne a
warre and what harmes,[1] losses and deth foloweth. T[h]erfore   40
th'apostle saith all that is wreton is wreton to our doctryne.
Whyche doctryne for the comyn wele, I beseche God, maye
be taken in suche place and tyme as shall be moste nedefull
in encrecyng of peas, love and charyte; whyche graunte us
he that suffryd for the same to be crucyfied on the rood-   45
tree, and saye we alle 'Amen' for charyte.

56. HOROLOGIUM SAPIENTIAE (*c.* 1491)

(a) *Incipit to Horologium Sapientiae*
These ben the chapitres of thys tretyse of the seven poyntes of
trewe love and everlastynge wysdom drawen oute of the
booke that is writen in Latyn and cleped *Orologium Sapiencie.*

(b) *Colophon to Horologium Sapientiae*
Thus endith the treatyse of the vii poyntes of true love and
everlastyng wysdom drawen of the boke that is wryten in
Laten named *Orologium Sapiencie.*
Emprynted at Westmynstre.
Qui legit, emendet; pressorem non reprehendat, Wyllelmum   5
Caxton, cui Deus alta tradat.

(c) *Prologue to Rule of St Benedict*
Here folowyth[2] a compendious abstracte translate into
Englysshe out of the holy rule of Saynte Benet for men and
wymmen of the habyte therof the whiche understonde lytyll
Laten or none to the entent that they maye often rede [and]
execute the hole rewll and the better kepe it than it is   5
accordyng to the abyte and their streyte professyon so that the

[1] hormes   [2] felowyth

welle of their sowlys and better ensample[1] of that holy rely-
gyon maye be the sooner had and knowen.

(d) *Conclusion*

Thus endeth this present boke composed of diverse fruytfull
ghostly maters of whiche the forseyde names folowen to
th'entent that wel-disposed persones that desiren to here or
rede ghostly informacions maye the sooner knowe by this
lityll intytelyng th'effectis of this sayd lytyll volume, in as   5
moche as the hole content of this lityll boke is not of one
mater oonly as hereafter ye maye knowe.

The fyrst treatise is named *Orologium Sapiencie* wyth vii
chapitours folowynge shewyng vii poyntes of true love of
everlastynge wisdom.   10

The seconde treatyse sheweth xii prouffytes of tribulacyon
wyth xii chapytours folowynge.

The thyrde treatise sheweth the holy rule of Saynt Benet
whiche is right necessary to be knowen to al men and
wymmen of religyon that understonde noo Laten whiche   15
sheweth xxxiii poyntes to be observed.

Emprynted at Westmynstre by desiryng of certeyn worshipfull persones.

59. HOUSE OF FAME (*c.* 1484)

(a) *Incipit*

The *Book of Fame* made by Gefferey Chaucer.

(b) *Conclusion*

And wyth the noyse of them [t]wo   Caxton
I sodeynly awoke anon tho
And remembryd what I had seen
And how hye and ferre I had been
In my ghoost, and had grete wonder   5
Of that the God of Thonder
Had lete me knowen, and began to wryte
Lyke as ye have herd me endyte;
Wherfor to studye and rede alway
I purpose to doo day by day.   10
Thus in dremyng and in game
Endeth thys lytyl *Book of Fame.*
                    Explicit

[1] emsample

I fynde no more of this werke tofore-sayde, for as fer as I
can understonde this noble man Gefferey Chaucer fynysshyd 15
at the sayd conclusion of the metyng of Iesyng and sothsawe,
where as yet they ben chekked and maye not departe. Whyche
werke, as me semeth, is craftyly made and dygne to be
wreton and knowen, for he towchyth in it ryght grete
wysedom and subtyll understondyng. And so in alle hys 20
werkys he excellyth in myn oppynyon alle other wryters in
our Englyssh, for he wrytteth no voyde wordes, but alle
hys mater is ful of hye and quycke sentence. To whom ought
to be gyven laude and preysyng for hys noble makyng and
wrytyng, for of hym alle other have borowed syth and taken 25
in alle theyr wel-sayeng and wrytyng.

And I humbly beseche and praye yow emonge your prayers
to remembre hys soule, on whyche and on alle Crysten soulis
I beseche Almyghty God to have mercy. Amen.

Emprynted by Wylliam Caxton. 30

71. JASON (c. 1477)

(a) *Prologue*

For as moche as late by the comaundement of the right hye
and noble princesse, my right redoubted lady, my Lady
Margarete by the grace of God Duchesse of Bourgoyne,
Brabant et cetera, I translated a boke out of Frensshe into
Englissh named *Recuyel of the Histories of Troye*, in whiche is 5
comprehended how Troye was thries destroyed, and also the
labours and histories of Saturnus, Tytan, Jubyter, Perseus
and Hercules, and other moo therin rehersed. But as to the
historie of Jason towchyng the conqueste of the Golden
Flese myn auctor hath not sett in his boke but brevely. And 10
the cause is for as moche as he hadde made before a boke of
the hoole lyf of Jason whyche he presented unto the noble
prynce in his dayes, Philippe Duc of Bourgoyne; and also the
sayde boke shulde have ben to grete if he had sett the saide
historie in his boke for it conteyneth thre bokes beside 15
th'istorie of Jason. Thenne for as moche as this sayd boke is
late newe made aparte of alle th'istories of the sayd Jason, and
the historie of him whiche that Dares Frigius and Guido de
Columpnys wrote in the begynnyng of their bokes touchyng
the conqueste of the sayd Golden Flese by occasion wherof 20
grewe the cause of the seconde destruccion of the sayd cite

of Troye is not sett in the sayd *Boke of Recuyel of th'Istories of Troye*, therefor under the proteccion and suffraunce of the most hyghe puissant and Cristen kyng, my most dradde naturel liege lord, Edward by the grace of God Kyng of Englond and of Fraunce and Lord of Irland, I entende to translate the sayd *Boke of th'Istories of Jason* folowyng myn auctor as nygh as I can or may, not chaungyng the sentence ne presumyng to adde ne mynusshe onything otherwyse than myne auctor hath made in Frensshe.

And in so moche as the grettest fame and renomme standeth and resteth in the conquest of the flese of gold, whereof is founded an ordre of knightes wherof oure sayd soverayne lord is one and hath taken the profession therof, howe well somme persones afferme and saye that the sayd ordre hath taken his orygynal of the flese of Gedeon, wherein I will not dispute. But well wote I that the noble Duc Philippe, firste foundeur of this sayd ordre, dyd doo maken a chambre in the castell of Hesdyn wherein was craftyly and curiously depeynted the conqueste of the Golden Flese by the sayd Jason; in whiche chambre I have ben and seen the sayde historie so depeynted. And in remembraunce of Medea and of her connyng and science, he had do make in the sayde chambre by subtil engyn that, whan he wolde, it shuld seme that it lightend and then thondre, snowe and rayne; and all within the sayde chambre as oftetymes and whan it shuld please him, which was al made for his singuler pleasir.

Thenne for the honour and worship of our sayd moost redoubted liege lorde whiche hath taken the sayde ordre, I have under the shadowe of his noble proteccion enterprised t'accomplissh this sayd litil boke; not presumyng to presente it unto his Highnesse for as moch as I doubte not his good grace hath it in Frensh which he wele understandeth. But not displesing his most noble grace I entende by his licence and congye and by the supportacion of our most redoubted liege lady, most exellent princesse the Quene, to presente this sayde boke unto the most fayr and my moost redoubted yong lorde, my Lord Prynce of Wales, our tocomyng soverayne lorde, whom I praye God save and encrease in vertue and bryng him unto as moche worship and goode renomme as ever had ony of his noble progenytours, to th'entent he may begynne to lerne rede Englissh, not for ony beaute or good endyting of our Englissh tonge that is therin but for the novelte of the histories whiche as I suppose hath not be had

bifore the translacion herof. Moost humblie besekyng my   65
sayd most drad soverayn and naturel liege lorde, the Kyng,
and also the Quene to pardon me so presumyng, and my
sayd tocomyng soverayne lord, my Lord the Prynce, to
receyve it in gree and thanke of me, his humble subgiett
and servaunte, and to pardone me of this my simple and rude   70
translacion; and all other that luste to rede or here it to
correcte where as they shalle finde defaulte.

Here endeth the prologue of the translatour.

(b) *Addendum to author's prologue*

Thus endeth myn auctor his prologe. And how wel that hit is
sayd afore this prologe that Eson was sone to Cacus, yet
Bochace saith in the *Genelagye of Goddes* that he was sone to
Erictheus, the xxix sone of Jupiter, as ye may see more
playnly in the xiii book of the *Genelagye of Goddes*, the xxiiii   5
chapytre.

(c) *Epilogue*

And howe be it that myn auctor writeth that he hath founde
no more of th'istorie of Jason, yet have I founden and red
in the boke that Bochace made of the genelagie of goddes
in his xiii boke that whan so was that Jason and Medea were
reconciled agayn togeder after that shee fled from Egeon that   5
he went with her into Colchos again. And whan he was comen
theder he founde the olde King Oetes, fader unto Medea,
bannissed and exiled out of his royame, whom he restored
and sette him by his valiaunce and puissaunce[1] in his kingdom agayn; and after went into Asie where he had victorie   10
in many batailes, and made so many conquestes with grete
magnificence in so moche that he was honoured and worshipped for a god. And were made and edefied diverce
temples in his name which after were destroied by the
commandment of King Alexander of Macedone, who   15
paraventure had envye of his glorie.

And also he saith that Thoant and Euneus where his sones
whom he begate on Ysiphile as he went to Colchos, where as
Stacius saith whiche were born[2] at ones. And for as moch
as it was not the custome in Lenos to fede and norisshe the   20
men-children, they were sent into another countrey for to be
nourysshed; wherfore the moder was put out of her royaume
and taken with pirates and theves and after sold unto

---

[1] puissaunte   [2] borñ

Lygurgis, King of Nemee. And after whan the sayde sones
waxe men they went with King Adrastus unto the Bataile of   25
Thebes. And as they went into the wode of Nemee they
herde of the sayd King Adrastus reherse her burth and the
caas of her moder, by which rehersayll they knew that she
was their moder; and in Kyng Lygurgis court they fonde her,
whenne Opheltes his sone was founde dede in the gardyn,   30
what time the lady that hadde charge of him went with the
Grekes to shew him the water, as in the *Siege of Thebes* it is
more plainly shewd. But what cam afterward of these two
sones it is incertayn. This saith Bochace in the xiii boke of the
Geneolagye of Goddes. And he saith he had another sone whos   35
name was Philemelus.

And more have I not red of the noble Jason, but this have
I founden more thenn myn auctor reherceth in his boke. And
therfore I make here an ende of this storie of Jason whom
diverce menn blame because that he left and repudied Medea.   40
But in this present boke ye may see the evydent causes why
he so dyd.

Prayng my said Lorde Prince t'accepte and take yt in gree
of me, his indigne serviteur; whom I beseche God Almighty
to save and encrece in vertu now in his tendre iongth that he   45
may come unto his parfait eage to his honour and worship
that his renomme maye perpetuelly be remembrid among the
most worthy; and after this present life everlasting life in
heven, who grant him and us that boughte us with his bloode,
blessyd Jhesus. Amen.   50

72. KING ARTHUR (31 July 1485)

(a) *Prologue*

After that I had accomplysshed and fynysshed dyvers
hystoryes, as wel of contemplacyon as of other hystoryal
and worldly actes of grete conquerours and prynces and also
certeyn bookes of ensaumples and doctryne, many noble and
dyvers gentylmen of thys royame of Englond camen and   5
demaunded me many and oftymes wherfore that I have not
do made and enprynte the noble hystorye of the Saynt Greal
and of the moost renomed Crysten kyng, fyrst and chyef of
the thre best Crysten and worthy, Kyng Arthur, whyche
ought moost to be remembred emonge us Englysshemen   10
tofore al other Crysten kynges. For it is notoyrly knowen

thorugh the unyversal world that there been ix worthy and
the best that ever were: that is to wete thre paynyms, thre
Jewes and thre Crysten men. As for the paynyms they were
tofore the incarnacyon of Cryst, whiche were named: the   15
fyrst, Hector of Troye of whome th'ystorye is comen bothe
in balade and in prose; the second, Alysaunder the grete; and
the thyrd, Julyus Cezar, Emperour of Rome, of whome
th'ystoryes ben wel kno and had. And as for the thre Jewes,
whyche also were tofore th'yncarnacyon of Our Lord, of   20
whome the fyrst was Duc Josue whyche brought the
chyldren of Israhel into the londe of byheste; the second,
Davyd Kyng of Jherusalem; and the thyrd, Judas Machabeus. Of these thre the Byble reherceth al theyr noble
hystoryes and actes. And sythe the sayd incarnacyon have   25
ben thre noble Crysten men stalled and admytted thorugh
the unyversal world into the nombre of the ix beste and
worthy. Of whome was fyrst the noble Arthur, whos noble
actes I purpose to wryte in thys present book here folowyng.
The second was Charlemayn or Charles the Grete, of whome   30
th'ystorye is had in many places bothe in Frensshe and
Englysshe. And the thyrd and last was Godefray of Boloyn,
of whos actes and lyf I made a book unto th'excellent prynce
and kyng of noble memorye, Kyng Edward the Fourth.

The sayd noble jentylmen instantly requyred me t'em-   35
prynte th'ystorye of the sayd noble kyng and conquerour,
Kyng Arthur, and of his knyghtes wyth th'ystorye of the
Saynt Greal and of the deth and endyng of the sayd Arthur,
affermyng that I ought rather t'enprynte his actes and noble
feates than of Godefroye of Boloyne or ony of the other   40
eyght, consyderyng that he was a man borne wythin this
royame and kyng and emperour of the same and that there
ben in Frensshe dyvers and many noble volumes of his actes
and also of his knyghtes. To whome I answerd that dyvers
men holde oppynyon that there was no suche Arthur and   45
that alle suche bookes as been maad of hym ben but fayned
and fables bycause that somme cronycles make of hym no
mencyon ne remembre hym noothynge ne of his knyghtes.
Wherto they answerd, and one in specyal sayd, that in hym
that shold say or thynke that there was never suche a kyng   50
callyd Arthur myght wel be aretted grete folye and blynde-
nesse, for he sayd that there were many evydences of the
contrarye.

Fyrst, ye may see his sepulture in the monasterye of Glast-

yngburye; and also, in *Polycronycon* in the v book, the syxte   55
chappytre and in the seventh book, the xxiii chappytre where
his body was buryed and after founden and translated into
the sayd monasterye. Ye shal se also in th'ystorye of Bochas,
in his book *De Casu Principum*, parte of his noble actes and
also of his falle; also, Galfrydus in his Brutysshe book   60
recounteth his lyf. And in dyvers places of Englond many
remembraunces ben yet of hym and shall remayne perpetuelly and also of his knyghtes. Fyrst, in the Abbey of Westmestre at Saynt Edwardes shryne remayneth the prynte of
his seal in reed waxe closed in beryll, in whych is wryton   65
Patricius Arthurus Britannie, Gallie, Germanie, Dacie Imperator.
Item, in the castel of Dover ye may see Gauwayn's skulle and
Cradok's mantel, at Wynchester the Rounde Table, in other
places Launcelottes swerde and many other thynges. Thenne
al these thynges consydered there can no man resonably   70
gaynsaye but there was a kyng of thys lande named Arthur,
for in al places Crysten and hethen he is reputed and taken for
one of the ix worthy and the fyrst of the thre Crysten men.
And also he is more spoken of beyonde the see, moo bookes[1]
made of his noble actes than there be in Englond, as wel in   75
Duche, Ytalyen, Spaynysshe and Grekysshe as in Frensshe.
And yet of record remayne in wytnesse of hym in Wales in
the toune of Camelot the grete stones and mervayllous
werkys of yron lyeng under the grounde and ryal vautes,
which dyvers now lyvyng hath seen. Wherfor it is a mervayl   80
why he is no more renomed in his owne contreye, sauf onelye
it accordeth to the word of God whyche sayth that no man is
accept for a prophete in his owne contreye. Thenne al these
thynges forsayd aledged, I coude not wel denye but that there
was suche a noble kyng named Arthur and reputed one of the   85
ix worthy, and fyrst and chyef of the Cristen men.

   And many noble volumes be made of hym and of his noble
knyghtes in Frensshe which I have seen and redde beyonde
the see, which been not had in our maternal tongue. But in
Walsshe ben many and also in Frensshe and somme in   90
Englysshe, but nowher nygh alle. Wherfore suche as have
late ben drawen oute bryefly into Englysshe, I have after the
symple connyng that God hath sente to me, under the favour
and correctyon of al noble lordes and gentylmen, enprysed
to enprynte a book of the noble hystoryes of the sayd Kynge   95
Arthur and of certeyn of his knyghtes after a copye unto me

---

[1] boookes

delyverd. Whyche copye Syr Thomas Malorye dyd take oute of certeyn bookes of Frensshe and reduced it into Englysshe. And I accordyng to my copye have doon sette it in enprynte to the entente that noble men may see and lerne the noble actes of chyvalrye, the jentyl and vertuous dedes that somme knyghtes used in tho dayes by whyche they came to honour, and how they that were vycious were punysshed and ofte put to shame and rebuke; humbly bysechyng al noble lordes and ladyes wyth al other estates of what estate or degree they been of that shal see and rede in this sayd book and werke that they take the good and honest actes in their remembrance and to folowe the same, wherin they shalle fynde many joyous and playsaunt hystoryes and noble and renomed actes of humanyte, gentylnesse and chyvalryes. For herein may be seen noble chyvalrye, curtosye, humanyte, frendlynesse, hardynesse, love, frendshyp, cowardyse, murdre, hate, vertue and synne. Doo after the good and leve the evyl and it shal brynge you to good fame and renommee. And for to passe the tyme thys book[1] shal be plesaunte to rede in. But for to gyve fayth and byleve that al is trewe that is conteyned herin, ye be at your lyberte. But al is wryton for our doctryne and for to beware that we falle not to vyce ne synne, but t'excersyse and folowe vertu, by whyche we may come and atteyne to good fame and renomme in thys lyf and after thys shorte and transytorye lyf to come unto everlastyng blysse in heven, the whyche he graunte us that reygneth in heven, the blessyd Trynyte. Amen.

Thenne to procede forth in thys sayd book whyche I dyrecte unto alle noble prynces, lordes and ladyes, gentylmen or gentylwymmen, that desyre to rede or here redde of the noble and joyous hystorye of the grete conquerour and excellent kyng, Kyng Arthur, somtyme kyng of thys noble royalme thenne callyd Brytaygne, I Wyllyam Caxton, symple persone, present thys book folowyng whyche I have enprysed t'enprynte; and treateth of the noble actes, feates of armes of chyvalrye, prowesse, hardynesse, humanyte, love, curtosye and veray gentylnesse, wyth many wonderful hystoryes and adventures. And for to understonde bryefly the contente of thys volume I have devyded it into xxi bookes, and every book chapytred as hereafter shal by Goddes grace folowe.

The fyrst book shal treate how Utherpendragon gate the noble conquerour Kyng Arthur and conteyneth xxviii

[1] boook

chappytres. The second book treateth of Balyn the noble
knyght and conteyneth xix chapytres. The thyrd book 140
treateth of the maryage of Kyng Arthur to Quene Guenever
wyth other maters, and conteyneth fyftene chappytres; the
fourth book how Merlyn was assotted, and of warre maad to
Kyng Arthur, and conteyneth xxix chappytres. The fyfthe
book treateth of the conqueste of Lucius th'Emperour and 145
conteyneth xii chappytres. The syxthe book treateth of Syr
Launcelot and Syr Lyonel and mervayllous adventures, and
conteyneth xviii chapytres. The seventh book treateth of a
noble knyght called Syr Gareth and named by Syr Kaye
'Beaumayns', and conteyneth xxxvi chapytres. The eyght 150
book treateth of the byrthe of Syr Trystram, the noble
knyght, and of hys actes and conteyneth xli chapytres. The
ix book treateth of a knyght named by Syr Kaye 'Le Cote
Male Taylle' and also of Syr Trystram, and conteyneth xliiii
chapytres. The x book treateth of Syr Trystram and other 155
mervayllous adventures, and conteyneth lxxxviii chappytres.
The xi book treateth of Syr Launcelot and Syr Galahad and
conteyneth xiiii chappytres. The xii book treateth of Syr
Launcelot and his madnesse and conteyneth xiiii chappytres.
The xiii book treateth how Galahad came fyrst to Kyng 160
Arthur's courte and the quest how the Sangreall was begonne,
and conteyneth xx chapytres. The xiiii book[1] treateth of the
queste of the Sangreal and conteyneth x chapytres. The xv
book treateth of Syr Launcelot and conteyneth vi chapytres.
The xvi book treateth of Syr Bors and Syr Lyonel, his 165
brother, and conteyneth xvii chapytres. The xvii book
treateth of the Sangreal and conteyneth xxiii chapytres. The
xviii book treateth of Syr Launcelot and the Quene, and
conteyneth xxv chapytres. The xix book treateth of Quene
Guenever and Launcelot, and conteyneth xiii chapytres. 170
The xx book treateth of the pyetous deth of Arthur and
conteyneth xxii chapytres. The xxi book treateth of his last
departyng and how Syr Launcelot came to revenge his dethe,
and conteyneth xiii chapytres. The somme is xxi bookes,
whyche conteyne the somme of v hondred and vii chapytres 175
as more playnly shal folowe herafter.

(b) *Epilogue*

Thus endeth thys noble and joyous book entytled *Le Morte
d'Arthur*, notwythstondyng it treateth of the byrth, lyf and

[1] boook

actes of the sayd Kyng Arthur, of his noble knyghtes of the
Rounde Table, theyr mervayllous enquestes and adventures,
th'achyevyng of the Sangreal, and in th'ende the dolorous deth   5
and departyng out of thys world of them al. Whiche book
was reduced into Englysshe by Syr Thomas Malory, knyght,
as afore is sayd, and by me devyded into xxi bookes,
chapytred and enprynted and fynysshed in th'Abbey [of]
Westmestre the last day of Juyl, the yere of Our Lord   10
MCCCClxxxv.

Caxton me fieri fecit.

73. KNIGHT OF THE TOWER (31 January 1484)

(a) *Prologue*

Alle vertuouse doctryne and techynge had and lerned of suche
as have endevoured them to leve for a remembraunce after
theyr dethe to us, by whiche we ben enfourmed in scyence,
wysedom and understandyng of knowleche hou we ought
to rewle ourself in this present lyf, have caused us to know   5
many good reules and vertuouse maners to be governed by.
Emonge al other this book is a special doctryne and techyng
by which al yong gentylwymen specially may lerne to bihave
themself vertuously as wel in their vyrgynyte as in their wedlok
and wedowhede, as al along shal be more playnly said in the   10
same. Which boke is comen to my handes by the request and
desyre of a noble lady which hath brought forth many noble
and fayr doughters which ben vertuously nourisshed and
lerned; and for very ziele and love that she hath alway had
to her fayr children and yet hath for to have more knouleche   15
in vertue to th'ende that they may alwey persevere in the
same, hath desired and required me to translate and reduce
this said book out of Frenssh into our vulgar Englissh to
th'ende that it may the better be understonde of al suche
as shal rede or here it. Wherfor atte contemplacion of her   20
good grace, after the lytel connyng that God hath sent me
I have endevoyryd me to obeye her noble desyre and request.
In whiche werk I fynd many vertuous good enseygnementis
and lernynges by evydent histories of auctorite and good
ensamples for al maner peple in generally, but in especial   25
for ladyes and gentilwymen, doughters to lordes and gentilmen. For whiche book al the gentilwymen now lyvyng and
herafter to come or shal be arn bounde to gyve laude,

praysyng and thankynges to the auctor of this book and also
to the lady that caused me to translate it, and to pray for her   30
long lyf and welfare; and when God wil calle her fro this
transitory lyf that she may regne in heven sempiternally
where as is joye and blysse without ende.

Thenne for as moche as this book is necessary to every
gentilwoman of what estate she be, I advyse every gentilman   35
or woman havyng such children, desyryng them to be
vertuously brought forth, to gete and have this book to
th'ende that they may lerne hou they ought to governe them
vertuously in this present lyf, by whiche they may the better
and hastlyer come to worship and good renommee. And I   40
desyre all them that shall lerne or see onythynge in this sayd
book by whiche they shal ben the wyser and better that they
gyve laude and thankyng to the sayd ladyes good grace and
also to praye for her. And where as ony defaulte shalle be
founde in the reducynge and translatynge into our Englysshe   45
tongue that it be arrettid to me, whiche am ignoraunt and not
expert in the werke, though so be that I have emprysed
heretofore to smatre me in suche translacions whiche I
confesse and knowleche me ignoraunt and therin to be
imperfect. Wherfore I humbly requyre and byseche my sayd   50
good lady to pardonne me of my symple and rude reducynge.
And yf onythynge be sayd or made unto her playsyre than I
thynke my labour wel employed, whome I humbly byseche
to receyve this lytel book in gree and thanke; and I shalle
pray to Almyghty God for her longe and good lyf and to send   55
to her after this shorte and transytory lyf everlastyng lyf in
heven. Amen. And alle other that be understandyng and
fyndyng ony defaute, I requyre and pray them of theyre
charyte to correcte and amende hit; and so doyng they shal
deserve thanke and meryte of God, to whome I shalle pray   60
for them.

Here foloweth the table of the rubryshes and the chapytres
of the booke of th'enseygnementes and techynge that the
Knyght of the Towre made to his doughters.

(b) *Colophon*

Here fynyssheth[1] the booke whiche the Knyght of the Toure
made to the enseygnement and techyng of his doughters,
translated oute of Frenssh into our maternall Englysshe

---

[1] fynysshed

tongue by me William Caxton. Whiche book was ended and
fynysshed the fyrst day of Juyn the yere of Oure Lord   5
MCCCClxxxiii and enprynted at Westmynstre the last day of
Janyver the fyrst yere of the regne of Kynge Rychard the
Thyrd.

74. LIFE OF OUR LADY (First Edition) (*c.* 1484)

Epilogue

Goo, lityl book, and submytte the
Unto al them that the shal rede
Or here, prayeng hem for charite
To pardon me of the rudehede
Of myn enpryntyng, not takyng hede.   5
And yf ought be doon to theyr plesyng
Say they thyse balades folowyng.

Sancte et individue Trinitati, Jhesu Cristi crucifixi humanitati,
gloriose Beate Marie Virgini sit sempiterna gloria ab omni
creatura per infinita seculorum secula. Amen.   10

Unto the holy and undevyded Trynyte,
Thre persones in one veray godhede,
To Jhesu Crist crucefyed humanyte,
And to our blessyd Ladyes maydenhede
Be gevyn laude and glorye in veray dede   15
Of every creature whatsomever he be
World withouten ende. Amen say al we.

Benedictum sit dulcissime nomen Jhesu Crysti et glorio-
sissime Marie, matris eius, in eternum et ultra; nos cum prole
pia benedicat Virgo Maria. Amen.   20

Blessid be the swettest name of Our Lord
Jhesu Crist and most glorious Marie,
His blessyd moder, with eternal accord
More than ever t'endure in glorye;
And with hir meke sone for memorye   25
Blesse us, Marie the most holy virgyne,
That we regne in heven with the ordres nyne.
Enpryntyd by Wyllyam Caxton.

75. MIRROR OF THE WORLD (First Edition) (8 March
1481)

(a) *Introduction and Prologue*

Here begynneth the table of the rubrices of this presente
volume named the *Mirrour of the World* or th'*Ymage* of the
same.

The prologue declareth to whom this volume apperteyneth
and at whos requeste it was translated out of Frenshe into   5
Englissh. After foloweth the prologue of the translatour
declaryng the substaunce of this present volume.

[Table of Contents]

Prologue declaryng to whom this book apperteyneth.
Consideryng that wordes ben perisshyng, vayne and forgete-
ful, and writynges duelle and abide permanent, as I rede   10
Vox audita perit, littera scripta manet; thise thinges have
caused that the faites and dedes of auncyent menn ben sette
by declaracion in fair and aourned volumes to th'ende that
science and artes, lerned and founden of thinges passed,
myght be had in perpetuel memorye and remembraunce. For   15
the hertes of nobles, in eschewyng of ydlenes at suche tyme
as they have none other vertuouse ocupacion on hande, ought
t'excersise them in redyng, studyng and visytyng the noble
faytes and dedes of the sage and wyse men, somtyme
travaillyng in prouffytable vertues. Of whom it happeth ofte   20
that som men ben enclyned to visyte the bookes treatyng of
sciences particuler, and other to rede and visyte bookes
spekyng of faytes of armes, of love, or of other mervaillous
histories. And emonge alle other this present booke whiche
is called the *Ymage* or *Myrrour of the World* ought to be   25
visyted, redde and knowen bycause it treateth of the world
and of the wondreful dyvision therof. In whiche book a man
resonable may see and understande[1] more clerer by the
visytyng and seeyng of it and the figures therin the situacion
and moevyng of the firmament and how the unyversal erthe   30
hangeth in the myddle of the same, as the chapitres here
folowyng shal more clerly shewe and declare to you.

Whiche said book was translated out of Latyn into
Frensshe by the ordynaunce of the noble duc, Johan of Berry
and Auvergne, the yere of Our Lord MCCxlv; and now at this   35
tyme rudely translated out of Frensshe into Englissh by me,

[1] undrrstande

symple persone William Caxton, at the request, desire, coste
and dispense of the honourable and worshipful man Hugh
Bryce, alderman and cytezeyn of London, entendyng to
present the same unto the vertuous, noble and puissaunt   40
lord, Wylliam Lord Hastynges, Lord Chamberlayn unto the
most Crysten kynge, Kynge Edward the Fourthe, Kynge of
England and of Fraunce, etc., and Lieutenaunt[1] for the same
of the toun of Calais and Marches there; whom he humbly
besecheth to resseyve in gree and thanke.   45

Whiche booke conteyneth in alle lxxvii chapitres and xxvii
figures without whiche it may not lightly be understande.
And for to declare more openly, it is ordeyned in thre parties:
of whiche the firste conteyneth xx chapitres and viii figures;
the seconde partie xxxiii chapitres and ix figures; and the   50
therde conteyneth xxiiii chapitres and x figures. Whiche was
engrossed and in alle poyntes ordeyned by chapitres and
figures in Frensshe in the toun of Bruggis, the yere of
th'yncarnacion of Our Lord MCCCClxiiii in the moneth of
Juyn; and emprised by me, ryght unable and of lytil connyng,   55
to translate and brynge it into our maternal tongue the
second day of the moneth of Janyver, the yer of our said
Lord MCCCClxxx, in th'Abbay of Westmestre by London.
Humbly requyryng alle them that shal fynde faulte to correcte
and amende where as they shal ony fynde; and of suche so   60
founden that they repute not the blame on me but on my
copie, whiche I am charged to folowe as nyghe as God wil
gyve me grace, whom I most humbly beseche to gyve me
scyence, connyng and lyf t'accomplysshe and wel to fynysshe
it, etc.   65

Thenne who so wylle comprise and understande the substaunce of this present volume for to lerne and knowe
specially the creacion of this world, the gretnes of the
firmament and lytilnes of th'erthe in regard to heven, how
the vii sciences were founden and what they bee, by whiche   70
he may the better avaylle in knowleche alle the dayes of his
lyf, thenne late hym rede this said volume treatably, avisedly
and ordynatly that in suche thing as he shal rede, he suffre
nothyng to passe but that he understonde it right well. And
so may he knowe and understonde it right well. And so may   75
he knowe and understonde veritably the declaracion of this
said volume. And he thenne that so wille obeye this commandement may by the contente of the same lerne grete

[1] lieuteññt

partie of the fourme and condicion of this worlde, and how
by the wyll of Our Lord it was by hym created, made and 80
accomplisshed. And the cause wherfor it was establisshid,
wherof the debonayr Lord hath don to us so grete grace
that we ever ben bounden to gyve hym lawde and worshyp or
ellys we had not ben of ony valew ne worth onythyng, no
more than unresonable beestis. Thenne late us praye the 85
maker and creatour of alle creatures, God Allmyghty, that
at the begynnyng of this book, it liste hym of his most
bounteuous grace to departe with us of the same that we may
lerne, and that lerned to reteyne, and that reteyned so teche,
that we may have so parfyght scyence and knowleche of God 90
that we may gete therby the helthe of our sowles and to be
partyners of his glorye permanent and without ende in
heven. Amen.

(b) *Book II chapter xi*

In Allemayne sourdeth a grete flood and ryvere named
Dunoe, the whiche stratcheth unto in Constantynople, and
there entreth into the see; but erst it traverseth vii grete
floodes by his radour and rennyng. And, as I have herd saye,
the hede of this Dunoe begynneth on one side of a montayne, 5
and that other side of the same montayne sourdeth another
grete ryver which is named the Riin, and renneth thurgh
Almayne by Basyle, Strawsburgh, Magounce, Covelence,
Coleyn and Nemyng, where fast by it departeth into iiii ryvers
and renneth thurgh the londes of Ghelres, Cleve and Holande 10
and so into the see. And yet er this ryver entre into the see he
entreth into another ryver named the Mase, and than loseth
he his name and is called the Mase, and Mase Depe xl myle
long in the see.

(c) *Book II ch. xii*

After thenne cometh Grece, Cypres, Cecyle, Toscane, Naples,
Lombardye, Gascoyne, Spayne, Cateloyne, Galyce, Navarre,
Portyngal and Aragon. And how be it that the auctour of
this book saye that thise contrees ben in Affryke yet, as I
understonde, alle thise ben within the lymytes and boundes 5
of Europe.

(d) *Book II ch. xiv*

Hit may wel be that of auncyent tyme it hath ben thus as afore
is wreton, as the storye of Tundale and other witnesse. But I
have spoken with dyverse men that have ben therin, and that

one of them was an Hye Chanon of Waterford whiche told
me that he had ben therin v or vi tymes and he sawe ne suffred   5
no suche thynges. He saith that with procession the relygious
men that ben there brynge hym into the hool and shette the
dore after hym, and than he walketh groping into it where, as
he said, ben places and maner of cowches to reste on. And
there he was alle the nyght in contemplacion and prayer, and   10
also slepte there; and on the morn he cam out agayn. Other-
while in their slepe[1] somme men have mervayllous dremes;
and other thyng sawe he not. And in lyke wyse tolde to me a
worshipful knyght of Bruggis named Sir John de Banste that
he had ben therin in lyke wyse and see none other thyng but as   15
afore is sayd.

(e) *Book II ch. xv*

Whan the she-ape hath two whelpes or fawnes, she loveth that
one moche better than that other. She berith hym that she
loveth best in her armes and that other she leteth goo whiche,
whan she is hunted, lepeth on the moder's backe and holdeth
her faste. And that other that she bereth in her armes she   5
leteth falle and is ofte constrayned to save herself.

(f) *Book III ch. xxiv*

Sith it speketh of thre maner of people that th'auncyent
philosophres put in the world, how nature werketh and what
she is, and how she dyversefyeth in everych of her werkes.
Also ye have herde of the facion of the world and of the
dyvvysion of the four elementes whiche ben round aboute and   5
holde them on the firmament, and how the erthe holdeth hym
within the firmament. Also ye have herde of the lytilnes of
th'erthe unto the regard of heven and also how the sonne
maketh his cours al aboute th'erthe and the other planettes in
lyke wyse. Alle this have ye herd in the first partye.   10

In the seconde partye is declared to yow whiche parte of
th'erthe is inhabyted and of the dyvvysion of Mappa Mundi.
And first it speketh of paradys terrestre, and of the contrees
and regyons of Ynde and of the dyversytees that ben ther: of
men, of bestes, of trees, of stones, of byrdes, and of somme   15
fysshes that ben there, and where helle the dolourous place is
and stondeth, and of the grete paynes that they endure that
ben dampned and ben there. After ye have herd of the
second element, that is of the water: of the flodes and of the

[1] shepe

117

fontaynes, hoot and colde, holsom and evyll, whiche ben in   20
dyverse contrees; and how the see bicometh salt; how the
erthe quaveth and synketh; and after of the ayer how hit
bloweth and rayneth: of tempestes and of thondres, of fyre,
of layte, and of the sterres whiche seme as they fylle; of pure
ayer and of the vii planettes; how the bysexte cometh; of the   25
firmament and of his tornyng, and of the sterres that ben
round aboute therin.

In the thirde partye ye have herde how the day and nyght
come, and of the mone and of the sonne how they rendre
their lyght and how eche of them leseth their clerenes by   30
nyght and by day somtyme, and of the eclipses that thenne
happe wherby the day bycometh derke; and of the grete
eclypse that fylle atte the deth of Our Lord Jhesu Cryste by
whiche Saynt Dionys was afterward converted; and of the
vertue of the firmament and of the sterres; and how the world   35
was mesured and the heven and th'erthe; of the kynge,
Tholomeus, and of his prudence; of Adam and of somme
other; and how clergye and the vii sciences were kepte ayenst
the Flood and how all this was founden agayn after the
Flood; and of the mervelles that Virgyle made by his wytte   40
and clergye, and for what cause moneye was so named and
establisshed; and of the philosophres that wente thurgh the
world for to lerne; what thinge is philosophye and what
Plato answerde therto; how moche the erthe, the mone and
the sonne have of gretenes, everych of hymself; and the stages   45
of the sterres, of their nombre, and of their ymages; the
heyght and gretenes of the firmament and of the blew heven
whiche is above that; and of the hevene crystalyn and of the
heven imperial.

(g) *Epilogue*

Thus fynysshith the boke called th'*Ymage* or *Myrrour of the
World*, the whiche in spekynge of God and of his werkes
inestymable hath begonne to entre in mater spekynge of hym
and of his hye puissances and domynacions and taketh here
an ende, for in alle begynnynges and in all operacions the   5
name of God ought to be called as on hym without whom
alle thinges ben nought. Thenne he so ottroye and graunte to
us so to bygynne, persevere and fynysshe that we may be
brought and receyvyd into his blessyd glorye in hevene unto
the blessyd Trynyte, Fader, Sone and Holy Gost, whiche   10
lyveth and regneth without ende *in secula seculorum*. Amen.

And where it is so that I have presumed and emprised this forsayd translacion into our Englissh and maternal tongue, in whiche I am not wel parfyght and yet lasse in Frensshe, yet I have endevourd me therin atte request and desyre, coste 15 and dispence of the honourable and worshipful man, Hughe Bryce, cytezeyn and alderman of London, whiche hath sayd to me that he entendeth to presente it unto the puissaunt, noble and vertuous lorde, my Lorde Hastynges, Chamberlayn unto our soverayn lord the Kynge, and his lieutenaunt of the toun 20 of Calays and Marches there. In whiche translacion I knowleche myself symple, rude and ygnoraunt, wherfor I humbly byseche my sayd Lord Chamberlayn to perdonne me of this rude and symple translacion. How be it I leye for myn excuse that I have to my power folowed my copye and, as nygh as to 25 me is possible, I have made it so playn that every man resonable may understonde it yf he advysedly and ententyfly rede or here it. And yf ther be faulte in mesuryng of the firmament, sonne, mone or of th'erthe or in ony other mervaylles herin conteyned, I beseche you not t'arette the defaulte in me but in 30 hym that made my copye.

Whiche book I began first to translate the second day of Janyver, the yere of Our Lord MCCCClxxx, and fynysshyd the viii day of Marche the same yere and the xxi yere of the regne of the most Crysten kynge, Kynge Edward the 35 Fourthe, under the shadowe of whos noble proteccion I have emprysed and fynysshed this sayd lytil werke and boke. Besechynge Almyghty God to be his protectour and defendour agayn alle his enemyes and gyve hym grace to subdue them, and in especiall them that have late enterprysed agayn 40 right and reson to make warre wythin his royamme; and also to preserve and mayntene hym in longe lyf and prosperous helthe; and after this short and transitorye lyf he brynge hym and us into his celestyal blysse in hevene. Amen.

77. MORAL PROVERBS (20 February 1478)

Epilogue

Go, thou litil quayer, and recommaund me
Unto the good grace of my special lorde,
Th'Erle Ryveris, for I have enprinted the
At his commandement, folowyng evry worde
His copye, as his secretaire can recorde,   5

At Westmestre, of Feverer the xx daye
And of Kyng Edward the xvii yere vraye.
Enprinted by Caxton
In Feverer, the colde season.

79. OF OLD AGE, OF FRIENDSHIP AND DECLAMATION OF NOBLESSE (12 August 1481)

(a) *Prologue to Of Old Age*

Here begynneth the prohemye upon the reducynge both out
of Latyn as of Frensshe into our Englyssh tongue of the
polytyque book named *Tullius: De Senectute*, whiche that
Tullius wrote upon the disputacions and commynycacions
made to the puissaunt Duc Cato, senatour of Rome, by   5
Scipion and Lelius, thenne beyng yong noble knyghtes and
also senatours of the said Rome, of the worshippe, recommendacyon and magnyfycence that shold be gyven to men of
olde age for theyr desertes and experyence in wysedom of
polytyque governaunce and blamed them that reproven or   10
lothen olde age; and how Caton exhorteth and counseilleth
olde men to be joyeful and bere pacyently olde age whan it
cometh to them; and how Tullius at reverence of Caton
declareth by waye of example how Enneus th'auncyent
philosophre purposeth and wryteth in thre verses com-   15
pendyously unto his frende Atticus,[1] also a senatour of Rome,
how he toke grete thought and charge for the governaunce
of the comyn prouffyght, for whiche he deserved grete lawde
and honoure in preferryng the same, named in Latyn *Res
publica*, kepyng the Romaynes prosperous and defendyng   20
them fro theyr adversaryes and rebelles.

Whiche book was translated and th'ystoryes openly
declared by the ordenaunce and desyre of the noble auncyent
knyght, Syr Johan Fastolf of the countee of Norfolk banerette, lyvyng the age of four score yere, excercisyng the warrys 25
in the royame of Fraunce and other countrees for the diffence and unyversal welfare of bothe royames of Englond
and Fraunce by fourty yeres enduryng, the fayte of armes
hauntyng, and in admynystryng justice and polytique governaunce under thre kynges, that is to wete Henry the Fourth,   30
Henry the Fyfthe, Henry the Syxthe; and was governour of
the Duchye of Angeou and the countee of Mayne, capytayn

[1] Attitus

120

of many townys, castellys and fortressys in the said royame
of Fraunce, havyng the charge and saufgarde of them dyverse
yeres, ocupyeng and rewlynge thre honderd speres and the   35
bowes acustomed thenne; and yeldyng good acompt of the
forsaid townes, castellys and fortresses to the seyd kynges and
to theyr lyeutenauntes, prynces of noble recomendacion, as
Johan Regent of Fraunce, Duc of Bedforde, Thomas Duc of
Excestre, Thomas Duc of Clarence, and other lyeutenauntes,   40
prayeng to take this reducyng pacyently and submyttyng me
to the amendyng and correction of the reder and understonder
that is disposed to rede or have ony contemplacion in
th'ystoryes of this book whiche were drawen and compyled
out of the bookes of th'auncyent phylosophers of Grece, as in   45
th'orygynal text of *Tullii: De Senectute* in Latyn is specyfyed [1]
compendyously, whiche is in maner harde the texte. But this
book reduced in Englyssh tongue is more ample expowned
and more swetter to the reder, kepyng the juste sentence of
the Latyn.   50

Thenne for as moche as this book thus reduced into our
Englyssh is with grete instaunce, labour and coste comen
into myn honde, which I advysedly have seen, overredde and
considered the noble, honeste and vertuous mater necessarily
requysite unto men stepte in age and to yong men for to lerne   55
how they owght to come to the same to whiche every man
naturelly desyreth to atteyne; and the mater and commynyca-
cion of this said book bytwene that wyse and noble man Cato
on that one parte and Scipio and Lelius, two yonge knyghtes,
on that other parte is moche behoefful to be knowen to every   60
man vertuous and wel-disposed, of whatsomeever eage
resonable that he be; thenne bycause I have not seen ony of
the same heretofore I have endevoured me to gete it with
grete difficulte, and so goten have put it in enprynte, and
dilygently aftir my lytil understandyng corrected it to   65
th'entente that noble, vertuous and wel-disposed men myght
have it to loke on and to understonde it. And this book is not
requysyte ne eke convenyent for every rude and symple man
whiche understandeth not of science ne connyng and for
suche as have not herde of the noble polycye and prudence of   70
the Romaynes, but for noble, wyse and grete lordes, gentilmen and marchauntes that have seen and dayly ben occupyed
in maters towchyng the publyque weal, and in especial unto
them that ben passed theyr grene yongthe and eke theyr

[1] specyfyced

myddle eage callyd virylyte and ben approchid unto senectute   75
callyd olde and auncyent eage, wherin they may see how to
suffre and bere the same pacyently and what surete and vertue
ben in the same; and have also cause to be joyous and glad
that they have escaped and passed the manyfolde peryllys and
doubteuous adventures that ben in juvente and yongthe, as   80
in this said booke here folowyng ye may more playnly see.
Whiche booke endyted and wrote in Latyn the noble philosopher and prynce of eloquence, Tullius, consul Romayn,
within the breste of whom phylosophye naturel and morall
had chosen her domycill, out of whiche it hath ben translated   85
into Frensh and aftir into our Englyssh tongue, as hieraftir
al alonge ye may see.

Also whan the said Tullius had made his book *De Senectute*
he aftir made another book callid *De Amicicia*, that is to saye
Of Frendship, in which he reherceth of two yong knyghtes of   90
Rome, that one named Sevola and that other Fannyus, bothe
sones-in-lawe unto Lelius, a noble senatour of Rome and
felawe and alyed in frendship with Scipio Affrycan whiche
within fewe dayes tofore was deed, how they desyred to
knowe of the frendship that was bytwene the said Scipio,   95
whyles he lyved, and Lelius, theyr said fader-in-lawe, and of
the disputacion in frendship as alle playnly it appiereth in the
same. Which book was translated by the vertuous and noble
erle, th'Erle of Wurcestre, into our Englyssh tongue.

And bycause it is accordyng and requysyte to have frend-   100
ship joyned to olde eage I have enprynted the said *Book of
Frendship* and annexed it to the *Book of Eage*, which *Book of
Frendship* is ful necessary and behoefful unto every estate and
degree. And aftir I have sette in this said book folowyng
them bothe a noble treatys of the declamacion of two noble   105
knyghtes Romaynes in makyng of two oracions tofore the
Senate to knowe wherin noblesse resteth. And thus this
volume is dyvyded into thre particuler werkes whiche ben of
grete wysedom in olde age, very love in frendship, and the
question wherin noblesse resteth.   110

Whiche lytil volume I have emprysed t'enprynte under the
umbre and shadowe of the noble proteccion of our moost
dradde soverayn and naturel lyege lord and moost Cristen
kyng, Kyng Edward the Fourth; to whom I moste humbly
byseche to receyve the said book of me William Caxton, his   115
moost humble subget and litil servaunt, and not to desdeyne
to take it of me so poure, ignoraunt and symple a persone;

and of his moost bountyuous grace to pardonne me so presumyng, bes[e]chyng Almyghty God to kepe, mayntene and
graunte to hym longe lyf and prosperous, and th'accom-　120
plysshement of his hye and noble desyres, and aftir this short
and transitorye lyf evirlastyng lyf and joye in heven. Amen.

Here foloweth a remembraunce of th'istoryes comprysed
and touchyd in this present book entitled *Tullius: De Senectute*,
'Tullye Of Olde Age', as in the redyng shal more playnly be　125
sayd al alonge.

[Contents]
Thus endeth the remembraunce of th'istoryes comprysed
and towchid in this lytil book entitled *Tullyus: De Senectute*.

(b) *Colophon to Of Old Age*
Thus endeth the *Boke of Tulle of Olde Age*, translated out of
Latyn into Frenshe by Laurence de Primo Facto at the
comaundement of the noble prynce Lowys Duc of Burbon,
and enprynted by me, symple person, William Caxton, into
Englysshe at the playsir, solace and reverence of men　5
growyng into olde age the xii day of August the yere of Our
Lord MCCCClxxxi.

(c) *Prologue to Of Friendship*
Here foloweth the said *Tullius: De Amicicia*, translated into
our maternall Englissh tongue by the noble, famous erle, the
Erle of Wurcestre, sone and heyer to the Lord Typtoft,
which in his tyme flowred in vertue and cunnyng, to whom I
knewe none lyke emonge the lordes of the temporalite in　5
science and moral vertue. I beseche Almyghty God to have
mercy on his sowle, and praye al them that shal here or rede
this lityl treatys, moch vertuous of frendship, in like wise of
your charyte to remembre his soule emong your prayers.
And bycause this werke was made by the prince of eloquence　10
Tullius, intitled *De Amycicia*, after that he had achevid his
boke *De Senectute* as hertofore ye maye more playnly see at
large, thenne me semeth it requisite and necessarye that I
sette in, folowing the said book, this book *De Amicicia* whiche
by Goddes grace shal playnly folowe.　15

(d) *Epilogue to Of Friendship*
Thus endeth this boke named *Tullius: De Amicicia* whiche
treateth of frendship, utterid and declared by a noble senatour
of Rome named Lelyus unto his two sones-in-lawe, also

noblemen of Rome named Fannyus and Sevola. In which
they desyred hym to enforme them of the frendship that was   5
bytwene the said Lelius and the noble prynce Scipio Affrican.
Wherin he hath answered and tolde to them the noble vertues
that ben in frendship. And withoute vertue veray frendship
may not be, as he prevyth by many exsamples and notable
conclusions as heretofore is moch playnly expressyd and said   10
all alonge. Whiche werke was translated by the vertuous and
noble lord and erle, th'Erle of Worcestre, on whoos sowle I
beseche[1] Almyghty God to have mercy; and alle ye that shal
rede or here this said werke of your charyte I beseche you to
praye for hym. And bycause this said book *De Amicicia* is ful 15
necessarye and requysyte to be had and knowen, I have putt
it in emprynte to th'entent that veray amyte and frendship
may be had as it ought to be in every estate and degree, and
vertue (withoute whiche frendship may not be had) may be
encreaced and vices eschewid.   20

Thenne whan I had enprynted the *Book of Olde Age*, whiche
the said Tullyus made, me semed it acordyng that this said
Booke of Frendship shold folowe bycause ther cannot be annexed to olde age a bettir thynge than good and very frendship. Which two said bokes heretofore wreton ben of grete   25
wisedom and auctoryte and full necessarye, behoeffull,[2] and
requysite unto every age, estate and degree. And that they
prouffyte in encreacyng of vertue, I beseche the blessyd
Trynyte to geve and graunte unto alle them that shal rede and
here thise bokes; and so to flee and eschewe vices and synnes   30
that by the merytes of vertuouse, honeste and good werkes
we may atteyne aftir this shorte, transytorye lyf the eternall,
blessyd lyf in heven where is joye and glorye withoute ende.
Amen.

(e) *Preface to Declamation of Noblesse*
Here foloweth the argument of the *Declamacyon*, which
laboureth to shewe wherin honoure sholde reste.

(f) *Epilogue to Declamation of Noblesse*
Thus endeth th'oracion of Gayus Flammyneus.

As touchyng the sentence dyffynytyf gyven by the Senate
aftir thise two noble knyghtes had purposed and shewed
theyr oracions, I fynde none as yet pronounced ne gyven of

---

[1] bechese   [2] bohoeffull

whiche myn auctour maketh ony mencion of in his book. 5
Thenne I wolde demaunde of theym that shal rede or here
this book whiche of thies tweyne, that is to saye Cornelius
Scipio and Gayus Flammyneus, was moost noble and in
whiche of theym bothe aftir the contente of theyr oracions
that noblesse resteth. And to hym juge ye this noble and 10
vertuous lady Lucresse to be maryed.

And here I make an ende of this mater for this tyme,
prayeng and requyryng all theym that in this sayd werke shal
have ony playsyre that ye wil remembre hym that translated it
into our maternal and Englyssh tongue, and not only this 15
said werke but the book of *Tullius: De Amicicia* heretofore
enprynted which[1] treateth so wel of frendship and amyte: I
mene the right vertuous and noble erle, th'Erle of Wurcestre,
whiche late pytously lost his lyf, whos soule I recommende
unto youre special prayers; and also in his tyme made many 20
other vertuous werkys whiche I have herd of.

O good, blessyd Lord God, what grete loss was it of that
noble, vertuous and wel-disposed lord! Whan I remembre
and advertyse his lyf, his science and his vertue, me thynketh
(God not displesyd) overgrete a losse of suche a man, con- 25
syderyng his estate and conning; and also th'excercise of the
same with the grete laboures in gooyng on pylgremage unto
Jherusalem, visytyng there the holy places that oure blessyd
Lord Jhesu Criste halowed with[2] his blessyd presence and
shedyng there his precious blood for oure redempcion and 30
from thens ascended unto his fader in heven. And what worship had he at Rome in the presence of oure Holy Fader the
Pope; and so in alle other places unto his deth. At whiche
deth every man that was there myght lerne to dye and take
his deth paciently, wherin I hope and doubte not but that 35
God receyved his soule into his evirlastyng blysse. For as I
am enformed he ryght advysedly ordeyned alle his thynges as
well for his last will of wordly goodes as for his sowle helthe,
and pacyently and holyly without grudchyng in charyte
tofore that he departed out of this world, whiche is gladsom 40
and joyous to here, thenne I here recommende his sowle unto
youre prayers and also that we at our departyng maye departe
in suche wyse that it maye please Our Lord God to receyve us
into his evirlastyng blysse. Amen.

Explicit per Caxton. 45

---

[1] whith   [2] thith

80. ORDER OF CHIVALRY (*c.* 1484)

Epilogue

Here endeth the book of th'*Ordre of Chyvalry*, whiche book is
translated oute of Frensshe into Englysshe at a requeste of a
gentyl and noble esquyer by me, William Caxton, dwellynge
in Westmynstre besyde London, in the most best wyse that
God hath suffred me and accordynge to the copye that the   5
sayd squyer delyverd to me. Whiche book is not requysyte
to every comyn man to have, but to noble gentylmen that by
their vertu entende to come and entre into the noble ordre of
chyvalry, the whiche in these late dayes hath [not] ben used
accordyng to this booke heretofore wreton, but forgeten,   10
and th'excersytees of chyvalry not used, honoured ne excer-
cysed as hit hath ben in auncyent tyme. At whiche tyme the
noble actes of the knyghtes of Englond that used chyvalry
were renomed thurgh the unyversal world. As for to speke
tofore th'yncarnacion of Jhesu Cryste where were there ever   15
ony lyke to Brenius and Belynus that from the grete Brytayne,
now called Englond, unto Rome and ferre beyonde conquered many royammes and londes, whos noble actes
remayne in th'old hystoryes of the Romayns? And syth the
incarnacion of Oure Lord byhold that noble Kyng of   20
Brytayne, Kyng Arthur, with al the noble knyghtes of the
Round Table, whos noble actes and noble chyvalry of his
knyghtes occupye soo many large volumes, that is a world or
as thyng incredyble to byleve.

O ye knyghtes of Englond, where is the custome and usage   25
of noble chyvalry that was used in tho dayes? What do ye
now but go to the baynes and playe atte dyse? And some not
wel advysed use not honest and good rule ageyn alle ordre of
knyghthode. Leve this. Leve it and rede the noble volumes of
Saynt Graal, of Lancelot, of Galaad, of Trystram, of Perse   30
Forest, of Percyval, of Gawayn and many mo. Ther shalle ye
see manhode, curtosye and gentylnesse. And loke in latter
dayes of the noble actes syth the conquest, as in Kyng
Rychard dayes Cuer du Lyon, Edward the Fyrste and the
Thyrd and his noble sones, Syre Robert Knolles, Syr Johan   35
Hawkwode, Syr Johan Chaundos and Syre Gaultier Mauny.
Rede Froissart. And also behold that vyctoryous and noble
kynge, Harry the Fyfthe, and the capytayns under hym, his
noble bretheren, th'Erle of Salysbury Montagu and many

other, whoos names shyne gloryously by their vertuous 40
noblesse and actes that they did in th'onour of th'ordre of
chyvalry.

Allas! what doo ye but slepe and take ease and ar al dis-
ordred fro chyvalry? I wold demaunde a question yf I shold
not displease. How many knyghtes ben ther now in Englond 45
that have th' use and th'excercyse of a knyghte, that is to wete
that he knoweth his hors and his hors hym, that is to saye he
beynge redy at a poynt to have al thyng that longeth to a
knyght, an hors that is accordyng and broken after his hand,
his armures and harnoys mete and syttyng and so forth et 50
cetera? I suppose and a due serche shold be made ther shold
be many founden that lacke, the more pyte is. I wold it pleasyd
oure soverayne lord that twyes or thryes in a yere or at the
lest ones he wold do crye justes of pees to th'ende that every
knyght shold have hors and harneys and also the use and 55
craft of a knyght, and also to tornoye one ageynste one or ii
ageynst ii and the best to have a prys, a dyamond or jewel,
suche as shold please the Prynce. This shold cause gentylmen
to resorte to th'auncyent custommes of chyvalry to grete fame
and renommee, and also to be alwey redy to serve theyr 60
prynce whan he shalle calle them or have nede. Thenne late
every man that is come of noble blood and entendeth to come
to the noble ordre of chyvalry rede this lytyl book and doo
therafter in kepyng the lore and commaundements therin
comprysed. And thenne I doubte not he shall atteyne to 65
th'ordre of chyvalry et cetera.

And thus thys lytyl book I presente to my redoubted,
naturel and most dradde soverayne lord, Kyng Rychard,
Kyng of Englond and of Fraunce, to th'ende that he commaunde this book to be had and redde unto other yong 70
lordes, knyghtes and gentylmen within this royame that the
noble ordre of chyvalrye be herafter better used and honoured
than hit hath ben in late dayes passed. And herin he shalle do
a noble and vertuouse dede. And I shalle pray Almyghty God
for his long lyf and prosperous welfare and that he may have 75
victory of al his enemyes and after this short and transitory
lyf to have everlastyng lyf in heven where as is joye and
blysse world without ende. Amen.

82 PARIS AND VIENNE (19 December 1485)

Colophon

Thus endeth th'ystorye of the noble and valyaunt knyght
Parys and the fayr Vyenne, doughter of the Doulphyn of
Vyennoys; translated out of Frensshe into Englysshe by
Wylliam Caxton at Westmestre, fynysshed the last day of
August the yere of Our Lord MCCCClxxxv and enprynted   5
the xix day of Decembre the same yere, and the fyrst yere of
the regne of Kyng Harry the seventh.
Explicit per Caxton.

85. PILGRIMAGE OF THE SOUL (6 June 1483)

(a) *Incipit*

This book is intytled the *Pylgremage of the Sowle*, translated
oute of Frensshe into Englysshe; whiche book is ful of
devoute maters touchyng the sowle and many questyons
assoyled to cause a man to lyve the better in this world; and it
conteyneth fyve bookes as it appereth herafter by chapytres.   5

(b) *Explicit*

Emprynted at Westmestre by William Caxton and fynysshed
the sixth day of Juyn the yere of Our Lord MCCCClxxxiii
and the first yere of the regne of Kynge Edward the Fyfthe.

86. POLYCHRONICON (2 July 1482)

(a) *Prohemye*

Grete thankynges, lawde and honoure we merytoryously ben
bounde to yelde and offre unto wryters of hystoryes, whiche
gretely have prouffyted oure mortal lyf, that shewe unto the
reders and herers by the ensamples of thynges passyd what
thynge is to be desyred and what is to be eschewed. For those   5
thynges whiche oure progenytours [dyde] by the taste of
bytternes and experyment of grete jeopardyes have en-
seygned, admonested and enformed us, excluded fro suche
peryllys, to knowe what is prouffytable to oure lyf and
acceptable and what is unprouffytable and to be refused. He   10
is, and ever hath ben, reputed the wysest whiche by the
experyence of adverse fortune hath byholden and seen the
noble cytees, maners and variaunt condycions of the people of

many dyverse regyons, for in hym is presupposed the lore of
wysedom and polycye by the experyment of jeopardyes and   15
peryllys, whiche have growen of folye in dyverse partyes and
contrayes. Yet he is more fortunat, and may be reputed as
wyse, yf he gyve attendaunce withoute[1] tastynge of the
stormes of adversyte, that may by the redyng of historyes
conteynyng dyverse customes, condycyons, lawes and actes   20
of sondry nacions come unto the knowleche of and understandynge of the same wysedome and polycye. In whiche
hystoryes so wreton in large and aourned volumes, he
syttynge in his chambre or studye maye rede, knowe and
understande the polytyke and noble actes of alle the worlde, 25
as of one cyte, and the conflyctes, errours, troubles and vexa-
cions done in the sayd unyversal worlde in suche wyse as he
had ben and seen them in the propre places where as they
were done. For certayne it is a greete beneurte unto a man
that can be reformed by other and straunge mennes hurtes   30
and scathes, and by the same to knowe what is requysyte and
prouffytable for his lyf and eschewe suche errours and inconvenytys, by whiche other men have ben hurte and lost theyr
felycyte. Therfore the counseylles of auncyent and whyte-
heeryd men, in whome olde age hath engendryd wysedome,   35
ben gretely preysed of yonger men; and yet hystoryes soo
moche more excelle them as the dyuturnyte or length of tyme
includeth moo ensamples of thynges and laudable actes than
th'age of one man may suffyse to see.

Historyes ought not only to be juged moost proffytable to   40
yonge men whiche by the lecture, redyng and understandyng
make them semblable and equale to men of greter age and to
old men, to whome longe lyf hath mynystred experymentes
of dyverse thynges, but also th'ystoryes able and make ryght
pryvate men digne and worthy to have the governaunce of   45
empyres and noble royammes. Historyes moeve and with-
drawe emperours and kynges fro vycious tyrannye, fro vecordyous sleuthe unto tryumphe and vyctorye in puyssaunt
batayiles. Historyes also have moeved ryght noble knyghtes
to deserve eternal laude, whiche foloweth them for their   50
vyctoryous merytes, and cause them more valyantly to entre
in jeopardyes of batayles for the defence and tuicion of their
countrey and publyke wele. Hystorye also affrayeth cruel
tyrauntys for drede of infamye and shame infynyte bycause
of the detestable actes of suche cruel personnes ben oftymes 55

[1] withouce

plantyd and regystred in cronykes unto theyr perpetuel obprobrye and dyvulgacion of theyr infamye, as th'actes of Nero
and suche other. Truly, many of hye and couragyous men of
grete empryse, desyryng theyr fame to be perpetuelly con-
servyd by lyteral[1] monumentis whiche ben the permanente 60
recordes of every vyrtuouse and noble acte, have buylded and
edefyed ryall and noble cytees, and for the conservacion of
the wele publycke have mynystred and establysshed dyscrete
and prouffytable lawes. And thus the pryncipal laude and
cause of delectable and amyable thynges in whiche mannes 65
felycyte stondeth and resteth ought and maye wel be attributed to hystoryes.

Whiche worde *historye* may be descryved thus. Historye is a
perpetuel conservatryce of thoos thynges that have be doone
before this presente tyme and also a cotydyan wytnesse of 70
bienfayttes, of malefaytes, grete actes, and tryumphal vyc-
toryes of all maner peple. And also yf the terryble, feyned
fables of poetes have moche styred and moeved men to pyte
and conservynge of justyce, how moche more is to be supposed that historye, assertryce of veryte and as moder of alle 75
philosophye moevynge our maners to vertue, reformeth and
reconcyleth ner hande alle thoos men whiche thurgh the in-
fyrmyte of oure mortal nature hath ledde the mooste parte of
theyr lyf in ocyosyte and myspended theyr tyme, passed ryght
soone oute of remembraunce; of whiche lyf and deth is egal 80
oblyvyon. The fruytes of vertue ben inmortall, specyally
whanne they ben wrapped in the benefyce of hystoryes.

Thenne it muste folowe that it is mooste fayre to men
mortalle to suffre labours and payne for glorye and fame
inmortalle. Hercules whan he lyved suffryd greete laboures 85
and peryllys, wylfully puttyng hymself in many terryble and
ferdful jeopardyes to obteyne of all peple the benefaytes of
inmortal laude and renommee. We rede of other noble men,
somme lordes and somme other of lower astates, reputed as
goddes in dyverse regyons, the whos famous actes and 90
excellent vertues only hystorye hath preservyd fro perysshyng
in eternal memorye. Other monymentes distributed in dyverse
chaunges enduren but for a short tyme or season, but the
vertu of historye, dyffused and spredd by the unyversal
worlde, hath tyme whiche consumeth all other thynges as 95
conservatryce and kepar of her werke.

Ferthermore, eloquence is soo precious and noble that

[1] lyberal

almooste noothyng can be founden more precious than it.
By eloquence the Grekes ben preferryd in contynuel honour
tofore the rude barbares. Oratours and lerned clerkes in like 100
wise excelle unlerned and brutyssh peple. Syth this eloquence
is suche that causeth men emonge themself somme t'excelle
other after the qualyte of the vertue and eloquence [it may]
be seyn to be of valew. For somme we juge to be good men,
digne of laude, whiche shewe to us the waye of vertue; and 105
other have taken another waye for t'enflamme more [to
pleasure] the courages of men by fables of poesye than to
prouffyte, and by the lawes and institutes more to punysshe
than to teche. Soo that of thyse thynges the utylyte is myxt
with harme, for somme sothly techyth to lye. But historye, 110
representynge the thynges lyke unto the wordes, enbraceth al
utylyte and prouffite. It sheweth honeste and maketh vyces
detestable. It enhaunceth noble men and depresseth wicked
men and fooles. Also thynges that historye descryveth by
experyence moche prouffyten unto a ryghtful lif. 115

Thenne syth historye is so precious and also prouffytable,
I have delybered to wryte twoo bookes notable, retenyng in
them many noble historyes as the lyves, myracles, passyons,
and deth of dyverse hooly sayntes, whiche shal be comprysed
by th'ayde and suffraunce of Almyghty God in one of them 120
whiche is named *Legenda Aurea*, that is the *Golden Legende*,
and that other book is named *Polycronycon*, in whiche book ben
comprised briefly many wonderful historyees: fyrst the
descripcion of the universal world as wel in lengthe as in
brede, with the divisions of countrees, royammes and 125
empyres, the noble cytees, hye mountayns, famous ryvers,
merveylles and wondres, and also the historial actes and
wonderful dedes syth the fyrst makyng of heven and erth unto
the begynnyng of the regne of Kyng Edward the Fourth and
unto the yere of Our Lord MCCCClx; as by th'ayde of 130
Almyghty God shal folowe al alonge after the composynge and
gaderynge of Dan Ranulph, monke of Chestre, fyrste auctour
of this book, and afterward englisshed by one Trevisa,
Vycarye of Barkley, which atte request of one Sir Thomas
Lord Barkley translated this sayd book, the Byble, and 135
Bartylmew *De Proprietatibus Rerum* out of Latyn into Englyssh; and now at this tyme symply emprynted and sette in
forme by me, William Caxton, and a lytel embelysshed fro
th'olde makyng. And also have added suche storyes as I
coude fynde fro th'ende that the said Ranulph fynysshed his 140

book, which was the yere of Our Lord MCCClvii, unto the
yere of the same MCCCClx, whiche ben an honderd and
thre yere.

Whiche werke I have finysshed under the noble protection
of my most drad, naturel and soverayne lord and moost 145
Cristen kynge, Kyng Edward the Fourth, humbly besechyng
his moost noble grace to pardone me yf ony thynge be sayd
therynne of ignoraunce or otherwyse than it ought to be; and
also requyryng al other to amende wher as ther is defaute,
wherin he or they may deserve thank and meryte. And I shal 150
praye for them that soo doo, for I knowleche myn ignoraunce
and also symplenes. And yf ther be thyng that may plese or
prouffite ony man I am glad that I have achieved it. And
folowynge this my prohemye I shal set a table shortly towchyd
of the moost parte of this book. And where the sayd auctor 155
hath alle his werke in seven bookes, I have sette that whiche
I have added to after aparte and have marked it the laste
booke, and have made chapytres acordyng to the other werke.
Of whiche accomplysshyng I thanke Almyghty God, to
whome be gyven honour, laude and glorye *in secula seculorum.* 160
Amen.

(b) *Epilogue after Book vii*

Thus endeth the book named *Proloconycon,* made and compiled by Ranulph, monk of Chestre, whiche ordeyned it in
Latyn; and atte request of the ryght worshipful lord, Thomas
Lord of Berkeley, it was translated into Englisshe by one
Trevisa, thenne vycarye of the paryssh of Barkley. And for 5
as moche as syth the accomplysshemente of this sayd booke
made by the sayd Ranulph, ended the yere of Oure Lord a
MCCClvii, many thynges have fallen whiche ben requysyte
to be added to this werke, bycause mennes wyttes in this
tyme ben oblyvyous and lyghtly forgoten many thyngys 10
dygne to be putte in memorye, and also there cannot be
founden in these dayes but fewe that wryte in theyr regystres
suche thynges as dayly happen and falle, therfore I William
Caxton, a symple persone, have endevoyred me to wryte fyrst
overall the sayd book of *Proloconycon* and somwhat have 15
chaunged the rude and old Englyssh, that is to wete certayn
wordes which in these dayes be neither usyd ne understanden.
And furthermore have put it in emprynte to th'ende that it
maye be had and the maters therin comprised to be knowen,
for the boke is general touchyng shortly many notable maters. 20

And also am avysed to make another booke after this sayd
werke, whiche shal be sett here after the same and shal have
his chapytres and his table aparte, for I dar not presume to
sette my booke ne joyne hit to his for dyverse causes. One is
for as moche as I have not ne can gete no bokes of auctoryte   25
treatyng of suche cronykes, except a lytel boke named
Fasciculus Temporum and another callyd *Aureus de Universo*, in
whiche bookes I fynde ryght lytel mater syth the sayde tyme.
And another cause is for as moche as my rude symplenesse
and ignorant makyng ought not to be compared, set ne   30
joyned to his boke. Thenne I shal by the grace of God set my
werke after aparte for to accomplysshe the yeres syth that
he fynysshed his book unto the yere of our Lord MCCCClx
and the fyrst yere of the regne of Kyng Edward the Fourthe,
whiche amounte to an honderd and thre yere.   35

(c) *Prologue to Liber Ultimus*

Thenne folowyng this forewreton booke of *Prolicronycon*, I
have emprysed to ordeyne this newe booke by the suffraunce
of Almyghty God to contynue the sayd werk bryefly and to
sette in hystoriall thynges, suche as I have conne gete from
the tyme that he lefte, that was in the yere of Oure Lord a   5
thousand three honderde and seven and fyfty, unto the yere
of our sayd Lord thousand four honderd and syxty and to the
fyrst yere of the regne of Kynge Edward the Fourth.

(d) *Epilogue to Liber Ultimus*

And here I make an ende of this lytel werke as nygh as I can
fynde after the forme of the werk tofore made by Ranulph
monk of Chestre. And where as ther is fawte I beseche them
that shal rede it to correcte it, for yf I coude have founden
moo storyes I wold have sette in hit moo. But the substaunce   5
that I can fynde and knowe I have shortly sette hem in this
book to th'entente that such thynges as have ben done syth
the deth or ende of the sayd boke of *Polycronycon* shold be had
in remembraunce and not putte in oblyvyon ne forgetynge.
Prayenge all them that shall see this symple werke to pardone   10
me of my symple and rude wrytynge.

Ended the second day of Juyll, the xxii yere of the regne
of Kynge Edward the Fourth, and of the incarnacion of Oure
Lord a thousand four honderd foure score and tweyne.

Fynysshed per Caxton.   15

91. REYNARD THE FOX (First Edition) (6 June 1481)

Colophon

Prayeng alle them that shal see this lytyl treatis to correcte and amende where they shal fynde faute; for I have not added ne mynusshed but have folowed as nyghe as I can my copye whiche was in Dutche, and by me, William Caxton, translated into this rude and symple Englyssh in th'Abbey of West-   5
mestre. Fynysshed the vi daye of Juyn, the yere of Our Lord MCCCClxxxi and the xxi yere of the regne of Kynge Edward the iiiith.

Here endeth the *Historye of Reynard the Foxe* etc.

93. ROYAL BOOK (*c.* 1484)

(a) *Prologue*

Whan I remembre and take hede of the conversacion of us that lyve in this wretched lyf in which is no surete ne stable abydyng and also the contynuel besynes of every man, how he is occupyed and dayly laboureth to bylde and edefye as though theyr habytacion and dwellyng here were permanent   5
and shold ever endure, and also practyse how they may gete temporalle possessyons, goodes and rychesses of whyche they are never contente ne satysfyed as for the moost partye, but contynuelly entende and laboure by many subtyl meanes how they may encreace theyr sayd possessyons and richesses for to   10
come and attayne to worldly honour and estate in whiche they wene be veray felycyte and blessydnes; and whan I have wel overseen and examyned these forsayd thynges and lyf, I fynde nothyng in them but vanyte of vanytees and all vanyte. And yet I merveylle moche of them that ben lerned, wyse and   15
noble men in the lawe that, notwithstondyng their rychesses and sure lyvyng as wel in spirituelte as in the temporalte, contynuelly laboure to be enhaunced and promoted to hye dygnytees and offyces as though therin were perpetuel felycyte, in whyche ye may see at eye that al is but vanyte   20
and they that men repute for wysest and gretest aboute prynces in a moment ben overthrowen and brought to nought. Notwithstondyng for the moost parte they of the spyrytuelte and also of the temporalte entende more to gete worldly honours, rychesses and possessyons for to satisfye   25
the appetyte of their inordynate desyre here in this tran-

sytorye lyf, which anone and hastely shal departe fro the
corruptyble body, than they do for th'eternal lyf which shal
ever endure in joye or in payne.

Thenne to th'ende that every man resonable remembre   30
hymself that he is mortal and shal withoute fayle departe out
of this lyf hastely and sone and ought while he is here lyvyng
to purveye and ordeyne for the perpetuel lyf to come and so
to lyve accordyng to the lawe and comandements of Our
Lord and ocupye hymself in vertuous operacyons and werkes   35
in eschewyng al vices and synnes and al the braunches of them
that they may after this short and transytorye lyf attayne and
com to the everlastyng lyf in heven, I purpose and attende by
the suffraunce of Almyghty God to translate a book late
delyverd to me and reduce it out of Frensshe into our comyn   40
Englysshe tonge, in whyche every man may be enformed how
he ought to kepe the lawe and comaundements of God to
folowe vertu and flee and eschewe vyces and to pourveye and
ordeyne for hym spyrituel rychesses in heven perpetuel and
permanent.[1]   45

Which book was made in Frensshe atte requeste of Phelip
le Bele Kyng of Fraunce in the yere of th'yncarnacion of Our
Lord MCClxxix and reduced into Englisshe at the request and
specyal desyre of a synguler frende of myn, a mercer of
London, the yere of our sayd Lord MiiiiClxxxiiii. Which   50
book is entytled and named in Frensshe *Le Lyvre Royal*,
whiche is to say in Englisshe *The Ryal Book* or *A Book for a
Kyng*. In whiche book ben comprysed the x comandements
of Our Lord, the xii artycles of the fayth, the vii dedely
synnes with their braunches, the vii petycions of the *Pater*   55
Noster, the seven yeftes of the Holy Ghoost, the vii vertues
and many other holy thynges and maters good and prouffytable for the wele of mannes soule. Thenne I exhorte and
desyre every man that entendeth to the prouffyt and salvacyon
of his soule to oversee this sayd book in whiche he shal fynde   60
good and prouffytable doctryne, by which he may the rather
attayne to come to everlastyng blysse. And alwaye what that
is wryton is under correctyon of lerned men, humbly besechyng them to correcte and amende where as is ony defaute, and
so doyng they shal doo a merytory dede. For as nyghe as God   65
hath gyven me connyng I have folowed the copye as nyghe as
I can. And I beseche Almyghty God that this sayd werk may
prouffyte the redars and that is the special cause that it is

_____
[1] permanent

made fore. That knoweth God to whome noothyng is hyd, whyche gyve us grace so to lyve vertuously in this short lyf   70 that after this lyf we may come to his everlastyng blysse in heven. Amen.

Here foloweth the table of the rubriches of thys presente book entytled and named *Ryal*, whiche speketh fyrst of the ten commandementes.   75

(b) *Epilogue*

This book was compyled and made atte requeste of Kyng Phelyp of Fraunce in the yere of th'yncarnacyon of Our Lord MCClxxix, and translated or reduced out of Frensshe into Englysshe by me, Wyllyam Caxton, atte requeste of a worshipful marchaunt and mercer of London, whyche instauntly   5 requyred me to reduce it for the wele of alle them that shal rede or here it as for a specyal book to knowe al vyces and braunches of them and also al vertues by whyche wel understonden and seen may dyrecte a persone to everlastyng blysse. Whyche book is callyd in Frensshe *Le Livre Royal*, that is to   10 say *The Ryal Book* or *A Book for a Kyng*. For the holy scrypture calleth every man a kyng whiche wysely and parfytly can governe and dyrecte hymself after vertu. And this book sheweth and enseygneth it so subtylly, so shortly, so perceyvyngly and so parfyghtly that for the short comprehencion   15 of the noble clergye and of the right grete substaunce which is comprysed therin, it may and ought to be called wel by ryght and quycke reason above al other bookes in Frensshe or in Englysshe *The Book Ryal* or *The Book for a Kyng*. And also bycause that it was made and ordeyned atte request of that   20 ryght noble kyng, Phelyp le Bele Kynge of Fraunce, ought it to be called *Ryall* as tofore is sayd.

Whiche translacion or reducyng oute of Frensshe into Englysshe was achyeved, fynysshed and accomplysshed the xiii day of Septembre in the yere of th'yncarnacyon of Our   25 Lord MCCCClxxxiiii and in the second yere of the regne of Kyng Rychard the Thyrd.

94. SAINT WINIFRED (*c.* 1485)

Conclusion

Thus endeth the decollacion, the lyf after, and the translacion of Saynte Wenefrede, virgyn and martir, whiche was reysed

after that her hede had be smyton of the space of xv yere;
reduced into Englysshe by me, William Caxton.

95. SEX EPISTOLAE (*c.* 1483)

Colophon

Finiunt sex quamelegantissime epistole quarum tria[1] a
Summo Pontifice Sixto Quarto et Sacro Cardinalium Collegio
ad Illustrissimum Venetiarum Ducem Joannem Mocenigum
totidemque ab ipso duce ad eundem pontificem et cardinales
ob Ferrariense bellum susceptum conscripte sunt. Impresse   5
per Willelmum Caxton et diligenter emendate per Petrum
Carmelianum poetarum laureatum in Westmonasterio.

Eloquii cultor sex has mercare tabellas
Que possunt Marco cum Cicerone loqui.
Ingeniis debent cultis ea scripta placere   10
In quibus ingenii copia magna viget.

96. SIEGE OF JERUSALEM (20 November 1481)

(a) *Prologue*

The hye couragyous faytes and valyaunt actes of noble,
illustrous and vertuous personnes ben digne to be recounted,
put in memorye and wreton to th'ende that ther may be
gyven to them name inmortal by soverayn laude and
preysyng, and also for to moeve and t'enflawme the hertes   5
of the redars and hierers for t'eschewe and flee werkes vycious,
dishonnest and vytuperable and for t'empryse and accomplysshe enterpryses honnestes and werkes of gloryous
meryte to lyve in remembraunce perpetuel. For as it is so
that th'ystoryagraphes have wreton many a noble hystorye as   10
wel in metre as in prose by whiche th'actes and noble fayttes
of th'auncyent conquerours ben had in remembraunce and remayne in grete, large and aourned volumes and so shal
abyde in perpetuel memorye to th'entente that gloryous
prynces and hye men of noble and vertuouse courage shold   15
take ensample t'empryse werkys leeful and honneste: fyrst,
for Goddes quarell in mayntenyng oure fayth and the
libertees of Holy Chirche, for the recuperacion of the Holy
Land whiche oure blessyd Lord Jhesu Criste hath halowed
by his blessyd presence humayne and by shedyng therin for   20

[1] tris

137

oure redempcion his precious blood, for the releef of suche
Cristen men as there dwelle in grete myserye and thraldomm,
and also for the defence of theyr royammes, londes, enherytages and subgettes; and for thyse causes t'endevoyre
theym in theyr noble persones with alle theyr puyssaunces and   25
power t'adresse and remyse theym in theyr auncyent fraun-
chyses and lyberte acordyng to that we fynde wreton in holy
scripture of many noble historyes, which were here overlong
to reherce. But in especial of thre noble and mooste worthy
of alle other, that is to wytte fyrst of Duc Josue, that noble   30
prynce whiche ladde and conduyted the childeren of Israhel,
the chosen people of God, oute of deserte into the londe of
promyssyon, the londe flowynge mylke and hony; secondly,[1]
of Davyd the Kynge and holy prophete, whome God chaas
after his herte, and achyevyd many grete batailles, governyng   35
the sayd chosen people of God by the space of fourty yeris;
and the thyrde, of the noble Judas Machabeus, how he
deffended the sayd people in fyghtyng many and merveyllous
batailles for veray zeele and love of his lawe, and mayntenyng
of the same unto the deth. For which causes aforsayd the names   40
of thyes thre abyde perpetuel for thre of the moste beste and
nobleste of the Jewys and in the nombre of the moost digne
and moost worthy.

And bycause valyaunce and prowesse is remembryd emong
the gentyles and paynems[2] as emong th'Ebrewes, I fynde   45
wreton of the incredible chevalrous prowesse of the noble and
valyaunt Hector of Troye, whos excellent actes wryten
Ovyde, Homer, Virgyle, Dares, Dyctes and other dyverse
and eche better than other, rehercyng[3] his noble vertues,
strengthe and humanyte; secondly, of Alysaundre the grete   50
Kynge of Macedone which domyned and had to hym
obeyssaunt the unyversal world; and the thyrde, the noble
Julyus Cezar, Emperour of Rome, whos noble actes ben
wreton by poetes, as Lucan, Stace and other, and dayly
remembryd as newe and fresshe as he yet lyvyd. Whiche thre   55
ben sette as for the moost worthy emong the gentyles and
paynems.

Now lete us thenne remembre what hystoryes ben wreton of
Cristen men, of whom ther be many wreton. But in especial as
for the best and worthyest I fynde fyrst the gloryous, most ex-   60
cellent in his tyme, and fyrst founder of the Round Table,
Kyng Arthur, Kyng of the Brytons, that tyme regnyng in

[1] socondly   [2] paynmes   [3] reherchyng

this royamme, of whos retenue were many noble kynges, pryntes, lordes and knyghtes, of which the noblest were knyghtes of the Round Table of whos actes and historyes there be large volumes and bookes grete plente and many. O blessyd Lord, whan I remembre the grete and many volumes of Seynt Graal, Ghalehot, and Launcelotte de Lake, Gawayn, Perceval, Lyonel, and Tristram, and many other of whom were overlonge to reherce and also to me unknowen. But th'ystorye of the sayd Arthur is so gloryous and shynyng that he is stalled in the fyrst place of the mooste noble, beste and worthyest of the Cristen men. Secondly, of Charlemayn, the grete Emperour[1] of Allemayne and Kyng of Fraunce, whos noble actes and conquestes ben wreton in large volumes with the noble faytes and actes of his douzepieres, that is to saye, Rowlond and Olyver with the other, whos name and renommee abydeth also perpetuel and is stalled in the second place emonge the most worthy of Cristen men. Of alle thyse historyes afor-reherced the bookes and volumes ben had in Latyn, Frenssh and Englysshe and other langage.

Thenne as for the thyrd of the Cristen pryntes taken, reputed and renommed for to be egal among thyse worthy and best that ever were, I mene the noble Godefroy of Boloyne whiche now but late, not yet four C yere syth, he flowred and was stalled in the thyrde stalle of the moost worthy of Cristen men. Whos hystorye is made and wreton in Latyn and Frensshe in large and grete volumes, and as not knowen emonge us here whiche ben adjacent and neyghbours to the place of his natyvyte; whos noble hystorye I late fonde in a booke of Frenssh al alonge of his noble actes, valyaunces, prowesses and accomplysshement of his hye empryses. In whiche I fynde very causes, as me semeth, moche semblable and lyke unto suche as we have nowe dayly tofore us by the mescreauntes and Turkes emprysed ayenst Cristendom; and yet moche more nowe than were in his dayes, for in his dayes the Turkes had conquerd upon Cristendom but unto the Braas of Seynt George by Constantynople and had no foote on this syde of the sayd Braas. But at this daye it is so that they have comen over and goten that imperial cyte Constantynople aforsayd and many royamme and countre to the grete dommage and hurte of alle Cristendom—to the resistence of whom as yet fewe Cristen pryntes have put theym in devoyr. Thenne I retorne agayn unto the conqueste at suche tyme as

[1] Epemrour

they were come to the sayd Braas that by the dylygent solici- 105
tude of a pour heremyte the sayd Godeffroy of Boloyne and
other dyverse prynces, lordes and comyn peple avowed the
croysyng and empryse to warre agayn the mescreauntes and
to recovere the holy cyte of Jherusalem; whiche afterward
they achyevyd and conquerd fro the sayd Braas unto the Holy 110
Lande and recoverd the holy cyte of Jherusalem, as in this
sayd book¹ al alonge and playnly shal appere. In whiche cyte
the sayd Godeffroy was elect and chosen for his vertue,
prowesse and blessyd disposicion to be kyng of the sayd
Jherusalem and the londe therabout. 115

Thenne I thus vysytyng this noble hystorye whiche is no
fable ne fayned thynge, but alle that is therin trewe, con-
siderynge also the grete puyssaunce of the Turke, grete
enemye of oure Cristen fayth, destroyar of Cristen blood and
usurpar of certayn empyres and many Cristen royammes and 120
countrees, and now late this sayd yere hath assaylled the cyte
and castel in the Isle of Rhodes, where valyantly he hath be resisted, but yet notwithstondyng he hath approched² more ner
and hath taken the cyte of Ydronte in Puylle, by whiche he hath
goten an entre to entre into the royamme of Naples, and fro 125
thens withoute he be resisted unto Rome and Ytalye, to whos
resistence I besche Almyghty God to provyde, yf it be his
wylle; thenne me semeth it necessary and expedyent for alle
Cristen prynces to make peas, amyte and allyaunce eche with
other and provyde by theyr wysedommes the resistence agayn 130
hym for the defense of our fayth and moder Holy Chirch and
also for the recuperacion of the Holy Londe and holy cyte of
Jherusalem, in whiche our blessyd Savyour, Jhesu Crist,
redemed us with his precious blood, and to doo as this noble
prynce Godeffroy of Boloyne dyde with other noble and hye 135
prynces in his companye. Thenne for th'exhortacion of alle
Cristen prynces, lordes, barons, knyghtes, gentilmen, marchauntes, and all the comyn peple of this noble royamme,
Walys and Yrlond, I have emprysed to translate this book of
the conquest of Jherusalem out of Frenssh into our maternal 140
tongue to th'entente t'encourage them by the redyng and
heeryng of the merveyllous historyes herin comprysed and
of the holy myracles shewyd that every man in his partye
endevoyre theym unto the resistence aforesayd and recuperacion of the sayd Holy Londe. 145

And for as moche as I knowe no Cristen kynge better

¹ boook   ² approchod

provyd in armes and for whom God hath shewed more
grace, and in alle his empryses gloryous vaynquysshour,
happy and eurous, than is our naturel, lawful and soverayn
lord and moost Cristen kynge, Edward by the grace of God 150
Kynge of Englond and of Fraunce and Lord of Yrlond, under
the shadowe of whos noble protection I have achyeved this
symple translacion, that he of his moost noble grace wold
adresse, styre or commaunde somme noble capytayn of his
subgettes to empryse this warre agayn the sayd Turke and 155
hethen peple, to whiche I can thynke that every man wyll put
hand to in theyr propre persones and in theyr mevable
goodes; thenne to hym, my moost drad, naturel and soverayn
lord, I adresse this symple and rude book, besechyng his moost
bounteuous and haboundaunt grace to receyve it of me, his in- 160
digne and humble subgette, William Caxton, and to pardonne
me so presumynge. Besechyng Almyghty God that this sayd
book may encourage, moeve and enflamme the hertes of
somme noble men that by the same the mescreauntes maye
be resisted and putte to rebuke, Cristen fayth encreaced and 165
enhaunced, and the Holy Lande with the blessyd cyte of
Jherusalem recoverd and may come agayn into Cristen men's
hondes. Thenne I exhorte alle noble men of hye courage to see
this booke and here it redde, by which ye shal see what wayes
were taken, what noble prowesses and valyaunces were 170
achyevyd by the noble companyes and especial by the said
noble prynce, Godeffroy of Boloyne, Duc of Loreyne, by
whiche he deservyd the name of one of the moost worthy that
ever were and ys stalled in the thyrd stalle of the Cristen conquerours and in the nynthe of the mooste worthy, where his 175
name and renomme shal remayne and abyde perpetuel. And for
to deserve the tenthe place I besche Almyghty God to graunte
and ottroye to our sayd soverayn lord or to one of his noble
progenye, I meane my Lord Prynce and my Lord Rychard
Duc of Yorke and Norfolke, to whom I humbly besche at 180
theyr leyzer and playsyr to see and here redde this symple
book, by which they may be encoraged to deserve lawde and
honour, and that their name and renomme may encreace and
remayne perpetuel, and after this lyf short and transytorye all
we may atteyne to come to the everlastyng lyf in heven where 185
is joye and reste withoute ende. Amen.

(b) *Epilogue*

Thus endeth this book intitled *The Laste Siege and Conquest of*

Jherusalem with many other historyes therin comprysed, fyrst
of Eracles and of the meseases of the Cristen men in the Holy
Londe and of their releef and conquest of Jherusalem and how
Godeffroy of Boloyne was first Kyng of the Latyns in that   5
royamme and of his deth, translated and reduced out of
Frensshe into Englysshe by me symple persone, Wylliam
Caxton, to th'ende that every Cristen man may be the better
encoraged t'enterprise warre for the defense of Cristendom
and to recover the sayd cyte of Jherusalem, in whiche oure   10
blessyd savyour Jhesu Criste suffred deth for al mankynde
and roose fro deth to lyf and fro the same Holy Londe ascended into heven, and also that Cristen peple, one unyed in a
veray peas, myght empryse to goo theder in pylgremage with
strong honde for to expelle the Sarasyns and Turkes out of   15
the same, that Our Lord myght be ther servyd and worshipped
of his chosen Cristen peple in that holy and blessyd londe in
which he was incarnate, and blissyd it with the presence of
his blessyd body whyles he was here in erthe emonge us. By
whiche conquest we myght deserve after this present, short   20
and transitorye lyf the celestial lyf, to dwelle in heven
eternally in joye without ende. Amen.

Which book I presente unto the mooste Cristen kynge,
Kynge Edward the Fourth, humbly besechyng his Hyenes to
take no displesyr at me so presumyng. Whiche book[1] I began   25
in Marche the xii daye and fynysshyd the vii day of Juyn the
yere of Our Lord MCCCClxxxi and the xxi yere of the regne
of our sayd soverayn[2] lord, Kyng Edward the Fourth, and
in this maner sette in forme and enprynted the xx day of
Novembre the yere aforsayd in th'Abbay of Westmester by   30
the sayd Wylliam Caxton.

103. VOCABULARY (*c.* 1480)

Colophon
Here endeth this doctrine,
At Westmestre by London
In fourmes enprinted,
In whiche one everich
May shortly lerne   5
Frenssh and Englissh.
The grace of the Holy Ghoost

[1] boook   [2] saverayn

Wylle enlyghte the hertes
Of them that shall lerne it,
And us gyve perseveraunce   10
In good werkes,
And after this lyf transitorie
The everlastyng joye and glorie.

106. OVID'S METAMORPHOSES

Colophon

Thus endeth Ovyde hys booke of Methamorphose, translated
and fynysshed by me William Caxton at Westmestre the xxii
day of Appryll the yere of Oure Lord M¹ iiiiC iiii×ˣ, and the xx
yere of the regne of Kynge Edward the Fourth.

Notes

1. ADVERTISEMENT

For details of the advertisement see Blake p. 223. The *pie* was a collection of rules regulating how one should deal with the coincidence of more than one office or commemoration on the same day. The Salisbury Use was the form of the liturgy developed at Salisbury Cathedral which had gradually been adopted by other churches and dioceses. It had become the most popular liturgical practice in England by the fifteenth century as Caxton's edition shows.

1. The explicit reference to clergy and laity here shows that Caxton expected what was to some extent a technical book to appeal to a wide range of buyers. Members of the nobility were interested in new feasts and the veneration of saints. For example, R. W. Pfaff, *New Liturgical Feasts in Later Medieval England* (Oxford, 1970), p. 47, notes that Elizabeth Woodville petitioned the pope about the Feast of the Visitation in 1480/1.

2–3. The Salisbury Use was printed in the same type as the advertisement (*after the forme of this present lettre*).

3. *whiche ben wel and truly correct:* this presumably refers back to the *pyes* of line 1. It would be important that the rules and tables were printed correctly so that the correct offices were sung. However, like most publishers Caxton makes claims which are sometimes exaggerated.

4. On the Almonry see Blake pp. 82–3. The Red Pale is not referred to outside Caxton's editions; it is not mentioned by de Worde. The invitation to customers to come to Caxton's shop is interesting in showing that in this case at least Caxton distributed his printed works through his own shop.

6. *Supplico stet cedula:* 'Please leave the handbill where it is.'

2. ÆSOP

(a) Caxton gives 1483 as the date of his translation here, but in the colophon the book is said to have been printed on 26 March 1484. For comments on the period between translation and printing of his texts see the Introduction.

1. *subtyl:* here in the sense 'skilfully composed'.

(b) How much of the conclusion of *Æsop* is Caxton's own writing is problematical. The final story of the two priests has long been accepted as Caxton's addition, as the *I wylle fynysshe* (l. 18) suggests. The tale of the widow, which is of a different character, may have been taken from some unidentified source. But R. H. Wilson, 'The Poggiana in Caxton's *Esope*,' *Philological Quarterly*, 30 (1951), 351, writes: 'Did Caxton's source also include the story of the widow? This is possible, but since that 'fable' is not assigned to any literary origin, it can most simply be attributed to Caxton's own composition based on a current anecdote, like the story of the worldly and unworldly priests which follows it.'

9. *suche a man:* a phrase suitable for recorded speech, but hardly for dialogue as here.

12. *peryllous man:* Cf. The Reeve's Tale I. A. 4189.

19. The informant has not been identified.

22. *coude putte hymself forth:* 'was able to push himself forward, attract attention'. Despite Caxton's religious feelings he is willing to retell a story which reflects the common attitude to the clergy then, that it consisted of two types: those on the make and those who did a proper job. The latter type is idealized in Chaucer's parson.

24-5. Benefices were parishes and the income obtained from them. Many holders of benefices simply took the income and employed a vicar at a smaller sum to conduct the services. Prebends were that part of a cathedral's or collegiate church's income allocated to individual canons. It was often more remunerative and less arduous to be a chaplain to a nobleman than to run a parish.

28. An annual priest said masses for a person's soul daily for a year. It was thus only a temporary position, whereas a parish priest enjoyed the usufruct of his benefice for life.

37. A *sowle preest* said masses for the souls of the dead; here it probably means the same thing as an annual priest.

54-5. *doo my parte longynge to my cure:* 'perform my parochial duties as well as I can'.

56. *or ony of them:* 'or if any of their souls are lost'.

59. *be the better:* 'behave in a more Christian way'.

5. ART OF DIEING

Several types of work go under the general title of *Art of Dieing*: some, generally the earlier ones, are designed to encourage people to lead better lives; others are in the nature of a battle between an angel and a devil for the soul of a dying man; and a third type consists of prayers for the dead. This last group is more common in the fifteenth century and is the one to which Caxton's translation belongs. Several of the works printed by Caxton at the end of his life, such as this one, the *Horologium Sapientiae* and the *Rule of St Benedict*, were abridged. While it is not certain if there is any significance in this detail, it is possible that it was an attempt to cut out some of the technical religious material to make the books more attractive to a wider audience.

(b) 3-4. *a M iiiC lxxxx:* that is, 1490.

6. BLANCHARDIN AND EGLANTINE

2. Margaret Beaufort (1443–1509) married Edmund Tudor, Earl of Richmond, the half-brother of Henry VI, in 1455. A son, the future Henry VII, was born after his father's death. Margaret then married Henry Stafford and finally Lord Stanley, though she spent most of her life in semi-retirement. Margaret was of a religious and orthodox disposition, as her patronage of the *Fifteen Oes* suggests, and it is interesting to find her the patroness of a romance.

8. *boke:* 'a manuscript'. The modern distinction between book and manuscript arose later. Caxton had sold Margaret a manuscript copy of the French romance, though it is impossible to estimate how long he meant by *longe tofore*.

14ff. Both here and elsewhere Caxton views love and knighthood in an ideal way: knights are to prove themselves by warfare and ladies are to remain constant in love.

7. BOETHIUS

Boethius, son of a noble Roman family, was only a boy when Theodoric conquered Italy in 489. He later served Theodoric, until the king's fears about the loyalty of his Italian subjects led him first to imprison and then to murder Boethius. Apart from his *De Consolatione Philosophiae*, written in prison, Boethius also translated some Aristotelian works and composed some writings on logic. The details of his life included in Caxton's epilogue could easily have been taken from Chaucer's translation, particularly bk I prose 4. It is unlikely that Caxton knew any of Boethius's other works (cf. ll. 10–13).

16. *to his power:* 'to the best of his ability, as much as he could'.

22–4. This praise of Chaucer is typical of Caxton's work and of the fifteenth century, see C. F. E. Spurgeon, *Five Hundred Years of Chaucer Criticism and Allusion*, I. *1357–1800* (London, 1914).

24–6. Chaucer made his translation about 1380, but he used a French version and not the original Latin.

31–2. *wherto every mann livyng in hit ought to entende:* 'to what goal every man in this world ought to aspire'.

33. Eight manuscripts of Chaucer's translation are extant, so the work cannot have been quite as rare as Caxton implies. His remark should be understood as a publisher's 'blurb'.

36. This friend may be William Pratt, see Blake pp. 87–8.

44–5. The *whiche shal endure perpetuelly* could refer to Chaucer's translation (*this sayde boke*) or to the language (*the sayd langage*) which he has enriched. It we consider Caxton's views on the transitoriness of English in his *Eneydos*, the former is more probable.

48–50. On the problems associated with Surigone's epitaph see N. F.

Blake, 'Caxton and Chaucer,' *Leeds Studies in English*, N.S. 1 (1967), 19–36. The epitaph is not reproduced here as it is not Caxton's, but the final four lines are. They may be translated: 'After your death, renowned poet Chaucer, the care of William Caxton was that you should live, for not only did he print your works in type but he also ordered these your praises to be placed here'.

9. BOOK OF GOOD MANNERS

(a) 4. For this proverb cf. W. G. Smith and J. E. Heseltine, *The Oxford Book of English Proverbs*, 2nd edn rev. by P. Harvey (Oxford, 1948), p. 404.

9. William Pratt, a mercer who was probably about the same age as Caxton, died in 1486. The first payments for Pratt's and Caxton's livery dues are recorded under the same year and they may have been friends as apprentices (cf. *of olde knowlege*, l. 20).

11. An edition in French was printed by P. le Rouge at Chablis in 1478 and this was Caxton's French original according to E. G. Duff, *William Caxton* (Chicago, 1905), p. 10.

13-14. *scrypture of the Byble:* 'writings in the Bible'.

(b) Henry VII's first regnal year extended from 22 August 1485 to 21 August 1486. There was apparently a long gap between the end of the translation and the appearance of the printed work; see Introduction.

11. CANTERBURY TALES

This prologue is printed and discussed in some detail in Blake pp. 161–9.

26–7. Caxton's *many a noble hystorye of every astate and degree* presumably means stories written by people of every rank and class.

30–1. The *wherin he fynysshyth thys sayd booke* refers to the Parson's Tale and to Chaucer's Retractions. It is an interesting comment on the importance attached to the conclusion by Chaucer's early readers. Caxton also comments at the end of his prologue on the efficacy of Chaucer's virtuous tales.

33. The *I fynde* is probably not a statement of much worth; note how Caxton claims he printed the first faulty edition *by ygnouraunce* (l. 53).

37. There is no evidence from Caxton's first edition of the *Canterbury Tales* that it was printed for a patron or from a copy lent to him. We may, I think, assume that the statement is correct and that it is not an attempt to transfer the blame to a fictitious patron.

40–1. *many and dyverse gentylmen:* Caxton is never specific about who bought his works.

15. CATON

(a) 2. *Caton* is a prose commentary based on the *Disticha Catonis* and its relation to the *Disticha* is suggested at ll. 81–6. Benedict Burgh had made a verse translation of the *Disticha* which Caxton printed as *Parvus Cato, Magnus Cato* (Blake No. 12–14); this work is much briefer. As Caxton himself translated *Caton* into English, his *whiche boke* must refer to 'the original form of the book'. It is strange that he should make no reference to his editions of Burgh's poem, which was popular since Caxton issued three editions between 1477 and 1481. Furthermore in his editions of *Parvus Cato, Magnus Cato* Caxton makes no reference to Burgh's authorship. Not a great deal more is known of Burgh than is mentioned here by Caxton.

5. *balade ryal:* the verse form particularly associated with Lydgate which was considered very fashionable in the fifteenth century.

6. Henry Bourchier was created Earl of Essex by Edward IV in 1461. His eldest son William, who married Anne Woodville, died before his father; hence Caxton's reference to *at that tyme*. Caxton as always shows himself very familiar with details of the Woodville family connexions, though the absence of specific references to the Woodvilles here may be due to the conditions prevailing in 1483.

14–15. For Caxton's life as a mercer see Blake p. 26ff. Although there may be particular reasons for Caxton's reference to London at this time (see Blake p. 92), it is interesting that he still feels himself to be intimately linked with London and the Mercers' Company.

19. *polecye:* here best understood as 'government, administration', from which its prosperity would partly come.

20–2. Little significance need be attached to this claim. It was, and is, common to look back to the past as a golden age.

28–9. Caxton's *th'actes of Romayns* may well be a general remark without specific reference to a particular book; see Introduction.

29–30. Publius Cornelius Scipio Africanus (236–184/3 BC) defeated Hannibal and saved Rome in the Second Punic War. His brother, Lucius Cornelius Scipio Asiaticus (consul in 190 BC), defeated Antichus III of Syria. *Actilius* is presumably Marcus Atilius Regulus, who was consul in 258 BC. He was reckoned by Cicero to be among one of the most famous Roman warriors because of a story current in Cicero's time. Atilius had been captured by the Carthaginians and allowed to go back to Rome provided he pleaded for peace. But in the Senate he urged the continuation of the war. Because of his oath, he returned to Carthage where he was cruelly murdered.

31. Marcus Porcius Cato censorius (234–149 BC) was a famous orator, statesman and prose writer. The *Disticha Catonis* date only from Roman imperial times, but they were attributed to Cato at an early date.

34–5. The popularity of the *Disticha Catonis* is attributable to its use as a school text. Indeed, Caxton may have printed *Caton* for use in schools, though he does point to its wider usefulness as an aid in inculcating morals.

60. This sub-title is found at the end of the book Caxton was printing in the form 'The Myrour of the Regyme and Governement of the Body and of the Soule' and he must have taken it from there.

61. On Poggio Bracciolini (1380–1459) see Blake p. 197. He is known particularly for his discovery of classical manuscripts. He wrote several moral works which may account for the linking of his name with *Caton*. Some of his *Facetiae* were included in the *Æsop* translated by Caxton. Poggio visited England in 1418–23, and on his return held positions in the Curia under the popes Eugenius IV (1431–47) and Nicholas V (1447–55). See Introduction.

87ff. The Latin here commented upon is included at the end of each section. The French version was divided into a prologue and the two major parts, of which the last part was divided into four books. So the division here is not made by Caxton who has merely quoted the first two or three words of each Latin chapter heading. When Caxton says the second part is in verse, he means the Latin headings are metrical, not his own translation which is all in prose.

16. CHARLES THE GREAT

(a) The early part of this prologue is modelled upon the French text of Garbin's *Fierabras*, printed at Geneva in 1483, which was Caxton's source. The *I* in this part refers to the French redactor; from l. 46 it refers to Caxton. Caxton seems to have been unconcerned about this confusion, though we should not think of it as an attempt to deceive.

11–13. This clause is difficult for Caxton has not kept close to the French, which reads 'Et aussi en racomptant histoires haultaines l'entendement commun est mieulx content a retenir pour la ymaginacion localle a laquelle il est subzmis'.

25. *a werk wel contemplatyf for to lyve wel*: this phrase is translated literally from the French; *contemplatyf* would seem to mean no more than 'moral, didactic'.

46ff. Caxton's edition of Malory's *Le Morte d'Arthur* (Blake No. 72) was printed on 31 July 1485, only four months before *Charles the Great*; his *Siege of Jerusalem*, the account of Godfrey of Bouillon (Blake No. 96), was issued on 20 November 1481. On the concept of the nine worthies see M. Y. Offord, *The Parlement of the Thre Ages*, EETS 246 (London, 1959), pp. xl–xlii. The nine were divided into three groups of three each: pagans, Jews and Christians. Chronologically Arthur was the first of the Christian kings, Charlemagne the second, and Godfrey the third.

51. *somme persones of noble estate and degree*: in the epilogue only Daubeney is mentioned as the propagator of the work. For a similar general statement cf. 72a :4–5; as these two prologues were written in 1485 it is

natural that some ideas and expressions are repeated. See also the Introduction.

55. *th'ystoryes, actes and lyves:* the use of the plural suggests Caxton was thinking of accounts of the three Christian kings.

56–8. It is difficult to know what weight to put on Caxton's statement that the majority of people do not know Latin and French. In general he does not publish for the majority of people, and in his prologue to *Jason* he notes that Edward IV knew French well and so did not need an English version.

71–2. Nothing is known of Caxton's schooling, see Blake pp. 24–5. The passage makes it clear that Caxton's parents were dead by this time.

72. The *by whyche* must refer to Caxton's schooling. He implies that at school he was educated, and because of his education he is able to translate books, by which he makes his living. It is probable that he did learn some French at school.

75. *dette:* 'sin'; i.e. the debt we accumulate for our sinful behaviour and which we must pay off before entry into paradise.

(b) 3. On Daubeney see Blake pp. 95–6.

16–17. Richard III died at Bosworth on 22 August 1485.

17. CHRONICLES OF ENGLAND

(a) This chronicle is based on a manuscript of the *Brut* which contained continuations down to 1461; see C. L. Kingsford, *English Historical Literature in the Fifteenth Century* (Oxford, 1913), pp. 113–15.

3. The patron or patrons have not been identified; see Introduction.

9. Albine, the daughter of Diocletian, King of 'Sirrie', was banished because of the murder of her husband. She landed in England, which was then desolate, and called it Albion after herself.

(b) This conclusion was added by Caxton to the account of Edward IV's succession which concluded his copytext of the *Brut*. The *whom* is Edward, and his *rightfull enheritaunce* France. There were no particular plans to invade France at this time and Caxton's remark may be taken as little more than a pious wish. Edward was in fact receiving a pension from Louis of France. But there was no final peace in Europe where relations between England, France and Burgundy remained fluid, and at the end of 1480 Edward was making preparations for a war against Scotland. However, Europe was worried about the advance of the Turks and talk of a crusade was often aired. In 1480 Giulio della Rovere visited Louis in the hope of gaining his help against the Turk. See further C. L. Scofield, *The Life and Reign of Edward IV* (London, 1923), II. 155ff.

3. *them:* i.e. England and France, his two kingdoms.

22. CONFESSIO AMANTIS

(a) No other source mentions that Gower was a squire or that he was born in Wales. We cannot say where Caxton got this information which has generally been ignored by modern scholars who prefer the view that Gower came from a Yorkshire or Kentish family, see J. H. Fisher, *John Gower, Moral Philosopher and Friend of Chaucer* (London, 1965). See also N. F. Blake, 'Caxton's Copytext of Gower's *Confessio Amantis*,' *Anglia*, 85 (1967), 282–93. The *Confessio Amantis* was written during the reign of Richard II, but the original dedication to him was changed by Gower to Henry Bolingbroke, the future Henry IV.

24. CORDIAL

Anthony Earl Rivers, the brother of Elizabeth Woodville the Queen, was one of Caxton's principal patrons; see Blake p. 84ff. Caxton had printed a French text of the *Cordial* while in Bruges (Blake No. 23) and it was this version which Rivers translated.

3. *Lord [of] Scales:* cf. 29a:5.

10. In modern reckoning the year is 1479.

13–14. Probably *the tyme of the grete tribulacion and adversite* for Earl Rivers was 1469–70. For then Warwick rebelled against Edward IV, beheaded River's father and brother, and caused Edward IV and Rivers to flee to the Low Countries and Elizabeth Woodville to take sanctuary in Westminster Abbey. If this interpretation is correct, it is interesting that so long after the rebellion Caxton should still refer to it so cautiously. Rivers himself in his own prologue to *Dicts or Sayings* mentions the storms of fortune to which he has been subjected. The information about Rivers's exploits must have come from the Earl himself. The places mentioned are all places of pilgrimage on account of the shrines there: Compostella (Spain) for the shrine of St James the Greater; Rome for the shrine of St Bartholomew; Amalfi (Italy) for the shrine of St Andrew; Salerno (Italy) for the shrine of St Matthew; and Bari (Italy) for the shrine of St Nicholas. According to his prologue in *Dicts or Sayings* Rivers sailed for Compostella from Southampton in 1473. Rivers's reception in Rome is mentioned by John Paston II in a letter to Margaret Paston of 21 March 1476; see N. Davis, *Paston Letters and Papers of the Fifteenth Century* (Oxford, 1971), I. 494.

20. Sixtus IV invested Rivers with the title of defender and director of papal courses in England.

20–1. The Chapel of Our Lady of the Pew adjoined St Stephen's College, and both were suppressed at the Dissolution. According to Stow's *Survey of London* (ed. C. L. Kingsford, Oxford, 1908) the chapel was burned down in 1452, but it was later rebuilt by Anthony Earl Rivers (II. 121). Earl Rivers in his will asked that his heart should be buried there.

24. *Scala celi* is the name of the church outside Rome where St Bernard had a vision of the souls, for whom he was saying mass, ascending by 'a ladder unto heaven'. An indulgence was attached to this church and

to all chapels and altars of the same dedication in England. There was a chapel of *Scala celi* in Westminister Abbey.

26–7. Rivers was appointed governor of the Prince of Wales, the future Edward v, in 1473 (cf. l. 5). The Prince of Wales was sent to live at Ludlow, which is probably what Caxton meant by *Wales*.

29. *as the fruit therof experimently sheweth:* 'as may be seen practically by the results'. What Rivers has given in time and trouble to the king and the prince may be seen from the results he has achieved.

32ff. These books are *Dicts or Sayings* (Blake No 29) and *Moral Proverbs* (Blake No 77). The balades against the seven deadly sins have not been identified, if they have survived. These balades were evidently not printed by Caxton.

47. *tyme of grace:* i.e. our life in this world, during which we may achieve salvation.

57. Earl Rivers's preface merely gives an account of the book's contents and stresses its value.

70. St Blaise was possibly a bishop in Armenia, but most accounts of him are late and unhistorical. The printing was started on 3 February 1479 and finished on 24 March 1479.

26. CURIAL

This book was given to Caxton by Earl Rivers, the *noble and vertuous Erle*; see Blake p. 93. Rivers was beheaded on 13 June 1483, and Caxton's edition is usually dated to 1484. This is the only printed book connected with Rivers which he did not translate himself. Alain Chartier (*c.* 1386–1457) was reputed to be an excellent orator and rhetorician; he may have translated his own work from Latin into French.

28. DESCRIPTION OF BRITAIN

(a) 1. It is doubtful whether Caxton has specific *places* in mind, but his statement does suggest that he knew copies of the *Brut* and other chronicles were common.

2. His edition of the *Chronicles* (Blake No. 17) was finished on 10 June 1480. As the *Description of Britain* was finished on 18 August of the same year, its printing must have been set in hand as soon as the *Chronicles* was finished. No doubt customers were urged to buy both together, and many extant copies of the *Description of Britain* are bound with *Chronicles of England*.

(b) 6. For Caxton's edition of *Polychronicon*, see No 86.

29. DICTS OR SAYINGS

(a) According to his own prologue Rivers was shown the French version of this work in 1473 on a voyage to Compostella by a

Gascon knight called Louis de Bretaylles, then in the service of England. He was much taken with it, but translated it later after he had been appointed governor of the Prince of Wales.

13–14. As the book was printed in 1477, soon after Caxton's return to England, his familiarity with the work must date from his time in Bruges. In fact French manuscripts of this text are common and a printed version was issued by Colard Mansion in Bruges. Caxton's use of the plural *bookes* may imply that several manuscripts had passed through his hands.

69–70. An interesting reminder that Caxton was aware manuscript copies could differ; cf. his remarks apropos of the *Canterbury Tales* (No 11).

77. Caxton's lengthy additions like this one are often added separately in the work with the result that attention is called to them. His smaller additions are included without notice in the texts and are more difficult to identify.

82–132. This passage is translated from the French.

93. *me:* the indefinite pronoun 'one'; cf. *one* 'a certain person' (l. 115).

138. Caxton foresees the possibility that those acquainted with the French text may also read the English version.

(b) This colophon is found only in the John Rylands Library copy of the first edition, though it is also included in what is usually considered as the second impression of the first edition.

34. DOCTRINAL OF SAPIENCE

The prologue is based directly on the French source Caxton used; he has merely adapted it for his own purposes. All the references and stories come from the French source. The addition (c) which is found only in the Windsor copy is the heading to the chapter dealing with misdemeanours at mass. Evidently Caxton meant that chapter to be seen only by clerical eyes. It shows that he produced books of this sort for both lay and clerical audiences, and it also reveals how sensitive he was in his publishing activities. He clearly did not wish to offend anyone.

(a) 4. *symple peple:* a traditional expression, in this case taken over from the French, which probably has little significance.

9. The Venerable Bede (673–735), author of the *Historia Ecclesiastica*.

19. Jacques de Vitry, a French cardinal who lived in the early thirteenth century, whose sermons helped to popularize the use of *exempla*.

26. St Augustine (354–430), Bishop of Hippo Regius in North Africa, from whose *Confessions* these details are taken.

36. ENEYDOS

(a) 2. I have argued elsewhere that this *studye* is best understood as Caxton's shop where he offered books (*paunflettis and bookys*) for sale;

see 'William Caxton: his Choice of Texts,' *Anglia*, 83 (1965), 289–307.

10. Æneas's son is called both Yolus and Ascanius in the text.

15. *honest:* little more than a general term of commendation.

21. The implication seems to be that although the book is old and had been used as a school text in Italy (though Caxton does not say how he acquired this information), it is neverthless fit reading for the English nobility.

32. Unfortunately Caxton does not tell us the age of this *olde boke*, but it need not have been older than the fourteenth century for he felt Trevisa's language needed modernizing when he published the *Polychronicon*. Cf. his use of *olde bookes* at 11:15–16.

35. The Abbot of Westminster was John Estney, who was abbot from 1474 to 1498. It is important to emphasize that Caxton was apparently on good terms with the abbot, whom he must by now have known for fifteen years at least, since Westminister possessed an important scriptorium. There was no dispute between the makers of books and those of manuscripts.

38. *Dutche:* 'Low German'. Since Caxton was able to translate *Reynard the Fox* from Dutch into English, his claim that he could not translate the abbot's legal documents may be taken with a pinch of salt.

40. The development in English between the fourteenth and fifteenth centuries was considerable, principally because of the Great Vowel Shift and of changes in vocabulary. However, such statements as these are traditional, cf. *Confessio Amantis*, prologue and *Troilus and Criseyde*, II 22–5 and V 1793–4.

48. The merchants would presumably have been sailing from London down the Thames to a port in Zeeland such as Middelburg. The *forlond* would be on the Kent or Essex coast. There was a mercer named John Sheffield who issued from his apprenticeship to Robert Hallom in 1456/7.

52. The form *eggys*, with a plosive *g*, is a development of Old Norse *egg*, and in the fifteenth century it was more characteristic of the North of England. *Eyren* is the Middle English development of Old English *æg*, with a palatal *g*. The plural is formed on the same pattern as *child: children*. The form *eyren* was more typically Southern.

60. Caxton's previous paragraph dealt with dialectal differences. This one is concerned with stylistic prejudices, which lead to differences in choice of vocabulary.

65. Caxton stands dismayed between two possible alternatives: barbarousness (*playn rude*) and ornateness (*curyous*). This probably meant for him the conflict between the English vocabulary of the alliterative style and the French vocabulary of the courtly style; see N. F. Blake, 'Caxton and Courtly Style', *Essays and Studies*, N.S. 21 (1968), 29–45. When finally Caxton said he would translate the book *in a meane bytwene bothe* and *in suche termes as shall be understanden by Goddys grace accordynge to my copye,* he no doubt wished to pacify both sides

while yet indicating his preference for the courtly style by adhering to the language of his copy.

75. 'And if any man starts reading it and finds such terms as he cannot understand, let him go and read and learn Vergil or Ovid's *Epistle* and there he will see and understand everything easily if he has a good reader and instructor (to help him at need)'.

81. *to clerkys:* perhaps a mistake for *for clerkys.*

86ff. If John Skelton (*c.* 1460–1529) translated Cicero's letters, his translation has not survived. His translation of Diodorus Siculus is edited by F. M. Salter and H. L. R. Edwards, *The Bibliotheca of Diodorus Siculus translated by John Skelton,* EETS O.S. 233 and 239 (London, 1950–4). The date of Skelton's laureation is unknown, but several people received this honour from Oxford at the turn of the century. Skelton's style is even more ornate than Caxton's so that the latter's praise of him suggests (despite his earlier remarks) that this was the style he wished to imitate.

98. *musicalle:* presumably 'of or pertaining to the Muses', cf. OED. *Musical, a.5.*

99. Helicon was a mountain in Bœotia dedicated to the Muses and its waters were used as an image of poetic inspiration. OED. *Helicon,* gives its first quotation for this use only from Skelton's *Against Garnesche,* *c.* 1529. But cf. Lydgate's *Troy Book,* III. 554–5.

106. *naturell:* probably used here and elsewhere in the sense 'legitimate'.

106. Arthur, the eldest son of Henry VII, died in 1502.

38. FEATS OF ARMS

1. Christine de Pisan was born in Venice in 1364, but her father went to live in France soon after her birth. He died in 1385, and Christine's husband in 1389. This encouraged her to start writing to earn her living. She dedicated her works, which were very popular, to members of the French aristocracy. She retired to a convent at Poisy in 1418. Caxton printed several translations of her books.

2–3. Flavius Vegetius Renatus wrote his *Instituta Rei Militaris* for the Emperor Valentian in the fourth century. It is a well-known military textbook in the Middle Ages. The *Arbre des Batailles,* 'Tree of Battles', by Honoré Bonet was a popular work written in the fourteenth century; it was translated into Scots by Sir Gilbert Hay.

8–9. That is, 23 January 1489.

16. John de Vere, thirteenth Earl of Oxford, was a staunch Lancastrian, who joined the future Henry VII on the Continent and gained an influential position after his accession.

31. It is natural to assume that by *next folowyng* Caxton meant 'immediately following'. It would of course be impossible to print a book within a week (8–14 July), so Caxton would have had to hand over each part to the printer as soon as he translated it. He may have wanted

to produce the volume quickly to impress his new patron. His use of *next* with *folowyng* and of *ful* with *fynyshyd*, which are unusual in his writings, implies a certain pride in the achievement.

46. Late in 1487 Parliament voted a subsidy in aid of Brittany which was threatened by the King of France, and some English troops left for Brittany. Later Henry sent soldiers to Flanders to help Maximilian harass the French.

49. It is not clear whether the subjects are in England or France. Henry faced several rebellions after his succession, which were generally put down fairly leniently.

50. *out of this londe:* 'abroad'.

43. FIFTEEN OES

Elizabeth, daughter of Elizabeth Woodville and Edward IV, had married Henry VII soon after his accession. The marriage helped to legitimize Henry's claim to the throne and it united the houses of York and Lancaster. For Margaret see 6:2.

44. FOUR SONS OF AYMON

(a) The only extant copy of Caxton's text lacks the beginning and end. His edition contained both prologue and epilogue since in the 1554 edition (which is a direct descendant of Caxton's edition) there are references to John de Vere Earl of Oxford for whom Caxton translated the work. However, the 1554 prologue and epilogue cannot represent Caxton's text word for word. If Caxton's prologue contained a reference to Aristotle's *Metaphysics* he must have borrowed it from some source since he is unlikely to have read it himself.

18–20. This translation (cf. Blake No 104) has not survived. Both the third and ninth Earls of Oxford were called Robert, but the life would almost certainly have been of the latter, who led a short but colourful life (1362–92). A favourite of Richard II, he was outlawed by the 'Merciless Parliament' in 1388. Froissart wrote of the events in England during Richard II's reign, and it is quite likely that an account of Robert's life was written in French. It may be significant that a life of the Earl, written originally in French, was translated into English at this time.

30. A French text was printed in Lyons in 1480, and this was probably the text Caxton used though manuscripts of the French version are common.

32–6. The Earl of Oxford was evidently slow to translate his patronage into cash. Hence Caxton stresses the cost of the edition (which can have been no greater than any other) and his hope of a fee. Such statements are the equivalent of begging poems, similar to those written by Lydgate and Hoccleve.

45. GAME OF CHESS (first edition)

(a) 2. George Duke of Clarence was the eldest of Edward IV's brothers. He had taken part in Warwick's rebellion of 1470, but he had repented and been forgiven.

7. The *victorye upon your enemyes* is probably a general reference without specific application.

14. *wyth guydyng of your hows:* 'under the leadership of your family', which included of course Edward IV and Margaret of Burgundy.

35. *unknowen:* Caxton was clearly unacquainted with Clarence and may have been encouraged to seek his patronage by Margaret of Burgundy.

(b) 4. The Observants were those Franciscan friars who observed the strict rule of the order as re-established in the early fifteenth century. The reference is the first one given under OED. *Observant*, B. *sb.* 2.

5–6. *I have ben conversant:* this ought to mean 'I have lived on terms of familiarity with', cf. OED. *Conversant*, A, adj. 2. If so, it may mean that when Caxton visited Ghent he was accustomed to stay with the White Friars. In view of his religious views, this is not improbable.

(c) 4. *ete:* here in the sense 'destroy, deprive of all their goods'.

8–9. These are various courts: the Chancery was the highest court of judicature; the King's Bench and Common Pleas were both superior courts of common law; the Exchequer and Receipt were both courts of revenue; and the Hell appears to have been part of the law courts at Westminister.

(e) 9. A reference presumably to English claims to France, for *bothe his royames* must be England and France; cf. 17b:2.

11–13. The emphasis upon the free conduct of merchandise reminds one of *The Libelle of English Policy*.

46. GAME OF CHESS (second edition)

(a) For the reasons for the new prologue, see Blake p. 93. Caxton opens by referring to St Paul's advice which was frequently quoted in the Middle Ages; cf. 50e:40–1, 72a:117 and the Nun's Priest's Tale (*Canterbury Tales* B² 4631–2).

8. Not a biblical quotation apparently.

13. The author was Jacobus de Cessolis, but Caxton's reference here is apparently to Jean de Vignay, the French translator, who in his translations often refers to himself as 'hospitalier de l'Ordre de saint Jacques du Haut Pas'. On de Vignay see C. Knowles, 'Jean de Vignay, un traducteur du XIVᵉ siécle,' *Romania*, 75 (1954), 353–83.

16–17. The first edition was printed in 1475, while Caxton was still in Bruges.
21. *The Game of Chess* was originally written in Latin, though Caxton used a French translation.
27. The second edition is provided with illustrations.

47. GOLDEN LEGEND

(a) The first part of this prologue (ll. 1–68) is based on the prologue in the French text, though Caxton has added many details.
4. Augustine's *De Opere Monachorum*, written in 401.
8. Not all the books Caxton mentions were translated for 'lords, ladies and gentlemen', though no doubt he wished to give the impression that they were.
11. There is no evidence that Caxton's version of the *Metamorphoses* was printed; but its inclusion in this list suggests he did not think it exceptional in any way. The problem is what he meant by *parfourmed and accomplisshed*. It would be natural to assume this meant 'printed' since he introduces the concept 'translated' later; see Introduction. The list contains most of the works Caxton translated before 1482 except *Reynard the Fox*, a translation from Dutch. It excludes works translated by others.
48. It is noteworthy that Caxton feels obliged to justify making a new translation. He does not claim that it is more literary or more accurate, but simply that it is fuller and differently arranged. On the various texts and their interrelationship, see Sister M. Jeremy, 'Caxton's *Golden Legend* and de Vignai's *Légende dorée*,' *Medieval Studies*, 8 (1946), 97–106 and 'Caxton's *Golden Legend* and Voragine's *Legenda Aurea*,' *Speculum*, 21 (1946), 212–21. The previous English translation is now often referred to as *Gilte Legende*.
55. For Caxton's different arrangements, see Blake pp. 117–23.
77. William Fitzalan Earl of Arundel played a minor role in government in the reigns of Edward IV and Richard III. There is no evidence that he ever met Caxton personally.
82. Nothing further is known of John Stanney.
(c). This section deals with the foreskin of Our Lord cut off at his circumcision, which was claimed to be in Antwerp.
13. *prepucium Domini*: 'foreskin of Our Lord'; cf. *Mandeville's Travels*, ch. xi.
(d) 1. *hym*: Joshua.
2–3. For Gideon, Jephthah and Sampson, see *The Book of Judges*.
6. *Book of Sapience*: The Wisdom of Solomon.
13. The Temporal was that part of the missal containing the daily offices arranged in the order of the ecclesiastical year.
(e) 11. Psalm 51 *Miserere mei Deus*, which David wrote in penance for

the death of Uriah, Bathsheba's husband, though the psalm has only nineteen verses.

28. *his sone:* Solomon.

(f) 1–2. *to wryte the curiosyte and werke of the temple and the necessaryes, the tables and cost:* 'to describe the intricacy and workmanship of the temple and its accoutrements, its inscriptions and decoration'.

5. *Paralipomenon:* Chronicles.

11. Solomon was credited with the authorship of several biblical books, though not all the attributions are accepted today.

13. *Canticles:* Song of Songs, so called from its Latin name *Canticum Canticorum*.

19. *folowed* may be a misprint for *flowed*.

(h) St Gregory the Great, pope from 590 to 604. His *Moralia* is a long and practical commentary on the Book of Job.

(i) 3–4. The Order of the Garter was founded by Edward III about 1348 under the patronage of St George. In 1415 his day (23 April) was made a festival of the highest rank in England. Sigismund became Holy Roman Emperor only in 1433, but he had been King of Germany since 1411. He visited England in 1416 and entered into an alliance with Henry V.

(j) 11. St Augustine's treatise *De Trinitate* (*Patrologia Latina* 42).

13. St Augustine was bishop of Hippo in North Africa.

32–6. It is possible, though perhaps unlikely, that Caxton had the Lollards in mind here. Caxton presumably meant 'slightly educated' by his *symple lettred*.

(k) 5. Caxton was in Cologne during 1471 and 1472 (see No 50) to learn the art of printing, though he may have paid other visits to the town in the course of his trading. It is worth noting that all the examples he adds to the *Golden Legend* are based on his experiences abroad.

30. *by:* 'through, by means of'.

50. HISTORY OF TROY

(a) This preface was printed in red ink in Caxton's edition.

4. Raoul Lefèvre who translated the Latin into French in 1464 appears to have been a kind of secretary to Duke Philip of Burgundy. Philip had died in 1467, hence Caxton's *in his tyme* (l. 6).

12. Margaret, Edward IV's sister, married Charles Duke of Burgundy in 1468.

19. *sixty and enleven:* a construction influenced by French *soixante onze*.

(b) 19. *blynde Bayard:* a proverbial expression; see OED. *Bayard*.

24ff. For a discussion of this passage see Blake p. 16ff. It is normally assumed that Caxton spent most of his time on the Continent in Bruges; but his trading and negotiating would have taken him to many other places in the Low Countries. Thus in his additions to *Golden Legend* he mentions he had been to Antwerp, Ghent and Brussels. He was also frequently in Holland and Zeeland, see W. J. B. Crotch,

The Prologues and Epilogues of William Caxton. EETS O.S. 176 (London, 1928), p. cxxxiiiff.

51. For a discussion of the meaning of *servant*, see N. F. Blake, 'Investigations into the prologues and epilogues by William Caxton,' *Bulletin of the John Rylands Library*, 49 (1966–7), 19–20.

57. '. . . that out of her goodness it please her to accept . . .'.

(d) 11. Caxton's *tyme of the troublous world* must refer in England's case to Warwick's rebellion with the consequent flight of Edward IV to the Low Countries.

19. John Lydgate (*c.* 1370–*c.* 1451) was the most popular poet of the fifteenth century. His *Troy-Book* starts with Jason and the Argonauts. It was commissioned by Henry V and proved to be a favourite work with the nobility, for many manuscripts are extant.

23. *contemplare:* see N. F. Blake, 'Word Borrowings in Caxton's Original Writings,' *English Language Notes*, 6 (1968), 87–8.

(e) 7. Caxton may have been in his early fifties when he wrote this. His comments on old age need not be taken too literally since it was a conventional theme; cf. *Troy-Book* I. 111.

16–17. That is, in printing all the first pages are printed together, as are all the final pages. Hence all copies are ready at the same time.

17–21. Margaret cannot have accepted the book already since, as Caxton has just informed us, all copies were finished at once. Either she had accepted it in principle or else she had accepted a manuscript presentation copy. The latter possibility could be supported by the existence of the manuscript of Caxton's Ovid.

27. Dictys Cretensis, whose *Ephemeris belli Trojani* was possibly written in the fourth century, and Dares Phrygius, the putative author of *Historia de excidio Trojae* from the sixth century, were the two best-known authors of the Trojan war in the Middle Ages. Both are mentioned in Raoul Lefèvre's version, where Caxton may have learned of them. Homer is not mentioned there, but he is frequently referred to as an authority on the war, as in Chaucer's *House of Fame*, 1466. On the history of the Trojan War see M. R. Scherer, *The Legends of Troy in Art and Literature* (New York and London, 1963).

32–4. This passage is a little difficult. The *somme oon name* must mean 'individual names'. *Equyvocacions* presumably signify 'forms, spellings', though this meaning (peculiar to Caxton) is not recorded in MED or OED. *They* denote contemporary writers in different countries who refer to the participants in the Trojan war.

56. HOROLOGIUM SAPIENTIAE

(b) 5–6. 'Let the reader make emendations, and do not blame the printer William Caxton, to whom may God send blessings.'

(c) This is the abbreviated form of the Rule of St Benedict. The translation of the Rule into English was not by Caxton, though it is possible that he made the shortened version.

(d) 1. No attempt is made to justify the union of such disparate material in one volume. These texts are the only ones Caxton printed from existing English versions instead of making his own translations. One naturally wonders therefore whether the volume was prepared for a religious house or order. The statement that the Rule of St Benedict is *necessary to be knowen to al men and wymmen of religyon* (l. 14) might support this view. Certainly one feels that the *certeyn worshipfull persones* (ll. 17–18) are more likely to be religious than lay people

59. HOUSE OF FAME

(b) For a discussion of Caxton's additions to and treatment of this text, see N. F. Blake, 'Caxton and Chaucer', *Leeds Studies in English*, N.S. 1 (1967), 19–36.

71. JASON

(a) 2ff. For Margaret, *History of Troy* and Raoul Lefèvre, see No 50.

7. The first books of History of Troy deal principally with Saturn (who is there not referred to by the Latinate form *Saturnus*), Titan and Jupiter, before going on to the accounts of Perseus and Hercules.

13–16. It is interesting to see that some people thought a book could be too big.

18. For Dares see 50e:27. Guido de Columnis (or delle Colonne) wrote his *Historia Destructionis Trojae*, a translation of Benôit's *Roman de Troie*, in 1287. Guido, however, constantly refers to Dares and Dictys rather than to Benôit.

33–4. The Order of the Golden Fleece was founded by Duke Philip of Burgundy in 1430; see Blake p. 217 and frontispiece. Although originally associated with Jason, the supposed founder of Burgundy, the order later traced its origin to Gideon's fleece to escape the pagan connexions of Jason.

39. Hesdin is a small town in N. France about 35 miles west of Arras.

53. It is possible that Caxton may have provided Edward IV with manuscripts.

58. The future Edward V.

(b) 3. Boccaccio's *De Genealogia Deorum* is an encyclopedic work dealing with the pagan gods. No English version was available at this time.

(c) 4ff. The story given here is somewhat muddled and perhaps Caxton was not very clear about it. Medea restored Aeëtes, her father, to his throne in his old age, but this was done without Jason. On his way to Colchis Jason landed at Lemnos where the women had killed their menfolk, except that Hypsipyle had spared her father Thoas. Jason lived with her and had twins by her, named Euneus and Nebrophonus. Hypsipyle was sold into slavery by the women of Lemnos for saving her father and then lived with Lycurgus, King of Nemea. When the seven against Thebes were passing through Nemea she showed them to a spring so that they could quench their thirst. But to do so she left unguarded the son of Lycurgus, Opheltes, who was in her care. During her absence he was killed by a snake.

17. *he . . . his:* i.e. Boccaccio and Jason's.

19. Statius (died AD 96) is the author of the *Thebaid* and the *Achilleid*, the former of which was a principal source for the account of war against Thebes. The *whiche* may here be interpreted as 'these two'.

32. Lydgate's *Siege of Thebes* is edited by A. Erdmann and E. Ekwall, EETS O.S. 108, 125 (London, 1911–30).

37. Caxton had presumably read both Boccaccio in the Latin and Lydgate's poem, though it is more doubtful whether he had actually read Statius (cf. 96a:54). This addition may be considered another example of Caxton's wanting to include all he knew, while keeping his own remarks separate from the main work.

72. KING ARTHUR

(a) 1ff. These works included *Golden Legend, Knight of the Tower, Order of Chivalry, Royal Book* and *Æsop*.

4. Caxton makes it seem as though many clients had asked for *King Arthur*, though he may have printed it particularly for the person who lent him the manuscript (cf. l. 96).

7. There is no English romance which is based solely on the *Queste del Sainte Graal*, though Malory's *Le Morte d'Arthur* contains many elements from it.

12. On the Nine Worthies see 16a:46ff.

16. Hector appears both in Lydgate's *Troy-Book* and in Caxton's *History of Troy*, but by *balade* and *prose* Caxton probably had authors like Dares and Dictys in mind.

17. See G. Cary, *The Medieval Alexander*, rev. edn. D. J. A. Ross (Cambridge, 1956).

18. For Julius Caesar cf. 96a:53, where Lucan and Statius are mentioned.

19–25. The histories of these three heroes are based on the Bible. The two Books of the Maccabees conclude the Apocrypha. For *londe of byheste*, cf. *londe of promyssyon* 96a:32–3.

30. Caxton printed *Charles the Great* (No 17) later in this same year; so it is surprising that no reference is made to it here. The *Siege of Jerusalem* (No 96) which deals with Godfrey's conquest of the Holy Land was issued in 1481.

46. The noun *bookes* is understood after *fayned*.

49. This *one in specyal* was presumably the person who lent Caxton the manuscript (cf. l. 96) and may have been Earl Rivers; see N. F. Blake,

'Investigations into the Prologues and Epilogues by William **Caxton**', *Bulletin of the John Rylands Library*, 49 (1966–7), 17-46.

55. For details of the *Polychronicon* see No 86.

59. Boccaccio's *De Casibus Virorum Illustrium* was used as a principal source by Lydgate in his *Fall of Princes*.

60. Geoffrey of Monmouth's *Historia Regum Britanniae* was finished about 1136 and was the principal source for most stories about Arthur.

67–8. Gawain, Arthur's cousin, and Cradock appear in several Arthurian romances.

68. This Round Table, which dates only from the fifteenth century, may still be seen in the Assize Court at Winchester.

76. It would be interesting to know if Caxton had seen versions of King Arthur in these languages. For various continental versions of Arthur see R. M. Loomis, *Arthurian Literature in the Middle Ages. A Collaborative History* (Oxford, 1959).

77–9. Probably a reference to the Roman remains at Caerleon in S. Wales.

82–3. Luke 4:24.

88–9. A reference to Caxton's stay in Bruges where, because of the influence of the French-speaking Dukes of Burgundy, many French books were produced.

90. For Welsh versions see R. M. Loomis, *op. cit.* p. 12ff.

98. For Sir Thomas Malory see E. Vinaver, *The Works of Sir Thomas Malory.* 2nd edn (Oxford, 1967), I. xii-xxviii. Even if he knew of it, Caxton makes no reference to Malory's use of an earlier English alliterative poem.

129–30. This use of *symple persone* reminds one of similar descriptions in colophons by authors and scribes and indicates Caxton's familiarity with this formula; cf. 34a:4.

(b). On the title of the book and its applicability, see Vinaver, *op. cit.*, p. 41ff.

73. KNIGHT OF THE TOWER

(a) 12. Probably Queen Elizabeth Woodville; see N. F. Blake, 'The "noble lady" in Caxton's *The Book of the Knyght of the Towre*,' *Notes and Queries*, 210 (1965), 92–3.

25. *in generally:* note the adverbial form; see further Introduction.

48. By this time Caxton had many translations to his credit.

(b) 4–8. The translation was finished on 1 June 1483 and printed on 31 January 1484. Richard III came to the throne only on 26 June 1483, but it is probable that the prologue as well as the epilogue was written after 1 June.

74. LIFE OF OUR LADY

It seems probable that Caxton composed these stanzas, particularly the first one. The latter two are poetic translations of the Latin and may have been in existence already.

Notes

1. A common formula, see Blake, p. 152.
5. *not takyng hede:* probably inserted simply to fill the line.
24. *more than ever:* for eternity and beyond; a translation of *in eternum et ultra.*
25. *for memorye:* in memory of your son and what he did for man. Another phrase probably inserted to fill in the line.
27. That is, the nine orders or choirs of heavenly beings.

75. MIRROR OF THE WORLD

(a) This prologue is based on that in Caxton's French source. Both are printed and discussed in Blake p. 155ff. See also N. F. Blake, 'The "Mirror of the World" and MS Royal 19 A ix,' *Notes and Queries,* 212 (1967), 86–7.
11. 'The spoken word dies, but the written letter lives on.' This proverbial expression, added by Caxton, was common; see H. Walther, *Carmina Medii Ævi Posterioris Latina* II/2 (Göttingen, 1964), 13903 and 13903a.
39. Hugh Bryce was a mercer who had been employed by Edward IV on several missions to the Low Countries. He was Mayor of London in 1494 and died in 1496. He was governor of the King's Mint in the Tower under Lord Hastings, which may account for his wishing to present a book to him.
41. William Lord Hastings was employed by Edward IV on diplomatic missions, including the negotiations leading to the marriage of Margaret to Charles of Burgundy. He was appointed master of the Mint in 1461 by Edward IV, in which capacity he may have come into contact with Bryce.
47. The *Mirror of the World* is decorated with woodcuts which are modelled on the illustrations in MS Royal 19 A ix.
(b) 2. The Danube rises in the Black Forest in Germany and flows into the Black Sea. First, at or near its source, 'it crosses seven great streams in its impetuous course' (lit. by its rapidity and running).
2. *unto in:* a construction that seems not otherwise to be recorded, the meaning of which is probably 'as far as and into'.
7. The Rhine rises in Switzerland some distance from the source of the Danube. It passes through Basle, Strasbourg, Mainz, Koblenz, Cologne and Nijmegen on its way to the sea. In the Netherlands it divides into two principal arms, the Oude Rijn and the Waal, the latter of which discharges into the North Sea by the River Maas. Gelderland, Cleves and Holland are provinces in the Netherlands.
13–14. 'and Maas Diep (is) forty miles long to the sea'.
(d) The *Vision of Tundale* is one of the best known of medieval visions. There are many copies of it in Latin, French and English versions. St Patrick's Purgatory, which this section deals with, was a kind of cave established by St Patrick in which the visitor was subjected to many torments.

4. The High Canon of Waterford has not been identified.

14. Caxton would have known Sir John de Banste in Bruges. We may remember that he may have acquired the French manuscript while in Bruges, and so he may have discussed it with friends there.

(f). This section, which simply provides a summary of the book or table of contents, is not in MS Royal 19 A ix.

12. Mappa Mundi: the map of the world, here used for the world itself. A medieval Mappa Mundi is still preserved in Hereford Cathedral.

34. St Dionysius or Denis, said to have been coverted by St Paul, later became the patron saint of France.

37. *Tholomeus:* Ptolemy, honoured by the Middle Ages as an astronomer.

48. *hevene crystalyn:* this is a technical term for the heavenly sphere between the primum mobile and the firmament in the Ptolemaic system. This is the only time that Caxton used this expression in his own writings, but he took it from the body of the *Mirror of the World*, in which the heavenly bodies are described.

(g) 34–5. Edward IV's regnal year started on 4 March. So that 8 March in his twenty-first year is 8 March 1481. The translation was commenced on 1 January 1481 and finished on 8 March 1481. As in other cases Caxton reckoned the calendar year from the end of March, so his January 1480 is our January 1481.

38–41. By 1481 Edward IV was enjoying relative peace in his kingdom. Caxton may have been referring again to Warwick's rebellion of 1469–70.

77. MORAL PROVERBS

1. Cf. 74:1.

5. Nothing is known of Earl Rivers's secretary and no other references to him occur. He may have been like John Stanney who undertook negotiations with Caxton for the *Golden Legend* on behalf of William Earl of Arundel. We need not assume that he proofread the text or in any way supervised the edition.

79. OLD AGE, OF FRIENDSHIP AND DECLAMATION OF NOBLESSE

(a) 1–2. The work was translated from Latin to French and then from French to English (cf. ll. 47–50).

3. Cicero's *Cato maior: De Senectute* is ostensibly a discussion between Marcus Porcius Cato and his two young friends, Publius Scipio Africanus Minor and Caius Laelius. In fact it is largely a monologue put into the mouth of Cato about old age.

14. Quintus Ennius (239–169 BC), a Roman poet who was much praised

by Cicero and whose *Annales* might be regarded as the Roman national poem until superseded by the *Æneid*.

16. Atticus was Cicero's friend to whom many of his letters were written. Caxton was confused here since Ennius must be the subject of *wryteth*. Cicero's *De Senectute* was dedicated to Atticus.

24. On Fastolfe see J. Crosland, *Sir John Fastolfe, A Medieval 'Man of Property'* (London, 1970).

26–7. *for the diffence and unyversal welfare of bothe royames:* this would seem to mean something like 'for the defence of the two kingdoms and yet for their ultimate benefit'.

36. *bowes acustomed thenne:* the archers who would accompany three hundred knights. According to Crosland, *op. cit*, p. 24, Fastolfe took ten men-at-arms and thirty archers to France.

39. John Duke of Bedford (1389–1435) was Henry IV's third son who became Regent of the English possessions in France on Henry V's death. On the death of Charles VI of France, Henry VI became King of France as well, and John was theoretically Regent of all France. Thomas Duke of Exeter was the youngest son of John of Gaunt and Catharine Swynford; he was thus a half-brother of Henry IV. He accompanied Henry V on his expeditions to France. Thomas Duke of Clarence was Henry IV's second son. He also took part in the French wars in which he was killed in 1421 at Beaugé.

46. *specyfyced*, the reading in Caxton's text, is not recorded elsewhere and is best taken as a misprint.

47–50. Caxton seems to have been confused here. He implies that the Latin of the original is somewhat difficult to read. Yet the English translation which reproduces the meaning of the Latin closely is fuller and more fluent. The English translation was in any case made from the French version.

52. Unfortunately Caxton does not specify what difficulties he overcame to acquire this text. Possibly his statement that he had not previously seen a copy may imply that manuscripts of this work were scarce.

55. *stepte in age:* cf. The Nun's Priest's Tale (*Canterbury Tales* B² 2821).

67. These remarks echo those in the epilogue of *Eneydos*.

89. Cicero's *Laelius De Amicitia* is a discussion on friendship between Gaius Laelius, Quintus Mucius Scaevola and Gaius Fannius.

99. On John Tiptoft Earl of Worcester see R. J. Mitchell, *John Tiptoft* (London, 1938), and R. Weiss, *Humanism in England during the Fifteenth Century*. 2nd edn (Oxford, 1957), pp. 112–22.

(b) 2. Laurence de Premierfait translated both *De Senectute* and *De Amicitia* at the command of Louis Duke of Bourbon in 1405. Laurence was noted for his many translations made in the late fourteenth and early fifteenth centuries. Caxton here uses a Latinized version of his name which he may have taken over from the copy he was reading.

(f) 6. A typical *demandio*.

17–20. Tiptoft was executed in 1469.

32. The pope then was Pius II, before whom Tiptoft delivered a Latin oration which, it is said, moved the Pope to tears.

80. ORDER OF CHIVALRY

3. The squire has not been identified. It is interesting that the book itself consists of the relation of a hermit to a squire of the requirements of chivalry.

16. Brenius and Belinus were two mythical kings of England who were said to have conquered most of Europe. They are both referred to in *Polychronicon* and *Le Morte d'Arthur*.

18–19. This is probably a general reference. Caxton may have been thinking of such writers as Dares and Dictys, though neither mentioned Brenius or Belinus.

25–6. It is unlikely that fifteenth-century knights did spend all their time visiting the baths, even assuming any were available in contemporary London. It seems probable that Caxton modelled this passage on some complaint with a classical origin.

30–1. These people or events are not all the subjects of individual romances in Middle English, though most are mentioned in *King Arthur* (No 72). Perceforet is the Indian hero of a romance set in pre-Arthurian England which was very popular at the court of the Dukes of Burgundy.

32ff. The *conquest* is the Norman Conquest. Richard I (1189–99) took part in the first crusade; Edward I (1272–1307) conquered Wales and campaigned in Scotland; and Edward III (1327–77) and his most famous son, the Black Prince, won famous victories in France. Knolles, Hawkwood, Chandos and Mauny all fought for Edward III in France and all appear in Froissart's *Chronicles*.

37. Froissart visited the court of Richard II and was regarded by many as a fashionable writer. His history of the Hundred Years' War was evidently familiar to Caxton, who may even have considered making a translation of it. It was finally translated by Lord Berners in the sixteenth century.

38ff. Henry V (1413–22), the victor at Agincourt, was regarded by many as the paragon of knighthood. John Duke of Bedford carried on the fight in France after his death (cf. 79a: 39). Thomas de Montacute, fourth Earl of Salisbury, took part in the Battle of Agincourt.

73. *in late dayes passed:* presumably since the death of Henry V.

76. *al his enemyes:* this may be a general reference, though Richard's short reign was not a quiet one.

86. POLYCHRONICON

(a) The first part of this prologue is based ultimately on the *Historical Library* by Diodorus Siculus, though Caxton took it from a lost French version. It was also used by Skelton and Berners; see Blake pp. 149–50.

1. *merytoryously:* presumably 'as a meritorious cause'; see Introduction.

8. *excluded fro suche peryllys:* 'without experience of similar dangers'.

12. *by the experyence of adverse fortune:* 'as a result of misfortune'.

80–1. 'They are neither noticed in their life time nor remembered after their death'.

85. A reference to the labours of Hercules.

92–3. 'Other monuments, scattered by various changes, last only a short time.'

121. For the *Golden Legend* see No 47.

122. The *Polychronicon* by Ranulph Higden was a history of the world up to his own times which began with geographical details of the world. See J. Taylor, *The Universal Chronicle of Ranulph Higden* (Oxford, 1966).

130. As Caxton makes clear later (ll. 139–43) he added the final continuation up to 1460 in his *Liber Ultimus*.

132. Ranulph Higden entered St Werbergh's monastery, Chester, about 1299. He died in 1364.

133. For John Trevisa see D. H. Fowler, 'John Trevisa and the English Bible', *Modern Philology*, 58 (1960–1), 81–98, and 'New Light on John Trevisa,' *Traditio*, 18 (1962), 289–317.

(b) 1. *Proloconycon:* this form has not been emended because similar ones are found at l. 15 and (c) l. 1.

16. On Caxton's changes see Blake pp. 181–3.

21. Caxton's continuation is based principally on his own *Chronicles of England*, which is itself a version of the *Brut*. For his sources see Blake p. 116.

(d) 4–5. Caxton was always willing to include everything he could lay hands on.

91. REYNARD THE FOX

4. This was Caxton's only translation from Dutch. His original was printed in Gouda in 1479.

93 ROYAL BOOK

1–29. It is possible that this passage was borrowed from some unidentified source.

46. The original French text was compiled by Lorens d'Orleans for Philip the Bold of France (1270–81). It had been translated into English several times already, see W. N. Francis, *The Book of Vices and Virtues*, EETS o.s. 217 (London, 1942), though Caxton seems not to have known any other English version.

49. This mercer may be William Pratt.

51. In French it is more usually known as *La Somme de Roi*.
53ff. The contents of this book formed the essential tenets of Christian belief, which accounts for its popularity.
(b) 8. One might have expected *whyche* alone, in the sense 'which, when they are well understood and observed, may guide a person'. Otherwise *by whyche* could be understood as 'through which', with 'one' as the subject of *may* understood; 'virtues, through which, when they are well understood and observed, one may guide a person'.

95. SEX EPISTOLAE

A translation of the Latin is given in G. Bullen and J. Hyatt, *Sex Quamelegantissimae Epistolae, printed by William Caxton in 1483* (London, 1892). The Latin may of course be the work of Pietro Carmeliano rather than of Caxton, though the verses include an invitation to purchase the book.

96. SIEGE OF JERUSALEM

(a) 29ff. The theme is that of the Nine Worthies again, cf. 16:46ff.
32. *flowynge mylke and honey:* the phrase is traditional, and in late Middle English it was commoner without a *with*.
48. Homer, Dictys and Dares are mentioned as sources for the Trojan War in 50e: 27. The works of Virgil and Ovid were well known in the Middle Ages and often referred to by Caxton.
50. It is interesting that in none of his comments about the Nine Worthies does Caxton produce any source for the story of Alexander; so presumably he was not familiar with any.
54. For Statius see 71c: 19. Lucan, the author of *Pharsalia*, was a Latin poet who was much admired in the Middle Ages.
68–9. This list is very like that of 80:30–1. Ghalehot is a Flemish form of Galahad, which indicates that Caxton may have been familiar with Flemish versions of the Arthurian story. He was later to print accounts of King Arthur (No 72) and Charlemagne (No 16).
76. The *douzepieres* or twelve companions of the French *chansons de geste* included twelve of the foremost nobles of France.
77. *whos:* Charlemagne's.
84. Godfrey of Bouillon, the second son of Eustache Count of Boulogne-sur-Mer, led the First Crusade and was elected King of Jerusalem in 1099. He died in 1100.
87–8. William Archbishop of Tyre wrote his *Historia Rerum in Partibus Transmarinis Gestarum*, an account of the First Crusade, in the latter half of the twelfth century. It had been translated into French within fifty years. Many manuscripts of the French version are extant.

90. *his:* Godfrey's

97–8. *Braas of Seynt George:* the Dardanelles, so called because of the church of St George outside Constantinople; Braas is from French *bras* 'an arm', here 'an arm of water'. Caxton took the name from the body of the text, though the name is also found in Mandeville.

100. Constantinople fell in 1453, and after its fall the Turks made considerable inroads into the Balkans.

106. Peter the hermit preached the First Crusade widely in France and Germany.

122. Rhodes belonged to Venice and the city was besieged by the Turks under Mohammed II in 1480. The Turks were repulsed with heavy loss. This reference shows how quickly news travelled.

124. Ydronte: Otranto in Apulia.

125. Sicily and the Southern part of Italy formed the Kingdom of Naples, which in the second half of the fifteenth century was ruled from Spain.

157. *in theyr propre persones and in theyr mevable goodes:* by going in person or by providing money for the expenses of the crusade.

180. The two sons of Edward IV, the future Edward V and his brother, who were murdered in the Tower in 1483.

(b) 3. The opening chapter of the *Siege of Jerusalem* deals with Heracles and the coming of Mahomet, which led to the conquest of the Holy Land by the Mohammedans and the enslavement of the Christians there.

Glossary

Vocalic y *is treated like* i; *but consonantal* y *follows* w.

abasshed, disconcerted; confounded

abyding, permanence

abyte, practice

accomplisshement, winning, fulfilment

accomplyssh, to finish, complete

accomplysshyng, finishing, completion

acompt, accomptes, accounts, reckoning

accord: fyll at –, came to an agreement

accord wyth, to agree with

accordaunt, suitable, fitting

accordyng, in agreement with; in harmony with

achyeve, to complete, finish; to win

achievement, accomplishment

acustomed, customary, usual

addresse, to correct, set in order; *refl.* to prepare oneself

adjoust, to propose, suggest

admonest, to admonish, advise

advertyse, to reflect upon

advysedly, carefully; prudently

affermed, attested to, confirmed

affraye, to frighten

afore, earlier, before

afor-reherced, mentioned above

after, afterwards

agayn, against

aledge, to confirm

amende, to correct, improve

amendyng, correction

amyable, pleasurable, pleasing

amyte, friendship

ample, copiously

aournate, rhetorical, elaborate

aourned, adorned, elaborate

apaire, to harm, corrupt

aparte, separately; to one side

aparteynyng, suitable, fitting

apparaylles, apparatus, requisites

apperceyve, to realize, recognize

appertinent, pertinent, applicable

appropre, to assign, attribute

ardaunt, zealous, eager

arette, to impute, ascribe

arraye, dress, attire

assertryce, advocate (fem.)

assoyled, resolved, explained

assotted, infatuated

assured, betrothed

astate, see estate

atedyacyon, attediation, rendering tedious

attemperat, moderate, restrained

attones, at the same time

auctoryte, wise saying, quotation

autentyke, authentic, authoritative

avaylle, to prosper, benefit

avale, to take off

avisedly, attentively, deliberately

avowe, to promise, make a vow

ayenst, in protection from

axyd, pret. asked

bagge-berars, those who carry bags with money in them

baynes, baths

balade, verse, poetry

174

banerette, knight entitled to bring vassals to field under his own banner

barbares, barbarians

behalve, respect, matter

behoefful, necessary

beholden, examined

behove, to befit, be proper

benefyce, advantage, benefit

benefyced, holding a benefice

beneurte, happiness

besines, busy-ness, activity

bet-bespoken, well spoken

bewayllynges, loud lamentation

bycause, in order that

bienfayttes, good deeds

bysexte, the intercalary day in a leap-year

bone, request

boundes, boundaries

brede, breath

brevely, shortly; succinctly

brood, vulgar, common

brought forth, *pret.* educated

brute, lacking reason

brutyssh, ignorant, irrational

caas: in lyke –, similarly

capytal, principal

carnel, fruit, corn

chaas, *pret.* chose

chapitred, made into chapters

charge, weight, duty; responsibility

charge, to order, direct

charyte, love

chekked, halted, arrested

chepe: good –, at a bargain price

cleped, called

clergye, learning

comynte, the people at large, commons

commynycacyon, information, communication

commysed, accomplished, perpetrated

compendious, concise

compyled, based on

comprise, to include; to understand

comune, in common ownership

con, conne, to know; to be able

conceive, to understand, grasp

condicions, personal qualities, manners

conduyte, to lead

confusyon, destruction, confounding

congye, permission

conjurye, a sworn member

connyng, intelligence, wit

connyngly, skilfully

conservatryce, preserver, guardian (fem.)

contemplacion, regard, consideration

contemplare, to consider

contemplatif, characterized by contemplation; moral, educative

convenient, suitable

conversacion, life, existence

conversaunt, living on familiar terms with

convict, found guilty of an offence

corage, spirit, heart

corporas, cloth on which the consecrated elements are placed during Mass

corrobre, to affirm, strengthen

cost, adornments

cotydyan, daily

countre, district, area

covetises, avariciousness

craftely, elegantly, skilfully

crafty, well-made

croysyng, crusade

cronyckes, chronicles, histories

cure, care, charge, parish, benefice

curiosyte, ornamentation, workmanship

curyous, elaborate, delicate

curiously, expertly, skilfully

dalf, *pret.* dug, buried; *pp. dolven*

dampned, condemned

debonayr, gracious

debuoir, devoyr, devour, duty; *put myself (me) in –*, do what I can

declaracion, contents, meaning; *by –*, explicitly

decollacion, decapitation

defawte, fault, sin

delybere, to consider; to determine

departe, to die; to share; to seperate; *– fro*, to part with

depeynted, painted, portrayed

depessh, to distribute, sell

depress, to suppress, destroy

descrive, to describe

desdaygne, to scorn, despise

deth, conclusion, end

dette, spiritual debt

devour, devoyr, see debuoir

dictes, sayings

dyffamyng, bringing into disrepute

diffence, defence

difficile, difficult

digne, fitting, worthy

dygnytees, offices, positions

dylygence, industry, application

dyscordaunt, at variance, disagreeing

dyscrete, judicious

dyscrease, to decrease, diminish

dyseases, misfortunes, troubles

dysjoyned, unrelated, scattered

disordre, to distract from, be out of touch with

dispense, expense

disputacions, debate

dyuturnyte, long duration of time

dyvercely, in different ways, variously

dyversefy, to produce variety

dyversytees, differences, varieties

dyvulgacion, propagation

do, to cause to (do something)

doctour, teacher

doctryne, instruction

dolorous, sad, grievous

dolven, see dalf

domyne, to conquer

doubteuous, terrible, fearful

douzepieres, Charlemagne's twelve peers or paladins

dradde, revered

drawen out, compiled from

dredefull, dangerous, perilous

duelle, to remain

eage, age

edefye, to build

effectis, contents

egal: – wyth, equal, equal to

empeshement, hindrance

empryse, chivalrous enterprise

empryse, enpryse, to undertake

enbelyssh, to improve, ornament

enbelissher, one who makes beautiful

encreace, to grow rich and powerful

ende: to th'– that, so that, in order that

endure unto, to continue to

enduryng, lasting, the space of

endyte, to compose

endytyng, composition

enflawme, to excite

enformacion, instruction, training

enformer, instructor

engendre, to induce

engyn, mechanical contrivance

englysshe, to translate into English

engross, to write, copy

enhaunce, to glorify, exalt

enherytages, inheritance, lands passed down by inheritance

enpoigne, to impugn, call in question, assail

enpovere, to impoverish

enpryntyng, printing

enpryse, see empryse

enquestes, quests, searches

ensamples, illustrative stories

enseygne, to teach

enseygnementis, instructions

entendement, understanding
entendyble, intelligible
entermete, to engage, take part (in)
enterprise, to undertake
equyvocacions, forms, spellings
erst, first
erudicion, instruction
eschewe, to avoid
eschewyng, avoiding
estate, rank, status; *pl.* social classes
ete, to destroy, consume
eurous, happy, prosperous
everych, each
evydences, writs, legal documents; proofs
exaltacyon, elevation in authority and dignity
excercising, prosecuting, taking part in
excercyse, practice, practical training
excersytees, practice, occupation
excyte, to prompt, urge
execute, to carry out, fulfil
experyment, experience
experimently, by experience
expowne, to expound, declare
eye: at –, visibly, clearly

facion, visible appearance
faire, beautiful, attractive
faytte, dead, act
falle, to befall, come to pass
fast by, nearby
feble, to enfeeble
fee, payment (in money or kind)
fele, to be familiar with
ferdful, terrible, frightening
ferforthe, far, to a great extent; *as – as*, as much as, as far as
fermelye, resolutely, steadfastly
ferre, distant
figure, image, likeness
flood, river
flowre, to flourish, live gloriously
forgetynge, oblivion

forlond, headland, promontory
forme, fourme, type
fortune, to happen
foundement, beginning, foundation
fourme, make-up, physical appearance
fraternyte, guild, company
fraunchyse, free will, freedom; privilege, legal exemption
frere, friar
fresshe, beautiful, bright
fruytfull, beneficial

gaye, beautiful
gate, *pret.* begot
genelagie, genealogy
gentylly, nobly
gentylnesse, courtesy, good manners
ghoost, spirit
ghostly, spiritual
governaunce, control
gree: in –, at –, with favour, graciously
gretnes, large size

haboundaunce, plenty
habounde, to proliferate
happe, fortune, fate
happe, to happen, befall
happely, by chance, indeed
hardynesse, bravery
hastely, quickly, soon
hastlyer, sooner
haultayne, valiant, great
haunt, to practise
hede, source
hie, hihe, noble, lofty, elevated
historial, historical
historiograph, historian
history, story, adventure
hole, whole, cured
holsomm, edifying
honest, commendable, worthy
how wel (that), although

ymage, representation
incongrue, inharmonious, vulgar

inconvenytys, harms, troubles
indigne, unworthy
informacions, instruction, edification
instance, urgent request
instantly, urgently, persistently
intytelyng, title
intituled, intitled, called
iongth, yonthe, youth

jentyl, courteous, chivalrous
jeopardye, danger
jeopardous, risky, hazardous
joyefull, producing pleasure
joyes, joyous, pleasant
justes of pees, tournaments
juvente, youth

kepe, to guard
knewe, pret. had intercourse
knowleche, to acknowledge

lade, to ladel, bale
layte, lightning
lange, longe, to belong
large: at –, at length, in full
largely, extensively
late, recently
laton, an alloy resembling bronze
laude, glory, praise
lecture, reading
leeful, lawful, permissible
legend, saint's life
lerne, to educate
lernynge, lesson, example
lese, to lose
lesyng, falsehood
lettred, educated
lettres missives, correspondence
lyberte, privilege, right
licence, approval
lychorous, tempting, dainty
lighten, to flash lightning
lyghter, easier
lyghtly, easily, conveniently
lymytes, boundaries, confines
liste, to be pleased with

lyteral, written
lytilnes, smallness
lyvyng, way of life, manner of life, behaviour
londe of byheste, promised land
londe of promyssyon, promised land
longynge, belonging to
lore, instruction
lothe, to hate, despise
lowely, humbly
luste, to have pleasure

magnyfycence, glory, reputation
malefaytes, evil deeds
maner, kinds
manhode, manliness, courage
maters, contents
meritory, meritorious
merytoryously, as a meritorious cause
mesease, hardship, affliction
mete, food
mete, suitable
myllyfluous, eloquent, sweet sounding
mynussh, to subtract, leave out; to diminish
mynystre, to provide, bestow
myscreaunts, wicked people; heathens, Turks
moeve, meve, to persuade, inspire
moevyng, movement
moo, more
mowe, to be able
musicalle, pertaining to the Muses

name, reputation
naturell, legitimate
naturelly, by human reason
ne but, except
necessaryes, indispensable parts
nedefull, necessary
ner hande, almost
nyste, pret. did not know
noblenes, quality
noblesse, nobility
norisshe, to bring up, educate

notable, noteworthy

nothyng, noothynge, in no way, not at all

notoyrly, well, notoriously

notorye, notable, well known

nourysshar, sustainer, forefather

obeyssaunt, obedient, subservient

oblyvyous, forgetful

obprobrye, shame, humiliation

ocyosyte, idleness

olders, forefathers

operacions, works

or, before

ordenaunce, command, arrangement

ordeyn, to order, arrange

ordynatly, properly

orygynal, origin

ornate, to embellish

otherwhyle, occasionally, now and then

ottroye, to grant

over, beyond, in addition to

overchargeable, too onerous

over-curyous, too fanciful, fastidious

overest, superior

overgret, too great

overmoche, excessive

overrede, to read through

over-rude, too vulgar

oversee, to examine

overthrow, to subvert, undermine

paynym, pagan

paraventure, perhaps

parfyght, perfect, adult, grown up

parysshen, parishioner

partie, part; region, area

penner, pencase

perceyvyngly, penetratingly

petycion, prayer, supplication

perte, adroit, forward

philosophe, philosopher

pyetous, lamentable

pyked, adorned, exquisite

plantyd, recorded

plentiuouse, abundant

pletar, pleader, advocate

polecye, government, administration

polysshed, refined, elaborate

politicque, prudent; political, dealing with politics

power: to my –, to the best of my ability

preysyng, praise

prescience, foreknowledge

proheme, prohemye, introduction

properly, fittingly, accurately

propre, individual, separate

propretees, qualities, characteristics

prouffyte, to prosper

prove wel, to succeed

puissaunce, military power; *pl.* powers

puyssaunt, mighty

purpose, to present, put forward

put forthe, to publish

quayer, book, pamphlet

quave, to shake, tremble

quench, to destroy, kill

quyck, energetic; lively, vigorous

race, to delete

radour, rapidity, force

reame, royame, kingdom

rebuke: putte to –, to bring to a shameful check

recommendacyon, honour, favour

record, witness, testimony

recovure, recovery, regaining

recuperacion, recovery, reconquest

redoubted, dreaded, respected

reduce, to translate; *– to, by*, to commit to

reducynge, translation

reedefy, to rebuild

refrayn, to refrain from, stop

regard: unto the – of, in comparison with

regyment, rule, government

regystre, index, table of contents; diary, commonplace book

reherce, to relate; to include, record; to recount, expand
rehercing, relating
rehersayll, recounting, recital
remembraunce, contents
remyse, to put back again, replace
rennyng, running, course
renomee, reputation, renown
replye agaynst, to speak ill of, repudiate
reporte, refl. to appeal to
repudie, to divorce, abandon
requyre, to desire, entreat
requysite, essential
rescowse, deliverances
reserved, excepted, save
reasonable, rational
reverence, deference, respect
ryall, royal, noble
rightful, just, proper
rypyng, maturity
rood-tree, cross
rubrysshe, rubric, heading; contents
rude, vulgar, inelegant
rudehede, barbarousness

saleweng, salutation, greeting
salutacion, greeting
sauf onelye, except (that)
savour, taste, liking
scathe, harm, misfortune
scyence, knowledge, learning
semblable, like, equal to
sempiternally, eternally
senectute, old age
sentence, meaning; judgement
sepulture, tomb
serviteur, subject
sette, composed
shyppe, to embark
short, quick, immediate
shortly, quickly, briefly
sign, to indicate, distinguish
symple, honest, unpretentious
symplenes, ignorance, simplicity

singuler, individual, particular
singulerly, particularly
syth, adv. afterwards; *prep.* after; — *that*, because
syttyng, fitting, suitable
sleyghtly, indifferently, without much interest
smatre, to dabble in
somtyme, once
sothe, truth
sothsawe, truth
sourd, to rise
soverayn, excellent, paramount
space, time
specifye of, to contain, deal with
spirituelte, the clergy
stalle, n. seat, place of honour; *vb.* to induct into a seat
startemele, infrequently, by starts
stepdame, stepmother
stepte, advanced
straytli, urgently
straunge, exotic, exceptional
streyte, strict, rigorous
submyse, to submit
submytte, to surrender (oneself) to the judgement (of others)
subtyl, difficult to understand, abstruse
subtylly, with fine distinctions
subtyltees, ingenious devices
supplye, to beg, entreat
supportacion, approval, support
sured, betrothed
surely, constantly

table, tablet
taken, captured; considered, reputed
tastynge, personal experience
temporalte, the laity
termes, expressions, words
terrestre, terrestrial
thankynges, thanks
therafter, in accordance with it
therof, of it
tho, a. those; *adv.* then

thought, solicitude
thraldomm, slavery
tocomynge, future
tofore, above
torne, to interpret
tornoye, to take part in a tournament
trayttye, treatise, pamphlet
treatably, carefully, deliberately
trete, to deal with, contain
tryumphal, victorious
tuicion, protection
tunge, language

umbre, shadow
unconnynge, ignorant
undefowled, pure, uncorrupted
undoubtably, without doubt
unyed, united
unyversal, whole, complete
unnethe, hardly
unparfyght, imperfect
unperfightnes, lack of knowledge
unreasonable, without intelligence
unstablenes, instability, mutability
uplondyssh, provincial, boorish
utile, useful

vaynquysshour, conqueror
valyaunces, noble deeds
valyauntnes, bravery
variaunt, diverse
vecordyous, foolish

veray, true
veritably, in truth
veryly, in truth, indeed
veryte, truth
vyandes, foodstuff
visit, to examine, look at
vytayller, one who provides supplies for an army
vytuperable, blameworthy, wicked
voyde, vain, empty
vraye, truly, indeed

wavergynge, changing
wedowhede, state of being a widow, widowhood
wele, well, benefit, welfare; prosperity, riches
wel-sayeng, eloquent writing
wene, to think
wenynge, thinking
werke, construction
wete: that is to –, namely
wilfull, voluntary
wylfully, deliberately
will, to wish, desire
wyll: be in –, to intend
wythal, therewith
wordly, temporal
worshyppe, renown, honour
worshipful, honourable
wretchydnesses, misfortunes

yeftes, gifts

Index of Names

卐卐卐卐卐卐